Lincoln Christian College

D1091197

THE THEOLOGY
OF
P. T. FORSYTH

THE THEOLOGY
OF
P. T. FORSYTH

The Cross of Christ and the
Revelation of God

BY

JOHN H. RODGERS

LONDON
INDEPENDENT PRESS
MEMORIAL HALL EC4

© INDEPENDENT PRESS LIMITED

First published 1965

All rights reserved

Genehmigt von der theologischen Fakultät auf Antrag der Herren Prof. Hendrik van Oyen, Referent, und Prof. Heinrich Ott, Koreferent.

Basel, den 3 Juli, 1963

Der Dekan: Herr Prof. Max Geiger

Made and printed in Great Britain by
The Garden City Press Limited
Letchworth, Hertfordshire

231.7
R69

CONTENTS

v

24845

vi

PREFACE

THE major themes of Peter Taylor Forsyth are expounded in this work. It came into being as an attempt to describe and evaluate the doctrine of revelation as it is presented by Forsyth. Included in the study is his treatment of initial assumptions usually discussed in connexion with the doctrine of revelation. In this way it is a statement and evaluation of Forsyth's central theology, which may serve as an introduction to all his theology.

We have seen fit to place the numerous footnotes to this study in a section immediately following the Appendix, and for ease of reference they are listed under the appropriate page numbers of this work. It should be noted that the page references of books quoted in footnotes relate to the editions listed in the Bibliography and may differ from earlier or subsequent editions.

Since the completion of this study several works which are pertinent to it have appeared: by Peter Taylor Forsyth, *Revelation Old and New*, editor John Huxtable, London, Independent Press Ltd, 1962; *The Church, the Gospel, and Society*, editor J. Forsyth Andrews, London, Independent Press Ltd, 1962; by A. M. Hunter, *Teaching and Preaching the New Testament*, SCM Press Ltd, 1963; and the articles by S. J. Mikolaski, 'The Theology of P. T. Forsyth,' in *The Evangelical Quarterly*, January-March and April-June issues 1964. While it has not been possible to incorporate these studies into the present work, we have read them and rejoice to find others who confirm our interpretation of Forsyth. Either of the small collections of Forsyth's writings listed overleaf provides an excellent introduction to his writings.

We would like to express our appreciation of the kindness shown us by Mr Bernard Honess, formerly of Independent Press, by his interest in this study and for reissuing Forsyth's major theological writings, to Mrs J. Forsyth Andrews for her frequent encouragement, and above all to Professor Hendrik van Oyen whose personal friendliness and wise theological counsel made this study a possibility and our stay in Basle the joy that it was. To him we dedicate this study.

For financial support we are most grateful to the Church Society for College Work, the Bell Fellowship of the Protestant Episcopal Theological Seminary in Virginia, the Woolfall Fund and the Swiss-American Friends Society.

Finally we would like to mention our appreciation for the time taken by Professors van Oyen and Ott of Basle, by Professor John Woolverton of the Protestant Episcopal Theological Seminary in Virginia, by the Rev. Harold Bickley of Somerset, England, and by the Rev. Peter R. Doyle of Leesburg, Virginia, who read this study in manuscript form and who offered suggestions which have greatly helped the author to make it more adequate. Our deepest gratitude is extended to Mr J. H. Goodwin, our librarian and colleague, who prepared the Index. Naturally we and not they must accept full responsibility for the many inadequacies which remain.

August 1964   J. H. R.
Alexandria, Virginia, U.S.A.

INTRODUCTION

I T is generally helpful, when studying the writings of an author, to be familiar with his life and his historical setting. Due to the intense relationship existing between Peter Taylor Forsyth's theological writings and the thought and events of his time, such historical orientation is particularly helpful. Forsyth believed that 'thought' did progress and therefore he was concerned to be critically modern; he kept close to the 'times.' But from Christ he knew as well the darkening, distorting effects of sin and set himself to fight all of the elements in modern theological thought which obscured and perverted the Gospel of Jesus Christ. Owing to this appreciative-critical attitude to his time, all of Forsyth's publications are written in conscious dialogue and receive a dialectical character. It is because of this that these words, written in reference to Augustine, apply to a study of Forsyth: 'Biography here is more than information; it is commentary and key.'[1]

This introductory section has as its purpose to provide an historical-theological orientation to Forsyth's life and writings. In this section the material is divided into three parts. The first part will provide a short sketch of Forsyth's life, limited only to those factors which most probably influenced his theological thought.[2] The second part has as its theme the nature, scope, and style of Forsyth's theological writings and the last part will present Forsyth's critique of English and Continental theological thought contemporary to him.

A Short Sketch of the Life of P. T. Forsyth

Who was this man of whom it was asked: 'Who is this P. T. Forsyth? He has recovered for us a word we had all but lost—the word Grace.' What more could be said of a man than that he sought to give to his generation a true grasp of the word 'Grace'? And what more tragic could be said of a generation than that they were in need of being introduced to that word? This brief sketch seeks to portray the particular ingredients placed in our human life by Providence in order that this man might shoulder the joyful burden of recovering the reality and true dimensions of the Grace of God for his generation. Indeed, who is this P. T. Forsyth?

Several things may be said to characterize young Peter Taylor Forsyth during his undergraduate days. First we note his courage and determination. Born in 1848 to sincere Christians of humble origin and slender financial resources, he was able through intellectual brilliance and hard work to win the necessary scholarships which made it possible for him to graduate with first-class honours in classical literature from Aberdeen University. This he accomplished in the year 1869.[3] We note in this connexion that this rigorous schedule placed permanent marks upon Forsyth's body as well as it helped in the education of his mind, marks which were to keep him in pain and sickness for the rest of his life. It is a tribute to the courage and determination of this man that he did not let his abiding frailty keep him from a full and amazingly productive life.

Also during this period we can see the openness, the personal curiosity characteristic of Forsyth. He was willing and able to embrace the new. His careful reading and rereading of the writings of the great Anglican theologian, F. D. Maurice (1805–72) illustrates this. Maurice's influence on Forsyth has been over-emphasized and perhaps even misunderstood,[4] but there can be little doubt that Forsyth's openness to the new liberal insights in theology, his appreciation of the solidarity of the whole human race in Christ, and his attention to the voice of contemporary philosophy and culture, were nurtured and furthered by Maurice. This openness to the new remained with Forsyth all his days, even when he was called to turn to the task of a new understanding of the old, of the abiding in Christ's Gospel.

After graduation from the university Forsyth's daring and openness showed themselves in his willingness to cross the Channel in order to sit at the feet of that great, almost overwhelming figure Albrecht Ritschl (1822–89). It had been the influence of Robertson Smith, the controversial pastor in Aberdeen who was seeking to bring the message of Biblical criticism into conservative Scottish theological circles, that led Forsyth to make this trip to Göttingen. Thus Forsyth's openness during his undergraduate days led him to a short, one semester period in the winter of 1869–70 which was determinative for the rest of his earthly ministry. One could, with reasonable accuracy, describe Forsyth's whole theological pilgrimage as an inner critique of Ritschlian theology. One should add immediately, however, that the critique was so radical and basic as to create a position which can only in the most qualified manner be referred to as Ritschlian. The resultant affinities and differences can be briefly suggested by comparing Forsyth with Wilhelm Herrmann (1846–1922) the most Kantian of Ritschl's followers. Herrmann remained deeply within the nineteenth-century anthropocentrism from which Forsyth sought to break away. Herrmann posited a moral norm within man which acted as a religious *a priori*, that is, which both approved of and was attracted to

3

the Biblical portrait of the inner life of Jesus. He remained anti-dogmatic and anti-metaphysical in his position. In strong contrast, Forsyth stressed the *kerygmatic* character of Christianity, the miraculous nature of man's reception of God's self-disclosure, and the real possibility of an evangelical metaphysic of the conscience. Here we see the profound differences in Forsyth's theological stance from that of Ritschlianism. However there are elements of continuity, elements of agreement between Forsyth and his contemporaries. We neither find sheer reaction, obscurantism, nor repristination in Forsyth. He stood with them in his stress on the role of experience in the Christian life, particularly is he at one with Ritschlianism in locating the seat of the 'evangelical experience' in the conscience. More detailed material concerning Forsyth's relation to Ritschlianism will appear throughout the study,[5] here we have been concerned to suggest the profound break-through to which Forsyth's inner critique of Ritschlianism led him.

Besides setting the whole tone and frame of Forsyth's theological pilgrimage, this time in Göttingen also began a life-long conversation with German theology for Forsyth. Forsyth's daughter, in the memoir she wrote of her father,[6] tells us that at least one-third of his theological library consisted of German books, and that he continued to read two German theological periodicals each week. His writings reflect this lively and intimate knowledge of German theology and philosophy. Nor was this simply for Forsyth a carrying out of a duty, a professional responsibility to keep abreast of new developments on the Continent. Forsyth grew to love Germany dearly. He liked to travel there and took a real delight in being mistaken for a native of the country. It was a cause of great sadness, though not complete surprise, to him when Germany took the steps which led to World War I.[7]

4

Still a young man Forsyth returned to England, to London, in order to study further at New College. This was a short and not too profitable experience. Perhaps the real value in it lay in the fact that Forsyth came to know J. Baldwin Brown and A. M. Fairbairn, the leading liberals in his still dominantly orthodox denomination. Through Brown's help he received in 1876 his first Congregational responsibility, a call to a congregation at Shipley, Yorkshire, and was ordained there by Brown and Principal Newth of New College. This first part of his ministry can best be characterized as that of a fighting, flamboyant liberal. Forsyth seems to have been something of a 'shocker' to his congregation and fellow-clergy. Both his dress and his theology were out of the ordinary. Who else would wear shepherd's plaid trousers capped off with a flaming red tie in the pulpit? Nor were he and his congregation admitted into the local Union of Independent Congregations due to suspicious innovations in his doctrine. Forsyth provides a description of his work at this time when in 1905, looking back, he wrote: 'When I began to preach the chief test was orthodoxy. And I had the honour to suffer something alongside those who have changed that.'[8] At the beginning of his ordained ministry Forsyth was fighting; he was fighting for the right and necessity to rethink theological formulae. And he was fighting for this right as a creative, impressive young liberal.

In 1878, the second year of this young man's ministry, the hand of God reached more directly and dramatically into his life. To courage, determination, intellectual brilliance, openness to the new and contemporary, and flamboyant individualism, something new was added: a profound awareness of pastoral responsibility. And in and through this sense of responsibility a new foundation was laid which gave a different direction, a different cast to the ministry of

5

this man. It was to be sure a conversion, sudden and profound. Fortunately we have Forsyth's own words to interpret the event for us:

> 'Might I venture here to speak of myself, and of more than thirty years given to progressive thought in connexion for the most part, with a pulpit and the care of souls. . . .
>
> 'There was a time when I was interested in the first degree with purely scientific criticism. Bred among academic scholarship of the classics and philosophy, I carried these habits to the Bible, and I found in the subject a new fascination, in proportion as the stakes were so much higher. But, fortunately for me, I was not condemned to the mere scholar's cloistered life. I could not treat the matter as an academic quest. I was kept close to practical conditions. I was in a relation of life, duty, and responsibility for others. 1 could not contemplate conclusions without asking how they would affect these people, and my word to them in doubt, death, grief, or repentance. I could not call on them to accept my verdict on points that came so near their souls. . . . It also pleased God by the revelation of his holiness and grace, which the great theologians taught me to find in the Bible, to bring home to me my sin in a way that submerged all the school questions in weight, urgency, and poignancy. I was turned from a Christian to a believer, from a lover of love to an object of grace. And so, whereas I first thought that what the Churches needed was enlightened instruction and liberal theology, I came to be sure that what they needed was evangelization in something more than the conventional sense of that word.'[9]

From a lover of love to an object of grace, what a turn was given this man, and what implications it had for his ministry. He was no longer able to follow the direction of the movement which he himself had helped to get started in his denomination. Without seeking to go behind liberalism he could no longer simply embrace liberalism. He had been 'turned' to new awareness of sin and the holiness of God's love. He was

6

thrust beyond liberalism to a recovery of a theology of grace. It was no longer possible for him to be simply a critic of the Bible,[10] he, himself, was criticized by the Bible's Gospel. But how could he convey what he was hearing through the Scripture? What words, what expressions, might he use, what themes must he treat? It took time for Forsyth to find adequate terms to express anew the centrality of grace. But seek he did, and write he did.

From this time forth Forsyth was to become more and more a separated and thus a lonely man. Perhaps in this he shared the fate of all of God's prophets. He became separated because he was claimed by the Gospel to stand against both of the dominant theological postures of the day; he was called to fight on two fronts. To the rationalistic orthodox he was a liberal; to the liberal he was dogmatic and obscure, still muttering dark words about sin and atonement. Why did he not join them in speaking of the brightness and attractiveness of God's love?

This new direction in Forsyth's thought became public through his writing and speaking. In 1893 he contributed an article, 'Revelation and the Person of Christ,' to a collection of Free Church essays entitled *Faith and Criticism*. In this essay we can already see the new recovery of the old struggling to find expression. It was in response to this essay that R. W. Dale asked the question with which we started this short sketch, 'Who is this P. T. Forsyth? He has recovered for us a word we had all but lost—the word Grace.'[11] By common consent Forsyth's article was considered one of the, if not the most, important contributions to the book. From this time on all of Forsyth's writings centre on Grace. While there is development and growing maturity in his writing we are not faced with a radical break. There is no earlier and later Forsyth in his

7

published theological writings as there is an earlier and later Schelling, for example.

Forsyth soon became one of the better-known figures in British Nonconformity. This, no doubt, was influential in his receiving a call in 1894 to Emmanuel Church in the university town of Cambridge. Two years later he preached his well-known sermon, 'Holy Father,' which was the first clear statement of the central category of his theology. It lies at the heart of all that he ever wrote. It was precisely here that Forsyth felt himself at odds with the major theological winds of the day. The Holy Father, the God of Holy Love, he is the author of grace and it was of holy love, of grace that Forsyth felt compelled to speak. As early as 1896 then we can say that the basic structure of Forsyth's theology was clear to him.

To the already mentioned qualities and to his newly found theological direction, was now added what we might call tragic popularity. That he became increasingly popular is indicated by the fact that he was asked to address the International Congregational Council held in Boston in September 1899. His address was entitled, 'The Evangelical Principle of Authority.'[12] It proved for many to be the high point of the meetings. The hearers responded to his address by rising and singing 'In the Cross of Christ I glory.' Another illustration of his growing recognition was his being requested by William Sanday to attend a conference on 'Priesthood and Sacrifice,' held the same year in Oxford. However we must term this growing appreciation as tragic, for Forsyth won few followers. Liberalism was on the wax and he could not stem the tide. In fact it was not long after his death that he was practically forgotten by most people. It has only been fairly recently that his writings and work have received the serious attention which they truly deserve.

We might term the period of his life beginning in

1901 and lasting until 1921 the period of amazing productivity. In 1901 after serving six congregations he accepted the position as principal of Hackney Theological College, London. There he remained until a year-long sickness terminating in November of 1921 ended his earthly ministry. During this period most of Forsyth's theological writings were produced and published. Eighteen of his twenty-five books were published and a good portion of his over 260 articles for periodicals.[13] Also he then contributed to some five of seven collections of essays. This productivity[14] becomes all the more amazing when we take into account that his health was poor, and that the College itself was in some ways a mixed blessing. He had the steady responsibility of the supervision of the school and of much of the teaching of the students. This he loved greatly.[15] But the College was in bad financial straits, and it fell upon Forsyth's already over-burdened shoulders to undertake to raise sufficient funds to keep the school going. In a relatively poor denomination this was no mean task. To make matters worse, during this period Forsyth was dragged into the Campbell controversy.

In 1907 R. J. Campbell published a book entitled *New Theology*;[16] it contained theology Hegelianized, popularized and made extremely superficial. It was a, not even thinly clad, emotional pantheism. Because of Forsyth's grasp of the holiness of God he reacted in print, and in a clear, forceful manner. No doubt because of Forsyth's awareness of God as the Holy One, Campbell singled him out among all of his critics[17] for virile and protracted counter-attack. This whole episode, which ultimately brought Campbell back to his senses, was time-consuming and exhausting for Forsyth. It was no ivory tower that he occupied at Hackney College. And despite all of the above we have this period to thank for the bulk of his literary output.

9

An amazing and dedicated man was this apostle of grace.

PART II

His Writings—their Scope, Nature, and Style

We have already mentioned the size of Forsyth's literary output, but what was its content, its scope? As one might expect from the background we have sketched above, the scope is broad, as broad as the culture in which Forsyth found himself. He was capable of writing in the fields of art, literature, philosophy, politics, ethics, history, and dogmatics. And he did in fact write in all of these areas. But if his scope was broad, his perspective was concentrated. He was no dilettante. He surveyed the broad scene for a purpose and from one point of view. All was seen from the Cross of Christ. It is true that Forsyth wrote no systematics from his Cross-centred perspective. He was not systematic. Even though he did cover and treat in one way or another all of the dogmatic *loci* in his writings, he seems to have felt no desire to present this material in an organized system.

Thus we might say that his writings are, by nature, closer to conversation, closer to occasional pieces, than they are to a theological textbook. There are some reasons for this dialogical nature of Forsyth's writings. First we must remember the huge demands upon his time. His writings are frequently a revision for the publisher of a series of lectures or addresses which he had given either at the College or elsewhere throughout the Church. Also, as we have indicated earlier, he was involved in an intense controversy with the theological tendencies of his day. His writings are in fact tracts-for-the-times and therefore they bear the marks, the lop-sidedness of battle. Also, and perhaps most importantly, Forsyth was fearful of a 'system' for theological reasons. He was wary of an exposition of man's relation to God which was controlled by the essentially monistic demand of man's logic. There is a profound dualism which must be expressed, a dualism felt in the conscience which was not being properly honoured either by rationalistic orthodoxy or by modern theological Hegelianism. The freshness of his battle with these forces kept Forsyth alert to the danger of a system in theology. We shall consider these factors in detail later in our study, at this point we are interested in them only as possible explanations of the rather conversational, occasional character of Forsyth's theological writings.

Forsyth's amazing unity of perspective, his material consistency together with the occasional nature of his writings are both the hope and the despair of anyone seeking to make a systematic study and presentation of one of his doctrines. Because he is in fact one of the most single-minded, unified men to have engaged in the theological enterprise, we are led to hope for a clear understanding of this unity. And the author hopes to be able to give clear expression to it in this study. But because Forsyth never gives systematic, formal expression to this unity, the danger is always present that the student will impose forms which are not adequate to the task at hand. We have, to the best of our ability, sought to avoid forcing Forsyth's thought into a mould of our own making. Rather, we have attempted to derive the very structure of this study, as well as its material content, from the movement of Forsyth's own thought.

There is one final subject that claims our attention here. It concerns the much discussed 'style' of Forsyth's writings. He has been praised and scolded for his style, and not without good reason on both sides. His is definitely not an easy style. He was aware of this himself and from time to time attempted to make it

11

simpler, more direct. However his style stayed with him. What is it like? Its most striking characteristic is its dramatic character. This is given to it by Forsyth's rich use of suggestive words, his feeling for the parabolic, but primarily by his epigrammatic manner of expression. Often we find a long concatenation of negations followed by an equally long one of affirmations. Or we come across single affirmations alternated with negations in rapid succession, sometimes lasting for a paragraph, finally to be summed up in the most masterful of sentences. It is a proclamatory style which involves the reader's imagination and emotions as well as his intellect. It calls for slow, deep, meditative reading. The following random selection gives us a touch of what we have just mentioned:

> 'Christ did not come as a grand spiritual personality, but as the Redeemer. It was not to spiritualize us that he came but to save us. Moral verve is bound to relax if the religion of the Cross become but a hallowed addition to life's spiritual interests or touching moods, if it do not carry the stamp of moral crisis and personal decision for death or life. . . . If in the Cross we have but the greatest of love's renunciations instead of the one establishment of God's holy will, if we have but the divine Kenosis and not also the divine Plerosis, then the sense of God's presence in the Cross, and in the Church, and in the world's moral war, is bound to fade.'[18]

Granted that Forsyth's style was not simple, should this be considered a purely negative factor? Surely the question of style is not to be decided by the canon of sheer simplicity but by the adequacy of the style to give expression to what the writer is attempting to communicate. The style must be appropriate to the message. And if it be true that the New Testament reflects the impact of its Gospel upon the usual styles of the day, it is not completely strange that Forsyth should also have his style affected by the message of

12

grace which he was called to proclaim. This most certainly was the case with Forsyth. For him, God's grace met man at the centre of his personality, in the guilty conscience and not primarily in the intellect. Therefore we find him seeking to find words and a mode of expression which could do justice to the complex relation between the human conscience and the historic cross of Christ. All is not forced under the laws of simplicity and precise definition. The miracle of grace engages the whole man, thus the suggestiveness, and even the paradoxical in his style. What Forsyth wrote of St Paul could well be applied to himself: 'To express a reality so unspeakable he strained language and tortured ideas, which he enlisted from any quarter where he could lay hands on them.'[19]

Perhaps it would help us to appreciate and even to studiously admire Forsyth's style, if we knew what it cost Forsyth to place these suggestive, luxuriant, complicated sentences before us. They did not come easily to him; they are not the easy rhetoric of one who enjoyed hearing himself talk. Rather they are his sacrificial offering to us. His daughter writes:

'At these times he was wrestling with thoughts almost beyond human expression; and he wrote with a physical and nervous intensity which shook the desk, and which after an hour or two left him utterly spent, stretched out white and still upon his study couch, until the Spirit drove him back to pen and paper. Of all his enormous output, every word was written by his own hand, and corrected and re-corrected. He could never dictate—he must feel the pen, he said.'[20]

We might, in summary, characterize Forsyth's style as a *kerygmatic* style. It is faith's apprehension of grace seeking to communicate that knowledge to and for faith. It is a dialogue from person to person and from kerygma to contemporary culture. Thus it is filled with the central Biblical categories, expressed and expounded anew. Ultimately the language of the time must come under the judgement of the *kerygma*, it must become expressive of the Gospel; the reverse is impossible:

> 'I cannot conceive a Christianity to hold the future without words like grace, sin, judgement, repentance, incarnation, atonement, redemption, justification, sacrifice, faith and eternal life. No words of less volume than these can do justice to the meaning of God, however easy their access to the minds of modern men.'[21]

Perhaps it would not be entirely amiss to say that the reason some found Forsyth's style too difficult was not simply its epigrammatic and suggestive character, but that they were not willing to enter into the moral dialogue which grace demands, and to which Forsyth's writings were dedicated.

PART III

Forsyth's Critique of the Dominant Theological Tendencies of his Time

Before letting Forsyth direct our eyes to the scene around him, it might be helpful if we paused for only the briefest historical orientation to the theological scene around 1900 in England. We cannot use very effectively the older party labels—low, broad, and high church, for the scene before us shows theological tendencies or directions which criss-cross all of the party lines. We will be better aided if we simply describe the sources and some of the main leaders of each of the three major theological directions: liberal, reformation, and 'catholic.'

English liberalism, as does all liberalism, finds its deepest roots in the influence of Kant, Schleiermacher, and Hegel. It was these men who moved the seat and perhaps the very source of religious authority decisively into the inner-life of the believing subject—be it in his moral sense, in his profound sense of dependence upon and unity with the universe, or in his rational intuition. Through this the element of directness, the existential element in Christian faith, was recovered, but it also had the effect of putting man and his religious affections or intuitions into the centre of the stage instead of into a gratis, albeit front-row seat. Further and most significantly, this shift of authority away from the historical allowed for a less anxious use, even an openness to historical criticism. The Bible and Christian origins in general became the object of much critical reconstruction. This tempted and led many liberals to seek a non-historical kernel to Christianity, a kernel which changes its outer husks like clothes follow the latest style. Even the 'Jesus of history' turned out to have essentially non-historic concerns: moral principles, eternal religious insights, or the heroic or romantic actualization of ideal manhood, etc. To the subjective and historical elements in liberalism we must add moral idealism and a concern for social justice. At the turn of the century Kantian and Hegelian idealism had captured the English scene. Men such as the Cairds and Green were its powerful representatives. This, along with the naturalism stemming from Darwin's evolutionism which was being made popular by Huxley and H. G. Wells, tended to give British liberalism a strongly incarnational emphasis. The immanence of God was its central theme. This moral idealism strengthened the growing social concern of the churches in the face of the huge social problems bequeathed to the new century by the Industrial Revolution. Put all of these influences together and we get some feel for the historic ingredients of British liberalism around the turn of the century. One might say that S. T. Coleridge is the father of British theological liberalism for it was he who seemed to first

15

sense and to introduce the influence of Kant, Schleier-macher and Hegel to the English scene. He passed it on to F. D. Maurice, who passed it on to such men writing at the turn of the century as A. M. Fairbairn—a more conservative, Christocentric liberal. But there were others more extreme: one thinks of the extremes of the Modernist movement with such a man as Campbell among the Protestants or a G. Tyrell of Roman persuasion—not to mention the openly Unitarian liberalism of a James Martineau. To this local literary activity we must add the liberal writings from Germany which were in translation. Especially influential were the writings of Adolph von Harnack, the most liberal of all the Ritschlians, and the writings of the Hegelian Pfleiderer.

A much smaller group was that group of men whom we would like to refer to as Reformation theologians. This title seems appropriate, because these men, like the Reformers, sought to stand rooted in the Bible. These men came to the Bible profoundly influenced by the Reformers themselves but they did not uncritic-ally reproduce the Reformers. In addition, they were not unmindful of the contemporary scene. They sought to address modern man. However it was their concern that the message which they brought to modern man had its norm in Holy Scripture, or in the Gospel. We think of such men as James Denney, James Orr, A. B. Bruce, Marcus Dods, and somewhat later H. R. Mackintosh. In this group, though perhaps a little less conscious of the modern scene, we would include Bishop H. C. G. Moule. From Germany we think of the influence of Martin Kähler and Adolph Schlatter. It needs to be said that there were also many 'evan-gelicals' who simply reacted. They attempted a repristination of Protestant Scholasticism, and thereby isolated themselves from the contemporary scene.

Lastly we must take note of the 'catholic' tendency

at the turn of the century. Since the Romantic movement raised up the noble image of King Arthur and his
Knights of the Round Table there has also been in
England the shining image of the first Seven Ecumeni-
cal Councils, that is of an Anglican Catholic Church.
This 'catholic' tendency was itself undergoing a
liberalizing at this time. In Lux Mundi (1889) we see
the marriage of traditional Romish, dogmatic and
sacramental piety with the 'results' of the newer
Biblical criticism. Bishop Charles Gore might well
serve us as the most able representative of this position
around 1900 and on into the first third of the twentieth
century.

Such then were the ingredients and the men among
which and with whom Forsyth lived. Before him he
saw an ever-rising liberal tide, with back eddies of
Reformation, Protestant scholastic, and pre-Reforma-
tion theology.

We have said that Forsyth lived in active encounter
with the thought of his time. What he found of value
we will consider in the following chapters; here we are
concerned to see what it was in nineteenth-century
religious thought that looked dangerous to him. We
want to know why he felt it to be the most dangerous
time since Gnosticism had threatened the canonical
and early post-canonical church.[22]

His basic objection (one that underlies all of his
specific dogmatic objections) is that the theological
thought of the time was anthropocentric. It was an
expression of humanity's egocentrism more than of
God's revelation. Man, even in his religion, was preoccupied with himself and not occupied with God.

> 'There is even what we might call a racial egoism, a
> self-engrossment of mankind with itself, a naïve and tacit
> assumption that God were no God if he cared for anything
> more than he did for his creatures. We tend to think of
> God as if man were his chief end, as if he had no right to

17

a supreme concern for his own holy name, as if his prodi-
gals were more to him than his only begotten Son in whom
he made the worlds and has all his delight. We think and
worship as if the only question was whether God loves us,
instead of whether his love has absolute power to give
itself eternal and righteous effect.'[23]

'But the God of the Church's revelation is not an anthropocentric God. Heaven is not humanity glorified, even by
a God. The public is not the tribunal of the Church. The
revelation in Christ entrusted to the Church reveals God
for whom man exists, rather than man for whom God
exists. What God does for man is to replace him in
absolute obedience to God—the obedience of entire trust
and communing love. The redemption is a redemption
from all the cultures, comforts, and happinesses, into the
worship and service of the Holy One who here and now
inhabits eternity. The Church is there not in the first place
for the service of man, but for his service, witness, and
worship of the God in whose holy love alone man comes
to himself and achieves his destiny.'[24]

This, of course, does not mean that anthropocentric
thought does not speak of God, nor that man ceases to
feel a need for God. God must still act if we are to
reach our fulfilment, but

'. . . the point is that this act is not a revolution in man,
not a new creation, not a regeneration, not an absolute
redemption, but only a release, an impulse from God, the
extrication of our best, a delivery of the innate spirituality
and goodness of man with which history is in travail until
now. It is not a salvation from death but only from scanty
life. . . . He is not in a real sense, but only in a figurative
sense, our Redeemer. . . . It should be clear that this is
another religion from that of redemption; and it has no
room or need for atonement.'[25]

The deepest danger of this religious tendency is that
it resides within the Church and speaks the language
of faith, but changes the contents of the terms in the

18

process. Anthropocentrism speaks of man's relation to God, it speaks of Christ and his Cross, it speaks of God as love, and of man as worshipper, but in all of these assertions it subtly distorts as it speaks. Having a centre, not in Christ's Cross but in man, in his desires and supposed needs, such language has but an outer similarity to a true response of faith.

Primarily, it misconstrues the Cross, understanding neither grace nor sin.

'Without such a cross and its atonement we come to a religion of much point but no atmosphere, much sympathy and no imagination, much kindness and no greatness, much charm and no force. . . . Religion becomes too aesthetic, too exclusively sympathetic, too bland, too naturalistic. Our very Christmas becomes the festival of babyhood, Good Friday the worship of grief, and Easter of spring and renewal instead of regeneration.'[26]

It is precisely here, in the misconception of redemption, that Forsyth saw the Gnostic danger reappearing in the nineteenth century. Gnosticism also knew of a longing for redemption, but it was a romantic-idealistic not a moral-historic salvation; it sought a deliverance from estrangement in the world and from the material aspect of existence, not deliverance from a guilty estrangement from God into communion with him in a new heaven and a new earth. 'It moved among spiritual processes rather than moral and historic acts.'[27] This same tendency to redefine redemption in terms ultimately less personal and less historical than that of grace and guilt, Forsyth saw as constituting the heart of idealistic theology, whether in its romantic phase of intuitive spirituality or in its classical phase of philosophical dogmatism.

Having misunderstood grace, the holy love of the Cross, liberalism found it easy to speak of the fatherhood of God and the brotherhood of man as if these were simply self-evident facts to be concluded from an observation of man's nature and that of the rest of creation. For Forsyth, these were assertions of faith only to be understood in the light of an atoning Cross. The great danger Forsyth saw in the prevailing doctrine of God was not anthropomorphism, as liberalism was asserting, but rather anthropopathism.[28]

'The love of God, for instance, has been removed from its New Testament setting. It has been treated as the mere superlative of romantic love. It has been detached from the idea of propitiation with which the Apostles identify it (1 John iv, 10), and regarded as an infinite dilation of human affection. . . . Accordingly, the moral action of love has been reduced to social conduct. . . . Thought is trivialized into interests neither universal nor fundamental, neither tragic nor glorious, but just drab or humdrum; so that adequate treatment of ultimate things is dismissed by the sentimentalists as obscurity. . . . Churches are frayed into ribbons of small but kindly endeavour.'[29]

'. . . there is in the conception of God's love, and especially in the more modern gospels of it, something one-sided, something over-obvious and therefore weak. God's love is too much a matter of course, too facile in him, to arrest people. It does not make them wonder and fear. It is just paternity transfigured, maternity taken up to heaven. There is a soft and cheap strain in it which unfits it for the moral task of seizing and rearing personality in a mighty history like man's. An element has gone out of it whose absence makes half the Bible meaningless—the element of holiness, majesty, and judgement. . . . Guilt comes to be felt as a disorder in us instead of a wound to the holy majesty of God. And the cross of Christ is treated as the great means of our peace, or of harmonizing our life by the spirit of sacrifice. . . .'[30]

There were those who were willing to admit the necessity of moving beyond a general immanent revelation of God in creation; they wished to speak of a special revelation in Christ. It might even be said that there was a genuine Christocentrism among some members of the liberal movement. Forsyth pointed out that it is not simply a matter of centring in Christ but that

'... some of the most dangerous challenges of Christianity are found amongst those who claim the Christian name. There are those who have a very real reverence for the character of Jesus Christ, and they can speak, and do speak, quite sincerely, with great devotion and warmth and beauty, about Christ, and about many of the ideas that are associated with apostolic Christianity. All the same, they are strongly and sometimes even violently, antagonistic to that redemption which is the very centre of the Christian faith; and they make denials and challenges which are bound to tell upon the existence of that faith before many generations are over.'[31]

Liberalism, putting its emphasis on what Christ graciously has in common with us, overlooked, even denied the evangelical stress on where he differs.[32] And, to disregard that, according to Forsyth, is to deny the gospel. For

'When Christ did what he did, it was not human nature doing it, it was God doing it. That is the great, absolutely unique and glorious thing. It is God in Christ reconciling. It was not human nature offering its very best to God. It was God offering his very best to man. That is the grand difference between the Church and civilization, even when civilization is religious.'[33]

Forsyth was also much distressed over the contemporary view of religion. All could not have been well with the liberals' understanding of religion, i.e. man's response to God's revelation, since revelation had been practically reduced to man's own spirituality. It is an indication of Forsyth's theological perceptiveness that he was perhaps the first English theologian to have appreciated Kierkegaard. He found Kierkegaard helpful in expressing his own feelings with regard to the popular understanding of religion.

'There is a timely saying of that searching Christian genius Kierkegaard—the great and melancholy Dane in whom Hamlet was mastered by Christ:

' "For long the tactics have been: use every means to move as many as you can—to move everybody if possible —to enter Christianity. Do not be too curious whether what they enter *is* Christianity. My tactics have been, with God's help, to use every means to make it clear what the demand of Christianity really is—if not one entered it."

'The statement is extreme; but that way lies the Church's salvation—in its ante-Nicene relation to the world, its pro-Constantinian, non-established, relation to the world, and devotion to the Word. Society is hopeless except for the Church. And the Church has nothing to live on but the Cross that faces and overcomes the world. It cannot live on a cross which is on easy terms with the world as the apotheosis of all its aesthetic religion, or the classic of all its ethical intuition.'[34]

In the above quotation, there is coupled with the sharp criticism of the popular view of religion, Forsyth's opinion that the proper relation between Church and culture is that of diastasis.[35] His view is not that of complete separation,[36] but rather that of an autonomy of the Church, grounded in Christ's accomplished work which separates the Church from the culture but which, at the same time, binds the Church in evangelical service to the culture. This view Forsyth maintained in the face of the fact that many of his contemporaries, quite consistent with their pragmatic view of religion, were judging the value of the Church solely by the norm of cultural benefit. Churches were to expend their major efforts in clearing out the slums, getting proper social legislation through Parliament and other such projects; it was an attitude which Forsyth once referred to as a 'kingdom-of-Godindustry.'[37] The awareness that the works arise from faith, or as it is expressed today, that the imperative of the Gospel lies in the indicative of the Gospel, had been lost sight of. Forsyth was most concerned that the Church bear political witness in the State, but he was also concerned that the flower of faith be not mistaken for its root. To him

'... the Churches can do nothing permanent and nothing final for human welfare till the soul gets its own. The Church is not "first of all a working Church." It is a communion of saints and lovers, a company of believers, a fellowship of spiritual realists. It is there first to feed the soul with eternal reality, to stablish, strengthen, and settle the soul upon the Rock of Ages. You cannot expect ill-fed people to devise much wisdom, or do much good.'[38]

There are other aspects of the religious temper of his time that were strongly criticized by Forsyth: the individualism,[39] the naïve extension of the biological concept of evolution into areas of experience and thought where it was inadequate, over-optimistic and harmful,[40] the loss of the sense of teleology or eschatology with its centre in Christ's Cross,[41] the prevalent moralism,[42] the concern for man's freedom independent of God's freedom,[43] the anti-dogmatic trend mentioned earlier,[44] and its implied subjectivism,[45] and the other extreme of rationalism, either from the side of orthodoxy or from Hegelian idealism.[46]

There can be no doubt that such a critique of the nineteenth-century[47] theology, which Forsyth began to express as early as 1893, was truly prophetic. As J. K. Mozley so aptly stated: 'The fact is that Forsyth was eminently what the mind of his time, not the least the Christian mind, needed, but not what it wanted.'[48] It was not fundamentally the personal spiritual insight of Forsyth that gave him the ability to look about him with critical eyes; Forsyth viewed all from the vantage point of Christ's Cross as the place where God's holi-

23

ness was revealed, in judgement on sin, and as grace to man. In the following chapters it will be our task to consider in detail Forsyth's positive effort to construct a doctrine of this revelation of the Cross and to deal with his answers to the various introductory problems (prolegomena) that are related to a doctrine of revelation.

CHAPTER I

The Cross as the Fulfilment of God's Redemptive-Revealing
Action in History

THE title of this chapter offers a concise summary of the contents to be found herein. The major emphasis lies on the action of God in revelation. We feel compelled to begin with this emphasis since it corresponds to the emphases found in Forsyth's writings. The threefold division, i.e. Chapter I: God's Action in Revelation; Chapter II: God's Interpretive Word within Revelation, and Chapter III: Man's Participation in Revelation, does not imply that there is a lack of unity in Forsyth's concept of revelation. On the contrary, these three chapters are discussing a unity or, as Forsyth refers to it, 'an eternal deed' in Jesus Christ. In actuality we are discussing one event with three moments or factors in it, all of which are included in what is termed in dogmatics, 'revelation.' We shall later find occasion to discuss more specifically the interrelatedness of these factors within the divine-human event or deed of revelation.[1] At this point it should merely be made clear that the order of exposition which we have adopted stems from what, according to Forsyth, must be first emphasized.

In order to deal with God's action in revelation, we will need to see what Forsyth understands by the term 'revelation,' to see precisely what in his doctrine of God and man gives direction to God's revealing action, to examine this action which he completes in the Cross of the Son, and to place this action in its context as the fulfilment of history.

A Description of the Concept of 'Revelation' as Used by Forsyth

'Revelation then may be defined as the free, final and effective act of God's self-communication in Jesus Christ for man's redemption. It is not simply an act of manifestation, or even of impressive representation, but is a historic and eternal act of deliverance, prolonged in an infinite number of acts *ejusdem generis* in the experience by Christian people of their redemption in Christ. It is a free act as being wholly marvellous and unbought. It is a final act because it embodies, in an aforesaid sense, the whole purpose of God with man. And it is effective because it is only completed by its return on itself in man's experience and response. A sound returns void, but not a word, not a revelation. A Christ is not a Christ without a kingdom. It is, moreover, the self-communication of God, because it is not a witness to God by his closest intimate even in Eternity, but God himself at work as our Redeemer. God so loved that he gave himself in his Son; not, God was so lovely that the Son could not help giving report of it to men. . . . It is impossible to separate revelation from redemption. Revelation has no real and final meaning except as the act of redemption to the experience of being redeemed. . . .'[2]

What we need first to notice in this description of revelation is Forsyth's stress on the personal, or better, the interpersonal character of revelation. It is God, opening himself to the man whom he has called into being. This personal character stresses the directness and vitality of God's act of revelation. Here we have to do with an act of self-revelation and not with revealed truths or doctrine. Here we are concerned with God's calling his creatures into communion with himself, not with the promulgation of a doctrine that they should be, or even that they are, in communion with him. Here all monologue is rejected, for when God reveals himself it is to another—to man; there is no revelation of God apart from one who receives his self-disclosure. Likewise there can be no thought of man knowing God apart from God's opening himself to man. This is excluded not simply by man's fallen condition, but by the fact that revelation is a personal *act* of God and as such, contingent upon God's will. The very fact that revelation is described by Forsyth as an act removes us from the realm of logical speculation in which there can be no room for contingent personal action but only for necessary conclusions, and places us in the interpersonal realm of contingent self-disclosure, the realm of communion. Due to the interpersonal character of revelation, it is incorrect to say that revelation occurs when self-communication is not effected, when communion does not arise; revelation is actual as self-communication which includes both God's self-disclosure to man and man's reception, by faith, of God's self-giving.[3]

This description of revelation as God's self-communication in Jesus Christ is of the deepest significance for it strikes a blow against the intellectualizing of revelation as it had occurred in orthodoxy[4] and at the same time it rejects the immanentism of liberalism by declaring all views of Jesus as the great moral Teacher or even Prophet-God to be woefully inadequate. In Jesus Christ we do not meet one who tells us about God, but in Jesus we find ourselves confronted by God, indeed, redeemed by him.

'God in Christ is the maker of his own revelation. It was God himself that came to us in Christ; it was nothing about God, even about his eternal essence or his excellent glory. It is God that is our salvation, and not the truth about God. And what Christ came to do was not to convince us even that God is love, but to be with us and in us as the loving God for ever and ever. He came not to preach the living God but to be God our life; yes, not to preach even the loving God but to be the love that God for ever is.'[5]

The fact that Forsyth wrote this when the thought of the time was epitomized in the writings of men like Troeltsch and Harnack will suffice to indicate the reason for the great stress which Forsyth placed on this last point.[6]

Another aspect included in Forsyth's description of revelation as interpersonal is the emphasis upon God's freedom in relation to history. The freedom of God or the sovereignty of God over himself and his creation cannot be expressed in the distinction between the infinite and the finite, but only in the relationship between the Creator and the creation. Only God is completely free to reveal himself in word and deed or to conceal himself in self-reserve. In that God exercises his freedom over his revelation with respect to man, he is related by acts to history. Perhaps it will be clearer to state that history is constituted by the relationship between the free God and man his creature. It is against this background that revelation is called final,[7] that is, final as effecting God's purpose for man, as setting up, establishing the Kingdom of God which is the communion between God and man. We shall be dealing with this in more detail later in this chapter; here we simply wish to show the connexion between the interpersonal character of revelation and its finality in history. Only this personal God is free to act finally in history, to establish man's destiny by an act of self-communication in Jesus Christ.

There is in Forsyth's definition of revelation a second factor alongside its interpersonal character which deserves special mention. God's act of self-disclosure to man in Jesus Christ is at the same time a deliverance.

To be final, revelation must not simply actualize man's undisturbed destiny but it must renew that destiny. It must re-establish man in communion with God; it must re-create[8] the soul of man to receive God's holy love. For the sinful heart of man is turned from God, at enmity with him. To reveal himself to man, God must redeem man; there is no revelation apart from redemption.

> '*Dat quod jubet.* It is the power *of the Spirit* not revealing alone, but redeeming us to take in the revelation. His spirit does not seize us but lives in us. The Saviour Son is revealed in us. Christ is our life who is also our Lord. His authority is not simply an external power, but a life-giving spirit within. We are redeemed into the power to know, to be, and to do what is revealed. And both the revelation and the redemption are one and the same act.'[9]

Here we can see the seriousness of sin. If revelation only reaches its fulfilment in Jesus Christ, which means in the Cross, then redemption is integral to revelation and sin is a deadly serious obstacle lying between God and man. Man separated from God by guilt and a perverted heart, caught in the bonds of Satan, is in no position to receive God's manifestation of himself unless God in his self-giving regenerates man, forgives his sin, and destroys Satan.

Forsyth knew himself to be standing against the liberal tendency of his day when he placed such heavy emphasis upon God's *redeeming* self-communication to sinful man. But an understanding of revelation which is derived from Christ's Cross as the act of revelation, can be described by Forsyth in no other way than as '. . . the free, final and effective act of God's self-communication in Jesus Christ for man's redemption.'[10]

God the Holy Father

Having considered Forsyth's definition of revelation, we are in a position to examine his view of the act of God in Christ. Before considering the Cross as the atoning confession of God's holiness made by the Son amid the conditions of sin, we must examine Forsyth's understanding of and emphasis upon the holiness of God. It is God the Father who acts in the Son in the power of the Holy Spirit. In terms of the path of knowledge, it is true that we know the Father through the Son by the Spirit, that is, we know God through his benefits as revealed in Christ. In considering the Holy Father first, we do not wish to imply that Forsyth is interested in speculation as to what sort of being God is apart from his revelation. For Forsyth, revelation is the sole and completely sufficient path to a knowledge of God. We discuss first God the Holy Father as the internal ground for the revealing-redeeming action in the Son and when we turn to the Cross as event, we shall then deal with the work of Christ.

There is no one point at which Forsyth stood so alone as in his conscious, explicit relating of all doctrine to a fundamental understanding of God as holy. His assertions as to the centrality of holiness in God's revelation of himself and as to the nature of this holiness, completely differentiated him from the Ritschlian school in which he had started,[11] and from liberal theological thought in general. It will become apparent, however, that Forsyth is not simply reaffirming the old orthodox position. The holiness of God is revealed in God's personal action and such metaphysical discussions and elucidations of God's holiness as we find in Protestant orthodoxy fall short of the real moral earnestness which they are trying to present simply because they lose the personal and the active in the deduction of God's attributes.[12] We will be in a better position to discuss Forsyth's criticism of the orthodox position when we deal with the atonement which is made to and by God's holiness.

a—THE NATURE OF THE FATHER'S HOLINESS

The first thing that must be said is that the Biblical witness to God is of him as the holy one.[13] Only after this is said and reflected upon can we properly understand St John's statement, 'God is love,'[14] for the love of God is a holy love.[15] This means, according to Forsyth, that at the burning centre of the Godhead is his holiness. The Old and New Testaments can be referred to as 'one grand holiness movement'[16] if we think of God's holiness and not of ours. Christ was first and foremost concerned with the Father's holiness, that he should hallow the Father's name; his death was a divine requirement of the Father's holy will.[17]

'The New Testament name and idea of God is not simply "Our Father," but "the God and Father of our Lord and Saviour Jesus Christ." And Christ's own prayer was "Holy Father." That was Christ's central thought of God, and he knew God as he *is*. The new revelation in the cross was more than "God is love." It was this "Holy Father." That is, God at his divinest, as he was *to* Christ, as he was *in* Christ.'[18]

Central to the Biblical witness,[19] seen as reaching its fulfilment in the Cross and resurrection of Christ, is the Holy Father, God as the Holy One. We must seek to gain a clearer understanding of what he means by the term 'holy' or 'holiness.'

'In the Bible, things, or places, or people are holy which are set apart for God; God is holy as he is set apart for himself. Things are holy as they are for God; he is holy as he is for himself. We are holy as belonging to him; he is

31

holy as belonging to himself, as absolute possessor of himself, by gift of none. . . . For the creature to be holy is *to be for God*; for God himself to be holy is *to be God*. His holiness is the complete accord of his will and his nature. It is not an attribute of God; it is his name, and being, and infinite value. But if the holiness do not go out to cover, imbue, conquer, and sanctify all things, if it do not give itself in love, it is the less holy. It is but partial and not absolute. As holy he must subdue all and bless all. God's holiness is the fundamental principle not of our worship only, but of his whole saving revelation and economy of love. It is the moral principle of both love and grace. It is love's content, it is what love brings or grace gives. . . . For only the holy can love for ever and for ever subdue the loveless; only the holy can thoroughly forgive so as to make his holiness dear.'[20]

The reader will have observed that we cannot discuss holiness without discussing its relationship to the entire movement of God toward man. This is true not only because we know holiness only in our relation to God, but because it is the holiness of God which is the foundation of this movement of God to man. 'Love is but its outgoing; sin is but its defiance; grace is but its action on sin; the cross is but its victory; faith is but its worship.'[21]

There are certain aspects in the above description of holiness which deserve our special consideration, particularly since a misunderstanding of Forsyth at this point will hamper our appreciation of his thought as we continue our study.

We note that the Biblical idea of 'separation,' or of God's transcendence is included and emphasized. Persons, places, and things are holy only in relation to him who in himself *is* holy. But it is inadequate to stop at this (as we know from Old Testament prophecy) for the ground and activeness, the personalness of God's transcendence is not yet in view. It would be all too easy to think in merely quantitative terms[22] if we

32

did not go on to speak of the personal, the moral *foundation* of this transcendence. God has revealed himself as the Lord, the Creator, and not as the absolute and the infinite. Forsyth refers to this by saying that God's holiness is the complete accord of his will and nature, that is to say, God's transcendence is not simply a static 'isness' but it is willed by God. God actively embraces his own nature; God is separate, exalted as Creator because he willed to create and because he wills that this particular separateness, this transcendence-immanence[23] be maintained. He *is* and remains the Lord of his people, the heavens and the earth, because he *wills* to be Lord and to have a people, a heaven and an earth.

At another point, Forsyth emphasizes this moral foundation by saying that God's holiness is the self-satisfaction of his own conscience.[24] This statement, of course, points us in the direction of the doctrines of the Trinity and the Atonement for it is the Son in whom the Father is well pleased, both eternally and in his atoning, satisfying life on earth.[25] This use of 'conscience' is, as far as the writer knows, unique to Forsyth. He uses it to shed light on the meaning of God's holiness in two ways. He asks us to remind ourselves that it is in our conscience that we are aware of standing under the claim of a universal, moral order. He goes on to say that faith's moral claim on us is

'God as self-complete and absolute moral personality, the universal and eternal holy God whose sufficiency is of himself, the self-contained, and self-determined moral reality of the universe, for which all things work together in a supreme *concursus*, which must endure if all else fail, and must be secured at any cost beside.'[26]

Forsyth is saying the same thing when he refers to the holiness of God as 'the whole concrete righteousness of existence,'[27] as 'absolute moral and personal

33

energy,'[28] and when he says, 'The holy law is not the creation of God but his nature, and . . . it cannot be denied or simply annulled unless he seem false to himself.'[29] In this usage of the term 'conscience' Forsyth is saying that the claim God makes upon us in revelation shows him to be 'absolute moral personality'; he is our Lord not simply by might but by right; indeed, he is the source of right. This leads to Forsyth's second usage of the term 'conscience' in connexion with God's holiness. It was referred to briefly above. Forsyth speaks of the 'conscience of God.' Here the stress is on God's faithfulness to himself, to his absolute possession of himself, to the utter seriousness with which God regards himself. To God's conscience there comes no claim from beyond, but his own claim upon himself, his self-determination. It becomes clear that we cannot picture God's love, *agape*, as selfless love, as forgetfulness of self in the service of his creation as it was being preached all around Forsyth, for God exists in the very act of self-regard, self-determination.[30] We creatures can lose ourselves in the love of God and neighbour, only to *find* ourselves precisely because we truly exist in such loving relationships. We are dependent but God exists truly in himself as absolute possessor of himself.

We can summarize Forsyth's view of God's holiness as follows: God is holy in his personal action of self-determination; it is from his self-determination that he freely wills to bring into being a creation and there stands over against his creatures an absolute, objective, moral claim which is nothing else than the personal Lordship of God over his creation. Or shorter still, the holiness of God is his absolute moral personality; God is holy.

Excursus: THE HOLY AND MORALITY

Before we consider the movement of holiness out of

34

itself, which is love or holy love, we must clarify the distinction which Forsyth makes between the Holy and Morality. To miss this distinction would lead the reader of Forsyth into a drastic misunderstanding, a de-personalizing and Kantianizing of his thought.

The danger of misunderstanding Forsyth at this point is increased by Forsyth himself, for he does from time to time use the terms 'moral' or 'the moral' as synonyms for 'the holy.' However, close attention to the context will make it clear that he is referring to the holy in most cases and not to morality.

Forsyth's understanding of the holy is such that the holy is deeper than, and yet the foundation of, morality. Holiness makes a total claim upon man, claiming all that he is, thinks, feels and does. God as the holy claims man's self in all its modes and expressions of existence and, as such, he demands man's conduct. The response to the holy God is the obedience of faith[31] and this obedience is a determination of man's whole existence and thereby also his conduct. Forsyth puts the relationship in the following manner:

'It (the religion that answers the Christian revelation) is one compendious act, into which the whole personality goes, responsive in kind to the one eternal act in which the whole person of the Revealer takes standing effect as Redeemer. All the best history of the Church was latent in the act of its salvation; and all the best in personal history and character lies hid in the act of faith wherein we pass from death to life.'[32]

Forsyth illustrates this distinction between holiness and morality with reference to justice. In the face of injustice, justice calls for penalty, for satisfaction, whereas holiness in the face of sin calls for a confession of holiness; that is, holiness calls for a positive appreciation of its own nature, for reverence amid the penalty and thus for a sharing of the burden of sin and not just shame.[33]

35

It will help to understand Forsyth at this point if we recall that God is the holy and that deeper than the morality of man is the moral or personal relation of man to God. Morality can be conceived of as impersonal, i.e. as conduct with regard to social norms, or self-given moral laws; but the holy demands and calls forth personal communion and this gives rise to a morality of interpersonal obedience out of the whole being.

It is important to keep this distinction in mind as we proceed with our study of Forsyth if we do not wish to reduce his deep voluntarism to shallow moralism.

b—THE HOLY LOVE OF GOD

The fact that we have first considered the nature of holiness and now come to examine its expression as holy love, is a witness to Forsyth's emphasis that God's love is unique. It is his love, differing from that of man who is both creature and fallen creature, which can only be understood as an expression of his holy self. Forsyth wrote at a time when the general tendency was to absolutize human love and to make it the norm under which God himself must stand. Indeed, Forsyth saw the tendency to subordinate holiness to love as the basic tendency of all aestheticism.[34] He opposed such anthropocentrism by a positive stress on the *holy* love of God:

'It is not enough to say that the Kingdom of God is identical with the spirit of sonship. For that might be compatible with a conception of fatherhood which eliminates all the holy majesty of love that was most distinctive of fatherhood in Christ's mind. His father was the Father in Heaven in such a sense that the whole prayer that so invokes him is preoccupied with his *kingdom*. It is remarkable that Christ, who spoke so incessantly of the Father, spoke no less incessantly of his kingdom and not of his family. . . . That means that the vital thing in father-hood for Christ was that holiness which made the Father royal. . . . That is to say, it was not a relation of love simply, but of love holy and yet gracious—which combination is a great miracle. The father in heaven meant for Christ the Holy Father. The sonship is the sonship of *holy* love. That is to say, the moral element in the love was of its essence, the ruling element and not only the sympathetic —thou *shalt* love.'[35]

We must first consider the inherent unity of holiness and love in God's love which is holy love. And before we turn to a second consideration, i.e. holy love in relation to its recipient, fallen man, we shall need to make a short excursus into Forsyth's theo-anthropology so that his understanding of sin is clear to us. We shall limit our remarks, however, for we will deal with the social nature of sin in the last section of this chapter when we consider God's revealing-redeeming act in Jesus Christ in the context of the fulfilment of God's action in history.

1. *Holiness and Love as a Unity in God's Holy Love*

We have quoted Forsyth above as saying, 'But if the holiness do not go out to cover, imbue, conquer, and sanctify all things, if it do not give itself in love, it is less than holy'[36] and 'Love is but its outgoing. . . .'[37] This means that love is the Holy One giving himself (as holy) into communion. Speaking in Trinitarian terms, this would mean that the Holy One wills to be and is in communion with himself, but the above quotation is obviously referring to a movement of holiness which proceeds from the Godhead outward. Here creation, and in particular, man who is created for communion with God, finds its place.[38] Holy love is God's movement toward his creature for the purpose of communion. Indeed, we must go further; it is God's successful, his free and sovereign movement to his

37

creature. Forsyth never wearies of telling us that the firm, the necessary, the triumphant element in God's love is its holiness. The steadiness of God's absolute moral personality, his personal determination to have communion with man, and his faithfulness to himself, is the rock on which our communion with him is founded.

> '... and it is only because he is holy that his Fatherhood is inexhaustible and our loves endure. Holiness is that in the love of God which fixes it and assures it for ever. If holiness fail not, then love cannot. If it cannot be put by, then love cannot fade.'[39]

Thus we might say that Forsyth stresses the theocentric character of God's love in opposition to the tendency around him to speak anthropocentrically by looking to man in his beauty and his need to be both the attraction of and the model of the 'divine' love.[40]

2. Holy Love as Grace to the Sinner

> 'God's holiness is the fundamental principle not of our worship only, but of his whole saving revelation and economy of love ... it is what love brings or grace gives. ... For only the holy can love for ever and for ever subdue the loveless; only the holy can thoroughly forgive so as to make his holiness dear.'[41]

The words 'saving,' 'subdue,' 'loveless,' 'forgive,' make us aware that when God in the act of revelation gives himself to his creature and calls the creature into communion with himself, there is rejection which has been overcome. What is this mysterious rejection on the part of God and man? What is involved in the action of holy love that it, in the form of grace or forgiveness, overcomes this rejection?

Excursus: SIN

Forsyth repudiates any attempt to discuss sin apart from its absolutely antagonistic relation to God.[42]

38

'God is fundamentally affected by sin. He is stung and to the core. It does not simply try him. It challenges his whole place in the moral world. It puts him on his trial as God. It is, in its nature, an assault on his life. Its total object is to unseat him. It has no part whatever in his purpose. It hates and kills him. It is his total negation and death. It is not his other but an other. It is the one thing in the world that lies outside reconciliation, whether you mean by that the process or the act. It cannot be taken up into the supreme unity. It can only be destroyed. It drives him not merely to action but to a passion of action, to action for his life, to action in suffering unto death.'[43]

Of what does this 'sin' consist which is enmity, antagonism to God? It is personal transgression and a state of guilt.

'There are many who recognize the power of sin, the misfortune of it; what they do not recognize is the thing that makes it most sinful, which makes it what it is before God, namely, guilt; which introduces something noxious and not merely deranged, malignant and not merely hostile; the fact that it is transgression against not simply God, not simply against a loving God, but against a holy God. Everything begins and ends in our Christian theology with the holiness of God.'[44]

We need to be careful at this point to notice Forsyth's emphasis on the personal. There can be no talk of God's hating the sin and loving the sinner. Forsyth refers to this as a 'meaningless phrase and a psychological anomaly. It separates sin from a sinning personality. . . .'[45] As an act of the whole person of man against the claim of the holiness (the whole moral person) of God, it goes deeper than conduct; '. . . it alters things for both parties. Guilt affected both God and man.'[46] Man, as sinner, stands in a personal relationship with God which can only be described in terms of rebellion, antagonism, and guilt. Sin is the rejection by the creature of God's movement toward

39

him in holy love, a rejection of God's holy purpose of communion. Forsyth can express the essence of sin thus: 'The nerve and marrow of sin was the rejection of Christ, because he was the nerve and marrow of the righteousness of God' or again, 'Sin, you note, is not measured by a law, or a nation, or a society of any kind but by a Person. . . . The essence of sin is exposed by the touchstone of his presence, by our attitude to him.'[47] Such statements are to be understood only when we understand Jesus Christ as the holy God's loving movement to man. Sin then consists of man's attitude to God's holy, loving presence; it is the personal guilt of a rebellious relationship. It is to live in active rejection of the Lord. And precisely because this personal rejection is against the very communion and person of God, the holy Lord whose claim is righteous, sin must be described as guilt.

> 'Sin is not, as the Greek idea of it goes, infection with a moral microbe . . . nor is sin, as the medieval idea, mere distance from God. It is what the Reformers declared it to be, guilt.'[48]

This guilt which is sin, is not equated by Forsyth with the empirical guilty conscience, with a *sense* of guilt. We note first that Forsyth has been referring to guilt as a relationship, as independent of one's sense of guilt. Secondly, Forsyth makes himself quite clear that he believes that it is only in revelation, in the act of being redeemed, in being drawn into communion with God through his saving revelation, that the sinner learns that he is a sinner and of the utter horror of sin. Apart from revelation, man is a blind sinner, blinded by the very sin in which he lives and which he does.[49]

> 'We can never know things at their worst till we stand where they are at their best. The worst of it is our sin; and that we can never realize till we have got the better of it in Christ, till we have made the best of it in God.

It is only as we share the redemption of Christ that we know what redemption is. Nor can we know that without gaining thereby a due knowledge of the horror from which we are redeemed. The moral horror of sin is more horrible than the extremes of suffering; and the disorder of it is more dismal than the aimless welter of a world that simply blunders upon mishap. There is much to appal the imagination in the spectacle of a stumbling universe which has hopelessly missed the happy way. There is plenty there to fascinate the genius of tragedy and the morality of compassion. But more terrible than a blundering universe is a will which has taken evil for its good, and more inveterate than ancient error is ingrained sin. And how inveterate it is, and how terrible, can be known to none but him who has overcome it, and in whom we are more than conquerors.'[50]

* * *

Keeping in mind the material of the excursus, we now return to our theme of holy love as grace. In the light of sin, God's holy love must establish itself as grace. For

'God's love then is love in holy action, in forgiveness, in redemption. It is the love for sinners of a God above all things *holy*, whose holiness makes sin damnable as sin and love active as grace. It can only act in a way that shall do justice to holiness, and restore it.'[51]

Here God's holiness stands in no contradiction to his grace, but the very opposite is true. It is the holiness of God which, in the face of sin, requires both the judgement of sin and the fulfilment of God's movement toward his creatures in holy love.

The following words of Forsyth serve to expand the phrase 'holiness makes . . . love active as grace' which we quoted earlier. He states:

'Grace was not an infusion of vital substance or supernal influence, but it was a relation of active persons . . .; it was the gracious will of the God of love acting on the soul . . . as a felt forgiveness and a power for goodness.'[52]

There has been a tendency in the sacramental thought of Roman Catholicism to objectify grace;[53] Forsyth shows that grace is the movement of the God of holy love in reaction to the personal act of sin against him. Therefore, grace is only to be understood as God's personal action in the face of sin.

We cannot, however, continue our discussion of grace in the abstract; for grace is not an abstract principle but God's act in Jesus Christ. Holy love works, acts, redeems in the Cross of Jesus Christ. It is he 'in whom the holiness goes out as love, suffers the judgement, and redeems as grace.'[54] To become more specific about grace, we must now turn to Forsyth's exposition of the Cross as God's gracious deed of revelation in Jesus Christ.

PART II

The Obedient Son—Jesus Christ

Forsyth sees the Cross most comprehensively as God's act of reconciliation. We have seen that God, who is holy love, must, if he be true to himself, act so as to destroy sin and establish loving communion with his creatures. The same holiness that demands the destruction of sin, demands that God receive the glory that is his. Man is able to give God the glory only as he responds in loving obedience to God's lordship; for such a response is the only one which adequately glorifies God as he is: the God of holy love. Thus the terrible situation called into being by sin demands that reconciliation be effected by God. A reconciliation, however, which deals with both parties in the relationship is called for. God must reconcile himself as well as man. Within God's act of reconciliation, Forsyth deals with the redemptive, the atoning and the regenerative aspects of Christ's work on the Cross.

The order of exposition which we shall follow in this

section is this: first, we shall examine more closely what Forsyth means by reconciliation; then we shall see what significance he attaches to each of the aspects of the Cross as mentioned above; and then we shall conclude this section with Forsyth's view of their interrelatedness.

a—CHRIST'S RECONCILIATION

Forsyth very conveniently summarizes for us the major considerations which he feels are necessary for a proper understanding of Christ's reconciling work.

> 'I place on the board before you five points as to Christ's reconciling work which I think vital:
> 1. It is between person and person.
> 2. Therefore it affects both sides.
> 3. It rests on atonement.
> 4. It is a reconciliation of the world as one whole.
> 5. It is final in its nature and effect.'[55]

The first two points belong together, i.e. the personal and therefore the mutual nature of reconciliation. The mutuality must not be confused with a synergistic type of mutuality in which man shares in his atonement. To be sure, Forsyth stresses that man is involved in reconciliation, and actively so, in response to what God has done and is doing in Jesus Christ, but this active response is not the ground of our reconciliation in any way.

> 'Now, let us own at the outset that the first things we must be sure about are the objective reality of our religion, its finality, and its initiative in God's free grace independent of act or desert of ours.'[56]

Having assured us that reconciliation has its beginning and sufficient ground in God himself, Forsyth can speak of the deep mutuality that is involved in the reconciliation between God and man.

43

'Bygones are actually explained and adjusted, they are not merely avoided or forgotten. Respect is superseded by love. . . . And there is a communion of spirit with spirit, and heart with heart, which binds the two parties in a bond more deep, lasting, and sacred than anything which held them before . . . they come to understand each other's heart and thought.'[57]

By the phrase, 'affects both sides,' Forsyth is further asserting, against the prevailing liberal view around him, that both parties (God as well as man) had need to be reconciled.

' "God was in Christ reconciling the world unto himself." As we are both living persons, that means that there was reconciliation on God's side as well as ours; but wherever it was, it was effected by God himself in himself.'[58]

This reconciliation of God by himself in himself is, in effect, point three above—the atonement.[59] We shall consider that in detail when we examine the three aspects of Christ's reconciling work on the Cross. Here it is only necessary to draw attention to the fact that it is God himself who is active in Christ. Forsyth will allow no thought that the Son could be more gracious than the Father.

'I said that the work of Christ meant not only an action on man, it meant an action on God. Yet I pointed out that it was more false than true to say that Christ and his death reconciled God to man. I said that we must in some way construe the matter as God reconciling himself. . . .'[60]

The last two points listed by Forsyth refer to the race-wide and the final nature of the reconciliation. These will be discussed as we consider the Cross in its teleological or historical context. The following statement by Forsyth will suffice at this point to show their connexion to reconciliation.

'Reconciliation was finished in Christ's death. Paul did

not preach a gradual reconciliation. He preached what the old divines used to call the finished work. He did not preach a gradual reconciliation which was to become the reconciliation of the world only piecemeal, as men were induced to accept it, or were affected by the Gospel. He preached something done once for all—a reconciliation which is the base of every soul's reconcilement, not an invitation only. What the Church has to do is to appropriate the thing that has been finally and universally done. We have to enter upon the reconciled position, on the new creation.'[61]

b—CHRIST'S THREEFOLD WORK ON THE CROSS

According to Forsyth's understanding, Christ on the Cross did a work of threefold significance, in order to bring about the reconciliation of God and man. He lists them in the following manner:

'There are three great aspects of the work of Christ which have in turn held the attention of the Church, and come home with special force to its spiritual situation at a special time. These are:
1. Its triumphant aspect;
2. Its satisfactionary aspect;
3. Its regenerative aspect.

The first emphasizes the finality of our Lord's victory over the evil power or devil; the second, the finality of his satisfaction, expiation, or atonement presented to the holy power of God; and the third the finality of his sanctifying or new-creative influence on the soul of man. The first marked the Early Church, the second the Medieval and Reformation Church, while the third marks the Modern Church.'[62]

1. The Triumphant Aspect of the Cross

The first aspect, *Christus Victor*, the triumphant aspect, was being ignored by Forsyth's contemporaries, for it was felt that it was irrelevant. 'Their belief in Christ is impaired for want of a belief in the Satan that

Christ felt it his supreme conflict to counter-work and destroy.'[63] This, of course, is to be expected from those whose eyes are not opened, who are still blinded by sin, but it represents a serious omission on the part of a Christian theologian. There is something very basic indicated when we call Christ our redeemer; there is included therein a confession to our having been enslaved, caught, helpless, lost. Forsyth states it as follows:

'Christ was little moved by a religion of moral excellence, such as many a Pharisee successfully pursued. He was all for a religion of salvation, in which the penitent went for more than the excellent. . . . God is not the world's greatest asset but its eternal Lord.'[64]

Faith knows of a broader triumph than only that of man's deliverance from the power of Satan.[65] 'Faith looks for a moral renovation not of the soul only but of the world, and it looks for it by redemptive catastrophe.'[66] This cosmic and historic perspective Forsyth finds fulfilled in principle in Christ's Cross, for:

'To treat the Cross as only priestly, and for single souls, is to lose power out of it. . . . It was priestly, but it was still more kingly, and therefore social and justiciary. . . . He died as King—he said he did—taking order for the Kingdom and its righteousness in the world . . . (fulfilling) his concern with history, with men in nations and realms.'[67]

We see that redemption points to Forsyth's view of history which we shall consider in part three of this chapter.

2. *The Satisfactionary Aspect of the Cross*

The second aspect of Christ's work on the Cross is referred to as its 'satisfactionary aspect.'[68] One of Forsyth's major emphases is that the work of Christ on the Cross[69] cannot be understood apart from its Godward action. Forsyth at one point, quite powerfully and

46

most simply, refers to the heart of the atonement as a prayer, that is, a dealing with God.[70] What we must learn from Forsyth is precisely what it is that constitutes Christ's dealing with God on the Cross and, further, what its value was to God. To do this we shall need to consider Forsyth's understanding of judgement, of sacrifice, and of Christ as our substitute and representative.

(a) *Judgement*—When Forsyth speaks of judgement, he is referring to God's judgement as accomplished in, and on the ground of, the Cross. The first thing which we should note with respect to this judgement is that it is good news. God's judgement is the destruction of sin, judged not in the sinner but in Christ.

> 'But as the second Adam and Man of men he attracts, accepts and absorbs in himself his own holy judgement; and he bears, in man and for man, the double crisis and agony of his own two-edged vision of purity and guilt.'[71]

Secondly, it is good news because it stems from God's holiness and re-establishes his holiness.

> 'Holiness and judgement are for ever inseparable. . . . God must either punish sin or expiate it, for the sake of his infrangibly holy nature. . . . And he chose the latter course, as honouring the law while saving the guilty. He took his own judgement. It was a course that produced more than all the effect of punishment, and in a better, holier way. It was vindicative and not vindictive. It re-established the holiness. . . . Expiation, therefore, is the very opposite of exacting punishment; it is assuming it.'[72]

Forsyth thereby places great emphasis upon judgement as the 'establishing and the securing of eternal righteousness and holiness. View punishment as an indirect and collateral necessity, like the surgical pains that make room for nature's curing power.'[73] Thus Forsyth changes the emphasis from judgement as punishment to judgement as the wrath[74] of God wiping out sin

47

and establishing holiness; or, as we have noted earlier, re-establishing man in communion with the God of holy love. Judgement is truly good news.

Thirdly, we note that God's judgement is personal action and also that in the Cross it is final judgement. Forsyth laid great stress on both the personal or contingent character of God's judgement and upon the fact of its finality in the Cross. Judgement is God's personal action; it is not a legal process. Judgement is God at work among men, judging, actively putting things right by his mighty deeds which find their fulfilment in the Cross.[75] As to the finality of the Cross (Forsyth refers to the Cross as the final judgement), this is best discussed in relation to Forsyth's view of history which we do later in this chapter. At this point it is sufficient to say that the judgement now actual in history is but a function of the Cross in which the destiny of the human race and of Satan was finally fixed.

We might summarize Forsyth's view of the judicial aspect of the atonement by pointing to the necessity[76] in God for a final act of judgement. In the face of sin, God's moral nature requires both a destruction of sin and a re-establishment of holiness, of his holy will for his creation. The good news of judgement is that God has chosen to destroy sin and hallow his name in such a way that man is re-established in communion with him. Forsyth states it in this manner:

'Judgement is not primarily punishment, nor is it a mere declaration of the state of the law, but it is the actual final establishment of righteousness upon the wreck of sin. The stroke of sin upon sanctity can only evoke judgement, which by the grace of Christ becomes salvation.'[77]

(b) Sacrifice—Christ's work was sacrificial. In this aspect of the atonement Forsyth sees its Godward movement. At this point we find Forsyth to be most original in his insight and exposition. His understanding of Christ's sacrifice is directly related to his understanding of God's judgement. The heart of Christ's sacrifice is his approving appreciation and joyful acceptance of God's judgement upon sin in himself. The sacrifice of Christ was this confession of God's holiness.

Such a view of sacrifice is so unusual and we have stated it so cryptically that, in order to appreciate his exposition, we must examine just how Forsyth came to this understanding of Christ's sacrifice.

First we must see why sacrifice is called confession. This becomes clear when we see that Forsyth understands the essence of Biblical sacrifice to lie not in the cultic action *per se*, but in man's obedience to God's will by obediently using the means of reconciliation which God has provided. The heart of sacrifice in Scripture lies in man's offering his will, in his obedient response to grace:

'... nowhere in the Old Testament does the value of the sacrificial blood lie in the blood itself. Nor does it lie in the suffering that might go with bloodshed. Nor does the final value lie even in the life symbolized by the blood, rich as we shall see that idea to be. We go behind and above even that to the obedience of faith answering God's will of grace.'[78]

The essence of sacrifice, therefore, is faith; the total self-giving of man in response to the Holy One's grace, his provision and claim.[79]

We have traced Forsyth's line of thought to the point where we have seen that faithful obedience is the heart of sacrifice. Now we must see how it is that Christ's faithful obedience unto death, his acceptance of the Cross, is the 'confession' of God's holiness which satisfies God. The connexion lies in the fact that the Cross is both God's judgement upon sin and man's confession of the holiness of God. In fact, man confesses God's holiness precisely in his acceptance of the Cross. This connexion becomes clearer when we understand the distinction Forsyth makes between the claim of holiness and that of honour. Holiness requires not simply a confession of proper respect as does honour, but the confession by man of a total, reverent recognition of the rightness and goodness of God's claim on his creation. Holiness demands a doxology. In relation to man in a sinful world and to God's judgement upon sin, this means that the confession of God's holiness must include a full appreciation and joyful acceptance of God's judgement upon sin in man. Jesus Christ accepted the Cross in just this willing, joyful, appreciative spirit; he, as man, thereby confessed God's holiness in a way well pleasing to the Father.[80]

The heart of Christ's confession of God's holiness lay, as we have seen, in the doxological spirit with which Christ accepted the Cross. The Cross, his act of obedience unto death, was the necessary mode of this confession. No confession by word would suffice, for man must confess God's holiness under the conditions of sin and death as judgement. As sin is an act of the whole man unto death, so must Christ confess God in a total act through death unto life:

'. . . it must be a practical confession, as practical as the sin. It must place itself as if it were active sin under the reaction of the divine holiness; . . . he bore this curse as God's judgement, praised it, hallowed it, absorbed it; and his resurrection showed that he exhausted it.'[81]

It is important to note that only the Son was in a position to make this 'confession,' for he alone possessed the 'two-edged vision of purity and guilt'[82] which perceived the Father's will in this judgement and rejoiced to see it come. Only Christ, the sinless one, was not blinded by sin; only he could see the ugliness of its guilt, the horror of its attack on God. Only he could rejoice to take the destruction of sin on himself, for only he is the Son of holy love, one with the Father.[83] Thus, in Christ's joyous acceptance of the Father's judgement, we have holiness answering holiness. We have man praising God for being the Holy One, no matter what this praising, this 'hallowing' entail. We have the fulfilment of the divine will for holy communion between God and man. We have man's justification of God in the Son. In Jesus Christ, man justifies, or glorifies God, but in such a manner that it is God's self-justification.

This leads us to the complementary aspect of Forsyth's understanding of sacrifice as part of the atonement. We have, in the discussion of man's confession of God's holiness given by Jesus Christ, stressed that the sacrifice or the confession was made by the *incarnate* Son, by man. Now we must emphasize that Christ's sacrifice is at the same time God's self-sacrifice to his own holy nature and person. '. . . in Christianity, atonement has meaning and value only as offered by God to himself.'[84]

What is the value and meaning which Forsyth sees in this aspect of the Cross? It is the *sola gratia* of the Cross, of the atonement, that is involved. Forsyth expresses this in two ways. He refers to this as being the objective aspect of the atonement and he refers to it as being the synthetic aspect of the atonement.

By 'objective' Forsyth means that atonement was done *extra nos*, that is, by God himself. God is satisfied, not apart from man for he is satisfied in man, but the objectivity lies in its being done by God in man. 'God is met with a love equally holy—a love, therefore, not rendered by sinful man, but by a function of his own love in man; . . .'[85] This objectivity is the rock on which man can stand, the fountain of grace that lies in God and in no sense in man himself.[86]

The second way in which Forsyth stresses God's action in the atonement is to point to the 'new thing' done which could not be done by sinful man. It is the self-atonement of God in Christ which has placed us in communion with him. It is *sola gratia*.

> 'It is the unique idea of atonement that makes the difference, God's atonement of himself in Christ. It is that which effects a communion so spiritual between God and his people, and between the people who live by it and in it. A revelation of atonement is a revelation really synthetic, i.e. it sets up a new relation; it is not merely analytic, i.e. expounding a standing relation. . . . It puts us together, the holy and the guilty, it does not show us how much closer we were than we thought.'[87]

We can summarize the sacrificial aspect of the atonement by saying that, in Christ, we have God in man, confessing and hallowing his holy name upon the Cross.

(c) *Substitution*—If we lay such stress, as we must, upon the self-wrought atonement of God, we are driven to ask: 'In what way was I involved in that act?' 'How is Christ related to me so that my sins are atoned?' Forsyth answers:

> 'Atonement is substitutionary, else it is none. . . . We may replace the word substitution by representation or identification, but the thing remains. Christ not only represents God to man but man to God. . . . Yet if the Sinless was judged it was not his own judgement he bore, but ours. It was not simply on our behalf, but in our stead—yet not quantitatively, but centrally.'[88]

Forsyth finds the most helpful key for understanding how we were involved in Christ's sacrifice in terms of our 'being in Christ.' Being in Christ does not mean that we are in him through our human nature, in some platonic sense of the word (i.e. Christ became 'Man' and since I am a man, I share in Christ). This

52

way of thinking is too amoral, too substantial to be adequate to the personal note which we have seen all through Forsyth's thought and in his understanding of Scripture. He sees an interpersonal or moral way in which we are involved in Christ's 'confession.'

> 'The thing of price done by Christ for God, must it not already include the thing done upon men? Does not Christ's confession of God's holiness include man's confession of his sin? . . . His offering of a holy obedience to God's judgement is therefore valuable to God for us just because of that moral solidarity with us which also makes him such a moral power upon us and in us. His creative regenerative action on us is a part of that same moral solidarity which also makes his acceptance of judgement stand to our good, and his confession of God's holiness to be the ground of ours. The same stroke on the one Christ went upward to God's heart and downward to ours. . . . Repentance is certainly a condition of forgiveness. But Christ could not repent. How then could he perfectly meet the conditions of salvation? The answer is that our repentance was latent in that holiness of his which alone could and must create it. . . . In presenting himself he offers implicitly and proleptically the new humanity his holy work creates. . . . He represents before God not a natural humanity that produces him as its spiritual classic, but the new penitent humanity that his influence creates.'[89]

We have quoted Forsyth on this topic at length for two reasons: firstly, this understanding of 'being in Christ' is typical of his interpersonal or moral approach to dogma which will appear in different connexions throughout our study and, secondly, because this understanding of the Cross is unique. Forsyth places the work of Christ and the work of the Spirit in the believer in a much more intimate, integral relationship than is usual in dogmatic theology.

We understand Forsyth to mean the following: Christ is our substitute in that he bore the judgement of sin which was ours and Christ is at the same time our representative in that his 'confession' of God's holiness is the gracious foundation or cause of our confession of God's holiness, i.e. our repentance and acceptance of grace. Christ could not, and did not, repent, which is a condition of our acceptance before God, but in his 'confession' he acted in such a way as to ensure our repentance. In fact, because our repentance is not our work but a response to grace, an aspect of faith, Forsyth can say that in his confession, Christ offered to God the faithful response of the men and women of the new humanity. He, while on the Cross, offered us, the children _ grace, proleptically to the Father.

So it is that Forsyth includes both the work of Christ on the Cross and of Christ the Spirit in the heart, in one work of grace. It is in this light that we shall come to hear Forsyth refer to the Cross as the 'eternal deed' of the Cross and to the 'Holy Spirit of the Cross.'

We have now examined all of the points which Forsyth presented in relation to the atoning aspect of the Cross. We have referred to the judicial, sacrificial and substitutional-representative elements which Forsyth includes as part of the atonement. While no short summary will serve to cover all that we have discussed, the following will serve to keep the main points before us. Atonement is that act of God in Christ whereby he judges sin unto destruction and satisfies his own holy nature in the sacrifice of the Son, doing this in such a way that man is placed again in communion with himself as a penitent recipient of grace.

We must now continue to our consideration of the third aspect of Christ's work on the Cross, the regenerative. We shall find that, as we consider the interrelatedness of these three aspects of Christ's work, each aspect will become clearer to us as we see it in its proper and complete setting.

3. The Regenerative Aspect of the Cross

What we have to say in this section is not essentially different from but rather a development of that which we considered under the representative element in Christ's work on the Cross. Forsyth places it as a separate aspect of Christ's work on the Cross in order to underline the fact that the work of the Spirit in men is a function of the Cross. If, in our discussion of Christ as our substitute, we laid emphasis upon his confession given under the conditions of sin and wrath which belonged to us, in this section we accent the response in us which his confession evokes. Here Forsyth emphasizes the fact that *our* confession really is included in Christ's, proleptically, and that it is a confession of repentance.

It remains for us in this section only to underline Forsyth's conviction that a repentant confession by the individual members of the new humanity of the Cross, is a necessity. That this confession is part of *Christ's* work in us, that is, that the *sola gratia* is preserved, we have already noted.

Forsyth first points out that even if we could not confess God's holiness due to our blindness and rebellion in sin, there does remain a confession which only we can confess:

'There is that in guilt which can only be confessed by the guilty. "I did it." That kind of confession Christ could never make That is the part of the confession that we make, and .ve cannot make it effectually until we are in union with Christ and his great lone work of perfectly and practically confessing the holiness of God. There is a racial confession that can only be made by the holy; and there is a personal confession that can only be made by the guilty.'[90]

Secondly, Forsyth points out that the end of Christ's work, reconciliation, or personal communion between God and man, calls for a repentance on the part of

55

man. Living communion with God can take place only when man's participation is that of thankful repentance. The holy nature of God expressed as his redemptive passion finds its satisfaction in the penitent return of the prodigal.

> '. . . the effect of that vicarious and loving sacrifice on men must bring them to a repentance and reconciliation which was the one thing that God's gracious love required for restored communion and complete forgiveness. He could now deal with them as he had felt from before the foundation of the world. It satisfied the claim and harmony of his holy nature, and it satisfied the redemptive passion of his gracious heart.'[91]

What Forsyth means by the regenerative aspect of the Cross is that Christ's 'great lone work' evokes this confession of repentance and joy in the believer, and that this confession is a necessary part of faith, of response to the Cross, of communion with God. The new humanity is regenerate in the Cross.

4. The Interrelatedness of the Three Aspects of the Cross

We conclude part two of this chapter by a consideration of the interrelatedness of Christ's work on the Cross. This will aid us by providing a summary but, more significantly, it will allow the full import of God's act in Jesus Christ to be expressed, for this is seen only in its unity. Each aspect (as Forsyth understands it), is fully understood only in its polar relationship to the other two.

> 'We cannot rest in unresolved views of reconciliation. As the reconciliation comes to pervade our whole being, and as we answer it with heart and strength and mind, we become more and more impatient of fragmentary ways of understanding it. We crave, and we move, to see that the first aspect (redemption) is the condition of the second (satisfaction), and the second of the third (regeneration),

56

and that they all condition each other in a living inter-action.'[92]

Forsyth goes on to tell us precisely what he means by this living interaction:

'Thus Christ's complete victory over the evil power or principle. His redemption (1), is the obverse of his regenerating and sanctifying effect on us (3). To deliver us from evil is not simply to take us out of hell, it is to take us into heaven. . . . So also we must see that the third —our regenerate sanctification—is the condition of the second—the complete satisfaction of God. The only complete satisfaction that can be made to a holy God from the sinful side is the sinner's restored obedience, his return to holiness.'[93]

The power of Satan is destroyed, he is judged by an act that robs him of his victims. The triumphant aspect of the Cross is just this overcoming of Satan. But this can only be understood in relation to the regenerating aspect of Christ's work on the Cross; for man is removed from the power of Satan by the power of his new obedient relationship with God, by his regenera-tion. There is no neutral point through which man passes from Satan on his way to God, there is only the enslavement to the Evil One or the freedom of the sons of God. But man can only enter into communion with the God of holy love if God's holiness be confessed by man and by man's repentant confession of his guilt. This can only take place in an act of the Son of God which renews man to such a faithful confession on the basis and in the gracious power of his confession. The satisfaction of God can only be met in the regeneration of man. So it is that each aspect of Christ's work deter-mines and interprets the other two.

We can now see the fundamental importance of Forsyth's emphasis upon the holiness of God. All through the interaction discussed above, it is decisive that the claims of holiness be met and that this can only take place by the restoration of communion between God and his fallen creatures. Whereas retributive justice could have been satisfied by punishment or destruction, and whereas sentimental, mystic love could have been satisfied by an amoral restoration of friendship, holiness culminated in an atoning Cross. It is precisely because God is the Holy One that he acts in the Son to redeem, to atone, and to regenerate unto holiness; it is precisely because God is personal that moral communion is his goal. God is not frustrated in purpose, not mocked in his nature. The obedience of the Son is the objective, accomplished justification of God by God and therein also the salvation of man into living communion with himself. Satan is destroyed by the act that restores the guilty to communion with the holy, by the creation of the new humanity, by the Kingdom of God actual on earth, which is faith working in love.

It is just this centring upon the holiness of God that Forsyth felt to be a new sharing in the Christian rediscovery of Paul. He places it in line with Augustinian and Lutheran Paulinism:

> 'The first great movement towards the rediscovery of Paul was by Augustine. . . . Augustine's rediscovery was this, justification by grace alone; Luther's side of the rediscovery was justification by faith alone—faith in the Cross, that is to say, faith in grace. What is our modern point of emphasis? Justification by holiness and for it alone. That is to say . . . reconciliation is something that comes from the whole holy God, and it covers the whole of life, and it is not exhausted by the idea of atonement only or redemption only. It is the new-created race being brought to permanent, vital, life-deep communion with the holy God.'[94]

We can best understand the heart of Forsyth's Paulinism so: God's righteousness is not simply placing

Christ in our stead to meet the claims of justice. It is rather his placing us, in Christ, in the holiness of faith. Faith, as a function of grace in us, is demanded and granted by the Holy God.

We have not yet examined the Cross, i.e. the fulfilment of God's revealing-redemptive action with men, in the light of its historical context. We have, to be sure, had hints of its historical actuality, but we have not stopped to explore them. This we must now do, for the Cross is an historical deed of revelation and cannot be understood, according to Forsyth, apart from history, that is, as separated from God's relation to his creation.[95]

PART III

The Cross as the Final Act of History

We can describe Forsyth's dominant theme in this third part of the chapter by saying that only a Christianity which is a response to God's final act on the Cross can have any interest in or understanding of history. Conversely, only the final historical act of God on the Cross is the revelation which calls forth the assurance of faith, that is, which establishes his Kingdom in history. Only such an act is revelation.

The best way for us to begin our consideration of Forsyth's understanding of the relation of revelation and history is to examine his understanding of the Kingdom of God as established on the Cross. The major characteristics of his understanding of the Kingdom can be summarized in the following manner: for Forsyth, the Kingdom of God

(a) is life lived under God as King,
(b) is completely a gift of God,
(c) has finally come,
(d) embodies proleptically the whole human race,

59

(e) is now working itself out as the ground and goal of history, and

(f) is only known in Jesus Christ.

We shall in turn briefly consider each of these characteristics.

a—THE KINGDOM OF GOD AS LIFE LIVED UNDER GOD AS KING

Forsyth stresses the fact that we have to do primarily with a living King when we think of the Kingdom of God.

> 'We get the idea by substituting for the word "king-dom" the word "sovereignty" or "lordship." . . . We cease to think of an order of society giving effect to certain principles . . . and we come to think of a state of things, in which God actually, and consciously, and experiment-ally rules in each soul. The particular social organization is a secondary affair . . . the kingdom of God rising socially from this act of love is not a matter of organization . . . it is a matter of spiritual re-creation.'[96]

Forsyth is cautioning us, when we think of the King-dom of God, to think primarily of God and man in personal relationship; of God as reigning in holy love and man as responding in joyful obedience. To think first of organization or to think first of man's response in any form, is to make the same moralistic mistake as that of placing conduct in the place of faith.[97] The organization, like the conduct, flows from the com-munion between the holy God and regenerate man.

b—THE KINGDOM OF GOD AS THE GIFT OF GOD

> 'There is nothing so prominent in Christ's teaching as the Kingdom of God. And about that Kingdom there was nothing to his mind so sure as that it was the gift of God. It came to the world from his grace, and not from effort of

60

ours. . . . We do not contribute to the Kingdom, we only work out a kingdom which is ours wholly because our God works it in.'[98]

In stressing that the Kingdom of God is a gift, we must not let ourselves be tempted into impersonal modes of thought and thereby forget that it is the gift of a relationship, that it is

'. . . a moral gift, i.e. that it is founded on the justifying grace which founds the Church, on Christ's fulfilment and satisfaction of the Father's holiness; . . . Its foundation is the soul's relation of sheer faith, loving obedience, and close communion with God both in piety and practice. It rests on that kind of morality which regards the holy, and takes shape in forgiveness and eternal life.'[99]

By emphasizing the Kingdom of God's gift, Forsyth avoids the immanentist danger of the 'progress doctrine' which was so alive around him. And by stressing that it was the gift of a renewed communion with the Holy God, he avoided any type of thinking which would simply ignore the active role which man does play in this Kingdom. Forsyth has in mind an actual act of God, calling forth an actual response among men.

c—THE KINGDOM OF GOD AS FINALLY COME

It follows, according to Forsyth, that if God gives us the Kingdom by his act on the Cross, we must say that the Kingdom has *come*—the Kingdom is *finally* established on the Cross. In fact, the historical actuality of the Kingdom lies at the very heart of the Gospel.

'Is the last victory won? Are all things already put under the feet of God's love and grace? Have we in the Cross of Christ the crisis of all spiritual existence? The Christian religion stands or falls with the answer of Yes to such questions. In his Cross, Resurrection and Pentecost,

61

Christ is the Son of God's love *with power*. . . . The thing is done, it is not to do. "Be of good cheer, I *have* overcome the world." "This is the victory which *has* overcome the world—your faith." '[100]

It is of the deepest significance that we should realize that the '. . . Cross of Christ is not the preliminary of the Kingdom; it is the Kingdom breaking in.'[101] To miss this fact is to rob the Cross of its atoning, its final, its once-for-all character. The 'given-ness' of the Kingdom is the fact that God has acted in self-atonement. To deny the presence of the Kingdom is to deny the finality of the Cross and, conversely, to deny the atoning finality of the Cross is to deny the effective establishment of God's Kingdom on earth. The Gospel, however, is insistent: the past tense is always used; 'he *gave* his only begotten son'; 'I *have* overcome the world.'[102] We will see shortly that Forsyth does not dissolve the eschatological tension that rises at this point, but rather he is concerned to establish one side, one pole of the tension. Here he wishes to stress the 'come' so that it may stand in relation to and as the foundation of, the 'coming.' It must be clearly and finally stated that the Cross as the *final* act of revelation means that, in Christ and in the response of the new humanity to him, God's Kingdom has come.

d—THE KINGDOM OF GOD AS INCLUDING THE HUMAN RACE

Light is thrown on the 'finality' of God's act in Christ when we mark Forsyth's statement that mankind was there dealt with as a 'racial unity.' The very finality of that act lies in its having dealt with all men and all men in their inescapable unity as historical persons. For Forsyth man is a social, historical unity. In essence, what we must do in this section is to seek to understand such statements by Forsyth as the following:

62

'... he (Christ) was, in his victory, the agent of the race. He did not overcome the world as a cloistered saint might, who conquers it in his solitary soul. . . . Christ was no mere lone individual and pioneer. He was the soul and conscience of the race. . . . If Christ died for all, all died in the act. We rise because he rose: and we rise not like him but in him. . . . We are the beneficiaries of his conquest by union with him.'[103]

'Individual men have to enter upon that reconciled position, that new covenant, that new relation, which already, in virtue of Christ's Cross, belonged to the race as a whole . . . the first bearing of Christ's work was upon the race as a totality. The first thing reconciliation does is to change man's corporate relation to God. Then when it is taken home individually it changes our present attitude. Christ, as it were, put us into the eternal Church; the Holy Spirit teaches us how to behave properly in the Church.'[104]

'. . . it was a race that Christ redeemed, and not a mere bouquet of believers. It was a Church he saved, and not a certain pale of souls. Each soul is saved in a universal and corporate salvation.'[105]

Forsyth is concerned to show that, as Christ acted on the Cross, he changed, once and for all, the relationship between God and the whole human race.[106] Christ's confession was a racial confession and the response of man to Christ, which is the Church, the Kingdom of God or the new humanity, is racial as well.

It is obvious that much depends on how this racial unity is conceived. Is Forsyth simply reintroducing the old realist, nominalist controversy? Does he destroy the significance of the individual soul? Is all personal decision made insignificant in a doctrine of universal salvation? To answer such questions, we must first become aware of Forsyth's singular understanding of man's racial unity.

For Forsyth, the most basic statement we can make

63

about man's racial unity is that it lies not in himself, not in his participation in 'reason' or 'nature' but in his personal relationship with God. We can see this if we compare two of his statements about man's unity.

> '. . . where does its unity lie? . . . The unity of the race is a moral unity. Therefore it is a unity of conscience.'[107]

> 'If there is a unity of the race, its source is the unity of God (that is, his moral holiness). . . . It is in his conscience then that man is one, and, above all, in what is done with his conscience by the power it owns supreme. Conscience is conscience because it owes to that power an obligation, which, as a matter of fact, is guilt. . . . Human unity is therefore one of deliverance. . . . The unity is a unity effected *by* God *in* conscience . . . by a holy grace.'[108]

The unity of the race is a social unity, a unity of relationship,[109] of communion with God and one another in redeemed consciences. This means that the human race stands in relationship to God either in guilt, as a Kingdom of Satan, or in grace, as the Kingdom of God. There is no neutral point, no ontological independence, no man in-and-for-himself possible, either for the race or for the individual members of it.[110] We can see that Forsyth is not simply reintroducing the realist-nominalist controversy, but rather that his use of 'race' is used to show that the race stands in communion with or in conflict with God. And due to the final act of God in Christ it now stands in communion with him as a totality, as a 'race.'

We will deal with the eschatological brackets which Forsyth puts around this finality in the next section. Here we must go on to answer our question as to whether or not, in his usage of 'race,' Forsyth has lost sight of the individual and of the significance of his personal response of faith or unfaith.

Forsyth views the individual within a social context. He takes as his point of departure for such a view the 'corporate personality' as seen in the Church or the Kingdom of God which is the true society.

> 'That notion of corporate personality with its implicates is a somewhat advanced and subtle one for the merely political or legal mind . . . it is really the result for the Church of its faith in the Holy Spirit. It is Christ indwelling by his Spirit that gives the Church its unique moral personality.'[111]

In the Church the members are not simply individual units in contact with one another but really become who they are in their relations one to another (as members of one another, of the same body, under the same Head). Forsyth seriously wishes to renounce all individualism:

> 'The reformers were as strong as their opponents about the necessity of the Church for the soul—though as its home, not its master. They were not individualists. Individualism is fatal to faith.'[112]

> 'We are not absolute, solitary individuals. We are in a society, an organism. . . . And our selfish, godless actions and influence go out, radiate, affect the organism as they could not do were we absolute units. . . . We are members one of another both for evil and for good.'[113]

Not even in the secret depths of our souls are we lone individuals; our very self is called into being by the Word of God and of our fellow man. Thus, for Forsyth, '. . . society is a living creature which has something in the nature of a personality.'[114]

We must note that Forsyth's accent on the social nature of manhood does not in any sense eliminate the self and the significance of the personal response of the self to God and his fellow man. If it is only in the Word of God and the word of his fellow man that the 'I' is called into being, there is an 'I' which *is* called into being, an 'I' which is ultimately aware and certain of

65

its reality and significance due to the presence of the Holy Spirit addressing it in and through the words of his fellow men, i.e. the mutual witness of the Church, and above all in and through the Incarnate Word, Christ the Lord of Scripture. Forsyth is just as concerned to lay stress on the personal as he is concerned to reject individualism; he is as concerned to emphasize the self in its social milieu as he is concerned to stress the organic society. 'As the soul is not a mere meeting point of converging influences, society is not a mere conglomerate of adjacent souls.[115] In fact, he can go so far as to say:

> 'There is no reality at last except soul, except personality. This alone has eternal meaning, power, and value, since this alone develops or hampers the eternal reality, the will of God. The universe has its being and its truth for a personality, but for one at last which transcends individual limits, i.e. for God.[116]

Such emphasis on the personality, coupled with his express statements protecting against any group-determinism,[117] make it evident that Forsyth did not forget for a moment that personal response is of decisive significance. He places us before the mystery of man, who is both a self and a self only in and through others, basically only a self in and through The Other, the creative, redemptive will of God. He places us, therefore, before the same mystery which St Paul points out in his statements: 'Then as one man's unrighteousness led to condemnation for all men, so one man's act of righteousness leads to acquittal and life for all men';[118] 'I have been crucified with Christ; it is no longer I who live, but Christ who lives in me.'[119] In these statements Paul places categorical emphasis on God's sovereign grace which has decisively dealt with *all* men and which Paul knows through his personal relation to Christ. But Paul finds no contradic-

66

tion as he continues: '. . . and the life I now live in the flesh I live by faith in the Son of God, who loved me and gave himself for me.'[120] Or, as he later writes to the Romans: 'To set the mind on the flesh is death, but to set the mind on the Spirit is life and peace.'[121] That there is a personal response of faith and that it is literally a matter of life and death are equally stressed by Paul.

It is to this same mystery of God's final act in Christ that Forsyth points in his use of the term 'race.' If we are saved in a racial salvation accomplished on the Cross, as indeed we must be if we *are* social selves before God, then this is the foundation of and not the denial of the fact that such a salvation must come home to us personally, evoking, by the work of the Holy Spirit, the personal response of faith in us. Forsyth underlines the urgency of faith in the following words: 'We are all predestined in love to life sooner or later, *if we will*.'[122] At another point he expresses the same thought thus:

'. . . all punishment is really corrective and educative. We cannot say that. There is plenty of punishment that hardens and hardens. That is why we are obliged to leave such questions as universal restoration unsolved.'[123]

Here we can go no further. We must leave our discussion of the Kingdom of God, as expressed in Forsyth's term 'racial,' where he left it. Forsyth has but pointed to the mystery and marked off its outline. It is a Kingdom *established* by sovereign grace, re-creating the human race into a new humanity, but doing so in such a manner that personal response is of decisive significance. For it is a personal communion with the Holy One which is salvation. Forsyth's description of revelation remains in effect: Revelation is both sovereign and personal.[124]

We have already mentioned that there are eschatological qualifications which Forsyth places on the term 'final.' In this section we must examine his understanding of God's reign as it relates to the temporal, interpersonal movement of history. Forsyth asserts that the Final Judgement has taken place upon the Cross, but he is also aware that God's Kingdom works in history by judgement and crises.[125] Here again we meet the mystery inherent in revelation of the 'final' and of the 'present,' indeed, of a present that points to the future as already present in the past. In this section, we will limit ourselves to such statements of Forsyth as will serve to make these assertions clear.

The first thing that should be noted is that Forsyth never considers history apart from God. In a sense it is false to say that God enters into history, as if history could be described as something independent of God. For Forsyth, history arises out of the relationship between God and his creation. Since the Fall, such a relationship is one of the judgement of grace,[126] of man's enslavement and guilt and of God's sovereign redemption, of God's victory and Satan's defeat. History, as the relationship between God and his creatures, is not a harmonious progress but antagonism overcome by gracious judgement.[127]

Forsyth felt that much had been lost in our understanding of revelation by the denial of Satan's work in history.

'To lose the sense of that kingdom of evil means, or it follows, the slackening of our sense of the Kingdom of God. . . . There is an incarnation of the evil one as well as of the Holy One; though its king has neither the moral power not the spiritual courage to appear as a historic person. For he cannot reduce himself to such limitation,

nor empty himself to the form of a servant. . . . We lower
the whole level and tension of the conflict if we discard a
war in heaven and think of God's antagonist as only
human, or only a principle. The Lord has a controversy
not with his people only but with a rival king and
strategy.'[128]

The Cross and its resultant Church are, in the above
view of history, the final defeat of Satan in such a way
that the Church or new humanity is the '. . . inchoate
stage of the new humanity and of the great history that
is to be.'[129] There is a sense in which Satan is still
active and judgement, as grace and righteousness, still
overcomes him. This on-going work of the judgement
of grace must be understood as the working out of the
final judgement which took place on the Cross.[130] It
was of this continuing judgement, as it burst forth in
the First World War, that Forsyth speaks in the following words:

> 'And now God enters the pulpit, and preaches in his
> own way by deeds. And his sermons are long and taxing,
> and they spoil the dinner. Clearly God's problem with the
> world is much more serious than we dreamed. We are
> having a revelation of the awful and desperate nature of
> evil. . . . We see more of the world Christ saw.'[131]

> 'It is all the judgement action of that kingdom of grace
> for which we pray. By terrible things in righteousness dost
> Thou answer us, O God of our salvation. When we pray
> for the kingdom to come, we know not what we ask.'[132]

In a small pamphlet, Forsyth sheds light on what he
means by the above comments and that 'War is a
revelation of man's evil on the one hand and God's
righteousness on the other.'[133]

> '. . . the course of history gets into tangles and knots at
> particular periods. . . . Grace enters to develop sin into
> transgression, to bring sin to the surface and make it overt.

69

Then comes the encounter, and the prince of the world is judged.

'These Armageddons are repeated in history, issuing in waves, as it were, from the central and absolute crisis of the Cross. And what we look down on from God's right hand is a great wager and waver of battle, a winning campaign of many swaying battles, progress by judgement, a rising scale of crises, working out in historic detail to an actual kingdom of God, with its strategic centre and eternal crisis in the death of Christ.'[134]

We note Forsyth's use of the phrase 'eternal crisis in the death of Christ.' His remarks at two other points are helpful in illuminating this phrase which is quite significant for an understanding of his eschatology or of the Cross as an eschatological act.

'A time process like progress, cannot be of first moment to the Eternal Spirit who has no after or before. What is of such moment to him is timeless acts like grace, redemption, faith, and love. . . . Eternity is a much more powerful factor in history than progress. At any rate, the value of an age or people for God (who is an Eternal Simultaneity) is not just what it contributes to other and later stages, but its own response and devotion to him. . . .'[135]

'In that eternal act (the Cross) . . . the Father's name is hallowed, his Kingdom come, and his will completely met on earth. . . . It is a solemn and fortifying thought that interior to all space, time, and history there is a world where God's name is perfectly hallowed, his will fully done, and his Kingdom already come.'[136]

We note three things: firstly, Forsyth makes a distinction between time and history. History is deeper than chronological time and includes such time within itself. Secondly, History is comprised essentially of 'eternal' acts. These timeless acts are not acts which do not occur in time, on the contrary, they do occur at a point in time, e.g. the Cross took place under Pontius

Pilate. But such acts, while occurring at a point in time, transcend time. They are acts involving God's movement to man and man's total response to God. Such acts, therefore, completely determine the persons involved in them; they are historical, that is, determinative for a relationship which is not exhausted by that moment of time. Thus they are not to be viewed on the same level as 'progress' which consists of acts which are not determinative for man's relation to God and thus do not reach the dimension of history but remain purely temporal. Thirdly, the Cross as an eternal act is that act which at a point of time, that is, within time and space, has finally determined the relationship between God and man, and therefore it is equally related to all the other acts which take place between God and man. It provides the basic significance or foundation for these acts. It is in this sense that '. . . time is related at every point to a holy Eternity.'[137] through the Cross. It is thus that the finality of the Cross is a '. . . finality working in history, not after it.'[138] The final judgement of grace is coming, is now active, only because it has already finally come. This assists us in understanding how Forsyth perceives the eschatological tension between the Cross as the Final Judgement, the judgement now being applied and the completion still to come. He summarizes this point beautifully in the following manner:

'Christ, in his victorious death and risen life, has power to unite the race to himself, and to work his complete holiness into its actual experience and history. He has power, by uniting us with him in his Spirit, to reduce time to acknowledge in act and fact his conclusive victory of eternity. . . . It is not enough to believe that he gained a victory at a historic point. Christ is the condensation of history. You must go on to think of his summary reconciliation as being worked out to cover the whole of history and enter each soul by the Spirit. . . . By uniting us to

71

himself and his resurrection in his Spirit he becomes the eternal guarantee of the historical consummation of all things some great day.'[139]

Forsyth does not often speak of a second coming, for his emphasis lies upon the finality of the Cross. However, he does not fail to see that God's working in history can be fully actualized only in a consummation. If Forsyth can say, 'The judgement *process* in history only unfolds the finality of the eternal judgement *act* which is in the Cross . . .'[140] he can also say

'And no conception of the Kingdom is anything but shallow . . . which does not realize its essential otherworldliness, its vastness so great that its consummation can only be beyond earthly history.'[141]

We must, however, keep in mind that the context of the last statement is that the consummation is the return of the Crucified, that is, the consummation is but the finality of the Cross brought home completely.

The limits of this study do not allow us to present this eschatological theme in detail. Briefly, Forsyth's application shows that the final judgement of the Cross as it comes home in history has a double effect. To the Church it is grace,

'. . . through the great judgement in the Cross, we do not escape all judgement; we escape into a new kind of judgement, from that of law to that of grace. We escape condemnation, for we are new creatures, but chastisement we do not escape.'[142]

To those who remain in rebellion, and also with regard to the relations between the social groupings (Forsyth was particularly concerned about the relevance of God's act on the Cross for international relations), the finality of the Cross comes home as public righteousness or justice.

'Righteousness is the form divine love takes between men

72

in nations, as it takes the form of affection between souls in a Church. It is the way love works in the grace of the Cross, whose great problem was the world's unrighteousness, not man's indifference (for Israel was a zealot) but man's wickedness. Love in the culture of the Church has one aspect, in the judgements of the world another. But it is love still.'[143]

In essence, Forsyth maintains that, since social collectives are only semi-personal, they cannot enter into the personal dimension of repentance and faith; they must live under God's holy love as under the form of divine law.

We can sum up this section regarding the eschatological nature of God's Kingdom thus: As the Cross is the eschatological Act, the eternal deed, which determines all history by its gracious judgement, so also the Kingdom it calls forth among men is an eschatological community in history, which has finally come but still lives under chastisement, longing for the consummation. The members of the Kingdom live in time, but in relation, at all points, to a 'Holy Eternity.' Or, more succinctly and keeping in mind Forsyth's use of the term 'history,' we can say, with Forsyth: 'History is no mere preparation for the Kingdom, it is the Kingdom in the making.'[144]

f—THE KINGDOM OF GOD AS KNOWN ONLY IN JESUS CHRIST

In our examination of Forsyth's view of the Cross, as the final act of history, we have chosen to approach its significance through his use of the term 'the Kingdom of God.' We have done this, for in no other way could Forsyth's view of the relationship of the Cross to history be indicated. This is the case because, according to Forsyth, the Cross as the act of God in Christ contains the Kingdom of God proleptically within itself. We became aware of this in our discussion

73

of Christ's work on the Cross; Christ offered the new humanity to God through his confession.

Up to this point we have seen that the Cross has called forth a Kingdom which is characterized by God's personal Lordship over the Church, the Kingdom; that this Kingdom is a gift of God's grace calling us into active communion with him; that in the Cross, the Kingdom has really come, the gift has been given and, indeed, given to all men, to the human race; that on the basis of the presence of the Kingdom, men and women are invited to enter it by their personal response of repentance and thanksgiving; that the Kingdom, precisely because it has come, is now coming and will ultimately be completely consummated. History is but the working out of God's will to holy communion with his creatures which he accomplished on the Cross. The Cross is the ground and the goal of history.[145]

It is fitting that we should close this section on the Cross as the final act of history, and indeed the whole first chapter dealing with the Cross as God's final redemptive-revealing deed in history, with Forsyth's assertion that the Kingdom of God, history as the Kingdom in the making, can only be understood in Jesus Christ.

Our task in this section is to make clear that the Cross is actually an act of revelation. That is, it cannot be understood apart from the faith which it calls forth. This becomes more inclusive when we recall from above that the Cross is the foundation and goal of history and '. . . history now transpires in him.'[146] If there is no understanding of the Cross apart from faith, there can be no understanding of history apart from faith. Therefore, every attempt to interpret history apart from faith leads to a perversion of history and a misunderstanding of Jesus Christ and his work.

Forsyth points out the fact that the Cross was a

historic deed of revelation basically in three ways. On the one hand he shows the inadequacy of all attempts to interpret history apart from faith, and on the other, he shows that non-faithful views of history lead to a denial of what faith knows to be the saving significance and the nature of Jesus Christ. He then exposits faith's assurance of providence as given in Jesus Christ. It is to be noted that Forsyth is speaking 'from faith to faith' since he assumes faith in Christ and a Christian view of history in his discussion.

1. The Inadequacy of non-faithful Interpretations of History

Forsyth indicates the impossibility of an inductive or positivistic historicism in three ways. This he presents in the context of a critique of trust in 'progress' or evolution. Firstly, historicism ignores the transcendent or Godly side of history.

'Scientific history cannot give us the super-historic in history. No induction can prove a miracle. Evidence could prove the fact, but not that it was a miracle, such as is God's creative relation to the world.'[147]

Secondly, 'Mere historicism does not even give us a standard by which we can tell what is progress and what is not.'[148] And lastly, even if inductive history could produce a norm of measurement for progress, which it cannot, it could not assure us that such an advancing movement which we perceive within the small part of history available to our study would continue and be victorious. He concludes:

'It is not in nature at all that we can find nature's end. Nor is it in living society that we find the sure word of prophecy as to the social goal. And if it be in history, it is not in history as a series. It is not an induction from the whole area of history (which we see not yet), or the abstraction of an apparent tendency.'[149]

If historicism leaves us without any final hope or

75

assurance in history, idealism, be it Hegelian or Kantian, fares no better.[150] Idealism is unable to overcome the gulf between the ideal and contingent reality.

'If our chief interest be but in the ideal future there is always some uncertainty. Has the ideal its own guarantee? Can it give itself effect, bring itself to pass, and not only evolve but redeem? ... How can faith in final good be absolute if all things are but on their way to the great goal, on their tentative way—if they are only working towards some great event and not working it out, if our last faith do not trust it is already done and secure in all but its actual effect with human wills?'[151]

Once again we are left without the certainty of faith. Forsyth summarizes his views in the following manner:

'We cannot discover a God of holy love in the career of history so far as gone, nor in the principles of a rational idealism; we can but meet him at the point where it pleased him to appear as Saviour, and greet him at the historic spot he chose, to set for ever his name and nature there.'[152]

2. *The Distortions of Christ which such views of History Produce*

Both historicism and idealism make the same basic mistake in interpreting the Cross, i.e. the person and work of Christ. They both evaluate him from the side of man. Since they had changed history from the divine-creature dialogue into a human monologue, it was inevitable that Jesus should be misinterpreted and that the New Testament witness to him would be, in crucial aspects, denied. Historicism could at best but recognize in Jesus of Nazareth the religious genius. It could even go so far as to assign to Jesus abiding cultic-sociological significance, as does Troeltsch.[153] Jesus is never seen to be more (except in degree) than what all men are; we are all religious.

If historicism had difficulty in seeing that Christ

actually 'came from the Father,' idealism could never take him seriously as a person, divine or human. He was the teacher of the eternal truth that all men were divine and human at once and his own life is the great symbol of his teaching. Again, he is no more than what we all are. In fact, since he taught in symbolic and not philosophic terms, he was less certain of his teaching than are the philosophers, for necessity is disclosed in philosophic speculation.

In both of the above views, the Cross plays a secondary and, at most, an illustrative role. It is either the death of a martyr or the symbol of the divine-human unity which, in its very being, declares that there is no creatural, sinful separation. Historicism's Jesus portrays the peak of developing man; idealism's Christ is the static truth of God-manhood; in neither description does faith recognize its encounter with Jesus Christ. We read Forsyth's rejection of the above views:

'... if history could explain itself, it could explain Christ as a part of it. And, if the general course of history could explain Christ, that would reduce Christ to be but a product of history. Whereas it is more true to say that history is the product of Christ, and Christ explains history as it can never explain him. .... History, man can only be understood by something which is final in history as well as beyond history, something in it but not of it, given to it but not rising from it, something that stands victorious and creative within it and says, "You are from below, I am from above. ... I bring God to explain man and complete him, as he can never explain or complete himself. I assure man of his eternal future because it is I who secure it. ... I bring the Creator with a new Creation. I am he." ... The key to history is the historic Christ above history and in command of it, and there is no other.'[154]

3. *Jesus Christ, the Key to History*
When Forsyth calls the historic Christ the 'key to

history,' he does not mean that the believer is given the ability to trace the ways of providence in history. We are talking about faith, not sight, and 'Providence cannot be proved from the course of history, only trusted from the positive revelation at certain crises, and at one centrally.'[155] At one point Forsyth echoes the Letter to the Hebrews by saying: 'We see not yet all things working out the Kingdom, but we see Jesus.'[156]

If faith is not sight, if it is but the faithful seeing of Jesus, how does that assure us that God will consummate history, will complete his plan? What precisely is the assurance which is faith? Forsyth answers: '. . ., it is a teleology only guaranteed by a soteriology.'[157] Faith finds its hope growing out of its present assurance. Faith is sure in the present light of the Cross as sealed in the resurrection, for faith is the

> '. . . power to trust ourselves and our world to his power. And not for what that power may do but for what it has done. . . . We must trust him for a Kingdom coming because come—sure, final, and eternal.'[158]

The Cross of accomplished reconciliation is the assurance of our forgiveness and the ground of our hope.

If we cannot trace the ways of God's providence, we can trust him to rule who has given us the goal of history at a central point within history. He gives history '. . . both its times and its means; and a good government of the world is what helps best in our circumstances to bring us there (to the Cross).'[159]

In this section we have seen that the Cross is truly the final act of God in history, but that such an assertion is only open to faith, for the Cross is final as revelation. Forsyth gathers together what we have been saying about the intimate relationship between the revelation of the Cross and history in these words:

'The authority in the history of the future is God at the

only point where he is indubitable, in his self-revelation and saving action, at the point of Christ in the history of the past. Real history must have an authority which is historically real.'[160]

We have now completed our exposition of Forsyth's understanding of the Cross as the final deed of revelation. We have seen it as the act of the holy God of love toward his sinful creatures, aimed at the sovereign re-establishment of personal communion. We have further seen that God, in so acting, has given all history its final determination. We must now consider the 'preaching of the Cross' as the prolongation of this final act of the Cross in time.

CHAPTER II

The Cross as the Word of Revelation

INTRODUCTION—*The Questioning of the Concept of Dogma*

I N Chapter I, Forsyth's understanding of revelation was presented as God's act in the historical
Cross, which calls forth a redeemed humanity, a
church, into living communion with himself. Such a
view, which places revelation in the dimension of interpersonal communion, requires a reformulation of the
significance, nature and possibility of statable knowledge in revelation. What can Dogma mean if it no
longer is supernaturally revealed truth which transcends the capability of finite reason? Can we speak
of the possibility or of the necessity of Dogma? What
is the relation of Dogma to the dogmas of the Church
or to the Church's confessional statements? Is there a
need to have a Confession or is it possible for the
Church to be Confessionless? How does the dogma
relate to the inspired Scripture of the Old and New
Testaments? Can we still speak of an inspired Scripture and, if so, how inspired, and to what purpose
inspired? What is the relation of Scripture to the
Church, to its common life and work, its teaching and
preaching? These are the questions which lie before us
in this chapter. They are unavoidably posed by the
shift of our understanding of the nature of revelation
from the dimension of revealed truths of faith (*credenda*)
to the self-revealing act of God (*credendus*).

It is significant to note that for large periods, perhaps for the predominant part of Church history, an intellectualistic view of revelation and thus of dogma, has been the dominant one. The Roman Catholic communion holds[1] and Protestant orthodoxy[2] held and in its modern form still holds, such a view. It was the liberal, relativistic attitude of the nineteenth century to the Scripture that caused many of the leading theologians to return to Scripture itself in order to find a more Biblical view of the function of Scripture and of the doctrine of revelation in general.

Forsyth was personally drawn into the search for a more adequate exposition of the doctrine of revelation. He felt that the question of revelation, authoritative and Biblical, was the central, burning issue of his day. It was to this task that Forsyth gave himself. His writings remain relevant today because of the seriousness with which he faced this problem and because the problem has not yet ceased to be central to the present theological scene.[3]

The material of this chapter will be presented in three major parts as follows: Part I. The Cross as Dogma; Part II. Dogma, the Holy Scripture and Preaching; Part III. Dogma and the Church. We follow this order because it is Forsyth's conviction that the Dogma called both the Church and the Scripture into being. This, as well as his answers to the questions which were posed at the beginning of this chapter, will become clear during the exposition.

PART I

The Cross as Dogma

We are concerned, in this part of the chapter, to examine Forsyth's understanding of the nature and necessity of Dogma. We shall include an historical excursus in which Forsyth defends, with an appeal to history, his understanding of Dogma. We will then conclude this part with a short transitional section on Forsyth's view of the Word of God which is important for an understanding of his view both of Dogma and of Scripture.

a—THE NATURE AND NECESSITY OF DOGMA

Since revelation is the God-given, God-sustained communion between himself and sinful man in Jesus Christ, Dogma is inevitable. Faith is man's relation to God in Christ, and all is centred on the 'content' that fills the word 'Christ.' 'Whom say ye that I am?' remains unavoidable in revelation, because it pleased God to reveal himself in the Son. Thus we might say that there is given in Christ both a positive and a negative necessity for Dogma, though the negative is dependent upon the reality of the positive.

Negatively, it is possible for man to misunderstand, to reinterpret, to distort the God-given content in the title 'Christ.' It is possible for men to see Jesus, but not as God's Christ, or to so conceive of a Christ as not to see him in Jesus. It is possible for a man to see Jesus as the Christ and to find him to be someone radically different than did the Apostles. Such distortions of one's knowledge of and response to Jesus Christ are extremely serious; for God is thereby not glorified and man is not forgiven. This possibility of idolatry, even in reference to Jesus Christ, is the negative necessity of Dogma. Forsyth expresses it thus:

> 'And it means little to the purpose now to say that we concentrate on Christ. A Christo-centric Christianity was the ideal of the late nineteenth century. . . . It is too vague. . . . The question is, on what Christ are we to concentrate?'[4]

The positive necessity also lies in the nature of God's

revelation. The positive necessity is, essentially, that the Word is the medium between God and man. Revelation is communion between persons and, as such, there is involved the definiteness, the purposive action and the rationality that is contained in mutual, personal recognition and communication. We shall come shortly to define the nature of Dogma and there we shall see the intimate connexion inherent between the Word, who is the crucified and risen Lord Jesus Christ, and the word which is the apostolic witness pointing to him. The Cross is the act of God's self-opening which includes within itself the word about the Cross.[5] In summary, the positive necessity of dogma lies in the fact that God's self-manifestation is dogmatic; it is filled with the content 'Jesus Christ,' as he is witnessed to in the Scriptures. He is the fulfilment of a long line of personal, purposive action done by God in history.

This will become clearer if we look at the way in which Forsyth uses the term 'Dogma.' Dogma usually calls to mind a statement, made by and recognized by the Church as a binding or official pronouncement which is constitutive of membership within the denomination or communion. This is not what Forsyth means by Dogma or Gospel. For Forsyth, Gospel or Dogma (we shall capitalize these words when they are used in this strict sense) means primarily Jesus Christ.[6] He, whom we know as the atoning Christ of the Cross, is the Gospel, the Dogma, the very norm of the Church's knowing and speaking about God and itself. We can say that the Cross is the Dogma, in order to differentiate between the Christ presented in the Scriptures and those 'non-dogmatic,' or, more accurately, 'differently-dogmatic' pictures of the Christ which men create and idolize. Forsyth makes clear that it is the living Christ of the Cross who is the dogmatic content of revelation in the following statements:

84

'Is it necessary to say that when I have to speak of creed I do not mean a document, but a gospel? It was no formula, that God gave in Christ, or Christ gave to us—no formula, either of belief or practice. By the divine deposit I mean the power and not the plan. I mean the *fait accompli* of redeeming grace. . . .'[7]

'We meet God in his coming in Christ, meet him there on his own tryst, and find there that we know only because we were first known.'[8]

'Nothing can create faith but God's actual coming in Son or Spirit, His actual contact and action in a soul. Nothing else can be a final authority for faith.'[9]

The Dogma which is authoritative for the Church is no pronouncement of the Church, no pronouncement at all, but rather God himself in the Son. It is God in his gracious turning to man in Jesus Christ. Jesus Christ, but, we must emphasize, only this crucified and resurrected Christ, is the Dogma or the Gospel. Dogma is this historic, contingent act and person, who becomes present in the Spirit.

Forsyth has concentrated all upon Jesus Christ. Only in Jesus Christ is the authority and power of God among men. There are no Dogmas; no usage of the plural is possible. This concentration of authority upon the Cross has implications for Biblical interpretation, as well as for Church unity; we will consider these later in this chapter. Now it is necessary for us to turn to a second usage of the term dogma, or gospel (sometimes spelled with small letters 'd' and 'g'), in Forsyth's writings.

We refer to the apostolic preaching of the Cross, the *kerygma*, the word of the Cross. Here we are no longer dealing with the Person and central act of Christ on the Cross, but we are dealing with statements, words preached, which point to the event and the significance of the Cross. The connexion between Christ as the

Dogma and the dogma, the *kerygma* as the preaching about Christ done by the Apostles, is very intimate and of great significance for Forsyth. He states the origin and the abiding value of the *kerygma* as follows:

'Revelation, indeed, is not there to convey supernatural truth, but it conveys God in an act which must be stated and cannot be stated except as such truth—truth not scientific but sacramental for God's access to the soul. . . . This first stated truth is moreover integral to the enacted truth of revelation; for a great word kindled by a great deed is also part of the whole deed. And it forms the element of continuity, identity, and tenacity in all the evolution of Christian thought. All future doctrine must take its departure from it, and refer to it as both fontal and normative.'[10]

The *kerygma* is connected to the Cross as evoked, as kindled by it. And it is the element of continuity in all Christian thought; it stands in the realm of Christian dogmatic statement as the source and the norm. The horizontal continuity of the Cross is the *kerygma* because the crucified and risen Lord is continually and primarily known in and through this apostolic testimony. Such testimony came from him; it continually witnesses to him. So Forsyth sees the origin and connexion, the abiding function of the *kerygma*. Faith comes by hearing, to be sure, but by the hearing of this word of the Cross; for only the Jesus Christ to whom it points can create faith in sinful man.

Thus it is that the apostolic *kerygma* is really a part of the fact of the Cross. It is a function of the Cross and the means of its eternal contact with each point of time. The deed of Christ, plus the preaching of the deed, form the primary Christian fact.

'It is the entire fact, not simply as a speechless occurrence, a statuesque phenomenon, but with something to say for itself, with its proper Word. The fact presents itself

in the New Testament inseparably with its own interpretation of itself.'[11]

We must pay particular attention to the transition
from act to statement, from Christ to *kerygma* or from
'Gospel as power' to 'gospel as truth,' as Forsyth
sometimes expresses it.[12] In the quotation above,
Forsyth stresses the significance and adequacy of this
transition; the continuity is there because this *kerygma*
is evoked by the Cross and therefore God can use this
proclamation to draw near to men in history. Here it
is obvious that we are at a critical point; we are called
to see the adequacy of the apostolic statement and at
the same time not to confuse the *kerygmatic* statement
per se with the personal act of God's coming in Christ.
We must be able to understand how Forsyth can affirm
both of the following statements:

> 'This (the *kerygma*) is not an article of theology, nor a
> tentative interpretation by apostles of a vast, vague
> spiritual impression that they felt, without positive
> features of its own; but it is their inspired statement of the
> Gospel of God's act and gift, the marrow of Christian
> religion, the object and content of faith.'[13]

> 'Dogma (the apostolic word about the Cross) is not
> religion, not faith; nor does it by itself create faith; it is
> the indispensable statement of that grace which does
> create faith, without which grace is dumb, not communic-
> able, and therefore not grace. No statement as such . . .
> can create faith.'[14]

Forsyth makes clear that we can in no sense equate
the Dogma with the dogmatic statement, the apostolic
kerygma; it is God who comes or else we overlook his
personal presence in the Holy Spirit. If we were to
equate the Dogma and the *kerygma* we would end in
supernaturalistic rationalism.[15] But on the other hand,
we cannot ignore the *kerygma* for it is through the

87

apostolic *kerygma* that God comes. This *kerygma* is not inadequate to the act it reports, which act still acts in it. In the *kerygma* we have '. . . no expectation of ours, no presumption in us of what a godlike God would do, no imagination of a God projected from our need.'[16] We have rather, the final account God gives of himself. The real author, the guarantor of the adequacy of the apostolic *kerygma* is God, not man. This confronts us with the fact of apostolic inspiration, the nature of which will be treated in part two of this chapter. Here we must concentrate strictly upon the relation of the *kerygma* to Dogma.

At this point we need to ask, what specifically does Forsyth mean by the apostolic *kerygma*? Does he refer to a particular phrase or text in the New Testament? Is he advocating a type of sacral thinking that simply repeats in errorless fashion, sacred sentences drawn from a holy Book?

Forsyth points out that we have to do with the meaning and not primarily with the form: 'No form is sacrosanct. But also to discard form is suicidal. . . . Here the form can never be independent of the content.'[17] It is the content, and precisely the apostolic content, that is significant. It is the centre of the apostolic preaching, the pointing to the Cross, that is intended. Forsyth suggests numerous passages in the New Testament, all quite differently formulated, which convey this meaning. He seems to prefer one such as:

> II Corinthians v: 'God hath given us the ministry of reconciliation, which is that God was in Christ, reconciling the world, not imputing their trespasses unto them. For (to meet the conscience that resents its easy forgiveness) he hath made him to be sin for us who knew no sin that we might be made the righteousness of God in him.'[18]

Other texts he suggests as particularly apt are: Romans i.16–17; Matthew xi.27 ff; and John iii.16.[19]

88

Forsyth even finds it possible to choose a statement formulated at a later period, such as one by Luther on justification by faith.[20] But no matter what form is chosen it must be a dogmatic statement '. . . on the scale of grace, on the one hand, and on the scale of the race on the other, and of the Church that confronts the race.'[21]

The heart of the matter lies in the Church finding the source, the continuity and the statable norm of its knowledge of God and of itself in the apostolic witness to Christ, which centres on the Cross. *Kerygma* is dogma in this sense because:

> 'What dogma is in its creative interior is not man's thought about God but God's treatment of man. It is preoccupied with the thing, the act, rather than the way of putting it. . . . Its subject-matter is God's revelation, God's gift, of himself; and its object is to state his purpose as summarily or as adequately as possible. It is not an account of the Christian consciousness but of God's revelation which creates that consciousness.'[22]

We can sum up the relation between the Dogma and the dogma, between Christ and the *kerygma* as: the relation between God's personal act and presence and the God-evoked verbal witness to that act and presence. In both cases we can only use the singular. There is One in whom God is with men and there is one apostolic *kerygma* which expresses the divine intention in the Cross. Together, the act of the Cross and the *kerygma* of the Cross form the fact of the Cross, in which God is eternally gracious to men. The deed without the *kerygma* would have been dumb, and no revelation, no calling of man into communion would have taken place.

In this giving verbal expression to God's purpose in the Cross lies the nature and the necessity of the dogma or the *kerygma*. The Dogma actualizes his presence and authority among men in the dogma. This is Forsyth's understanding of Dogma, in which he seeks to express both the personal act and presence of God and the necessity for a normative apostolic *kerygma*.

At this point let us turn to Forsyth's appeal to the history of the Church's use of the term 'Dogma' as a defence of the accuracy, even the necessity, of understanding and using the term 'Dogma' as he has just explained it.

Excursus: THE TERM 'DOGMA'; ITS VALUE AND
HISTORICAL DEVELOPMENT

Forsyth is convinced of the value of the term 'dogma' and does not wish to give it up. He believes that the history of the use of the term shows a development toward his own understanding of the term as against that of the Roman Catholic or Protestant orthodox usage.

One must note, however, that Forsyth is willing to give up the term if, in the minds of his readers, it is inevitably bound up with a rationalistic idea of dogma. He is not a linguistic purist, more concerned for terminology than for the practical significance of the term in the life of the Church. This he makes clear:

'... if the word dogma is incurably bound up with its use in Catholicism, I am not wedded to it. I am willing to take another word. ... If I were driven from the word dogma, I would try to escape into the word *Kerygma* for instance, which is the scriptural term to express the thing preached, the thing which makes Christianity Christian. It is the thing preached that matters; the word for it is secondary. There is for Christianity a statable, creative and unique act of God, cosmic and eternal, and germinal of all the Church and its truth. But I do not want to drop the word dogma.'[23]

It is our task to find out precisely why Forsyth did not wish to '... drop the word dogma.' He outlines his answer for us in the following words:

'. . . for two reasons. One is aesthetic; I would not part with any great and venerable term which has played a stirring part in the spiritual history of Christendom, so long as I could keep it with a due regard to its honest use, and one true to its historic evolution. Which leads me to my second reason. The word has already a long and not stationary past. It has a history and an evolution. And it will be a part of my business to show . . . that we are historically entitled, and even committed, to reduce it from an elaborate and statutory plexus of theology to the brief pregnant statement of the one creative Gospel posing itself in its intelligible content, which is also the intelligible base of the Church.'[24]

By presenting the historical development of the usage of the term 'dogma,' Forsyth feels that both the aesthetic and the theological foundations for his interpretation of 'dogma' will become apparent. We are most interested in the fact that Forsyth feels that such historical data as he presents not only allows us, but even commits us, *requires* us, to use the term as he does.

Forsyth notes three broad stages in the historical development of the Church's understanding of the meaning of dogma.

'It has run through an evolution of three stages according as the standard of its decision has been the Church, the Bible or the Gospel, according as Catholicism has been Roman, Protestant, or Evangelical. The use I make of it would justify as the latest stage of that evolution as it reverts to the New Testament type; as the necessary form taken by the idea of dogma, if the standard is the Gospel and not a book or a theology.'[25]

The three stages are characterized by their standard or norm for dogma. Roman Catholicism formulates dogma under the norm of the inspired Church consciousness or theology, whereas in Protestantism (here Forsyth is thinking primarily of Protestant orthodoxy) the norm for dogma was the Bible. In the third stage, which was emerging during Forsyth's time and was also held in New Testament times, the Gospel, Jesus Christ crucified and risen, is the norm of dogma, i.e. the *kerygma*.

Let us see if, in a more detailed statement of each stage, Forsyth can lend support to his claim. We shall present his description of all three stages first and then make what additional comments are necessary.

1. THEOLOGICAL TRUTHS AND DOGMA

'For the Byzantinism of the Eastern Church, dogma, as the sum of saving knowledge, was decided by the Councils, and ratified by the Emperor as it is now ratified by the Pope. For the Roman Church it was fixed by the Councils alone, of which the Pope became Emperor.'[26]

2. THE BIBLE AND DOGMA

'From the Councils Protestantism turned to appeal to the written word, and sought a reasoned word from the Bible. From decrees of Councils, accessible and intelligible to the few, it referred itself to the Bible, which it placed in the hands of all, and whose statements were held to be clear to all. The authority passed from an infallible Church to an infallible Book. Dogma was the co-ordination and exposition of all the doctrinal statements in the Bible. It was a compendium of Biblical theology. It was to contain all the truth in Scripture, and nothing which could not be proved from Scripture. So much of the old conciliar dogma was retained as could stand the test. . . . Its orthodoxy tended to become intellectualist, tended to continue the medieval intellectualism (only working in a new material), especially as the fires of Luther's inspiration died down.'[27]

3. THE GOSPEL AND DOGMA

'. . . amid the confused but recuperative movements of the nineteenth century there was slowly emerging a new positivity adjusted to the new conditions. . . . The dogmatic element began to recover from its swoon, and its eyes opened to two things. First it realized that its

positivity was as indispensable as ever (since natural
dogma challenges the Church for a supernatural); and,
second, it recognized that it must become more portable;
it must undergo a great reduction from the old range of
dogmatic truth. The Bible was not the wreck that the first
confident critics supposed they had made of it. . . . The
positive revelation, which all could verify, was there even
if the infallible book of the orthodox was gone. The Bible
was there for the Gospel, which it conveyed sacramentally
rather than stated categorically. . . . The historic salvation
was still there by grace through faith. . . . Disentangled,
but not severed, from both Church and Bible, the Gospel
stood out as the new authority for the human soul, as real
and fontal for theology as Nature is for science. Wherever
you have a real authority, you have something dogmatic
in its nature. And with a new authority you have a new
dogma.

'Once more then the idea of dogma changes its form to
secure its identity. It becomes different in order to remain
the same.'[28]

So it is that this last usage of dogma, as the *kerygma*
which is sacramental to the presence of the crucified
Lord, returns to the New Testament usage.

Forsyth is aware that within the New Testament
itself, the term 'dogma' is little used and that the term
'*kerygma*' is used there for the word of the Cross. However, the early fathers such as Ignatius, Clement,
Origen, Chrysostom and Eusebius, took over the term
'dogma' from the Stoics.[29] Seneca and Marcus
Aurelius used 'dogma' to refer to things ultimate and
given, things not demonstrated or inferred. In like
manner, these early fathers used dogma to point to the
ultimate, given, non-deducible character of the interpretation of the Cross found in the apostolic writings.
The term 'dogma,' as it was first used to replace the
Biblical term '*kerygma*,' signified finality, givenness. It
is to this original sense of the term that Forsyth feels
the Church has returned. It has returned to the

'. . . indubitable claim by the New Testament of finality for its distinctive Gospel, . . . (which is) God's central act, purpose and principle with the world. The nature of that act it states in such passages as I have named. It crystallizes there its message, its meaning, and its ground for being—its dogma.'[30]

Just as Forsyth feels that he has shown, in the history of the whole Church's usage of the term 'dogma,' a tendency to return to the short, final statement of the Gospel, so too he feels that this development can be illustrated even in the history of such a conservative-intellectualistic communion as the Roman Catholic.[31] Even within its understanding of revelation as revealed truths, Rome was not able to avoid the drive to a practical, or existential concentration of dogmatic authority. In a very real sense the historic influences of the nineteenth century helped Rome to compress all authoritative statement into one dogma. In fact, Forsyth feels this to be particularly evident in Rome's case.

'. . . no single institution has, on the whole, drawn so much profit out of the manifold ferment and even turbulence of the nineteenth century as the Roman Church.'[32]

He goes on to enumerate the influences which helped make such a concentration possible: Rome's sacramental mysticism was fed by the romantic movement; it gained influence as a place of dogmatic refuge amid a time of relativism; the rise of the historic sense and evolutionary development gave strength to its claims to be the one Church and the sole living expositor of a historic revelation (Forsyth points to the writings of Görres, Möhler and Newman); it was able to embody the dynamic of individualism within itself. These influences, together with earlier ones, did not act diffusely but quite specifically: they found their form and embodiment in ultramontanism.

94

'The Vatican Council of 1870 crowned a long doctrinal evolution by practically compressing the whole of Catholicism into one dogma—belief in the authority of the Church as concentrated in the Pope.'[33]

For all men, be they clergy or laity, '. . . all dogma has been, I will not say, reduced, but compressed into one —"I believe in the Church infallible in the Pope." '[34] Forsyth does not mean that the believer stops at this point but rather that trust in the Pope includes all else as *fides implicita*. The believer's authoritative centre is here and only through this centre can he move on to the certainty of the other dogmas. Here, according to Forsyth, is the dogma which stands practically as the creative ground of the authority of the other dogmas in the Roman Church.

Forsyth is aware that this development of papal authority has received a variety of interpretations from the Protestant world. He would that we look more deeply than those who see in this historical development nothing but the chicanery of power-mad priests and that we observe '. . . the summit of a long series of spiritual development, whether we think it is the right line or not.'[35] That is, despite its distortion due to the errors of Rome, Forsyth wishes to point out a principle of development that arises from the Christian revelation, from personal communion between God and man in Jesus Christ. He defines the development thus:

'As the Church aims at being a spiritual empire, it gravitates to personal rule, with its unity and effectiveness. All dogmas reduced to one, the Church, and that one incarnated in a living person, actual, accessible and historic for every age, dogma made pithy, personal, and social—that way lies the secret and principle of the great revival of the Roman Church. . . . But we must concentrate and dogmatize on the Gospel as Rome does on the Church.'[36]

Dogma must become pithy, personal, and social, that is, it must be the foundation of the Church; it must be personally accessible to every member of the Church in a living person and it must be concentrated into some one point. This is what Forsyth sees has happened within the Roman communion, centring in the Pope. Or, one can say that all in Rome centres in the Church, for the Pope is but the incarnation of the Church's authority. Protestants too must have an authority, absolute, incarnate in a person, available, actual and historic (objective) and this one Dogma it does have: in the Incarnate One, in the Christ of the Gospel. This same line of development is truly Christian only when it finds its fulfilment in the living God, active and personally authoritative in the statement of his final act on the Cross. Thus it is that Forsyth feels that an appeal to Church history supports his understanding of the Dogma.

The following statement summarizes his conclusions as discussed in this excursus:

'Our only hope lies in having for our central dogma one more Christian than Rome's, more evangelical than sacramental. It is not in scorning the dogmatic idea. Christianity cannot continue to live without a Church. And the Church cannot live without a positive, final, creative centre, which cannot be a rite but must be an act of moral redemption set forth in all its words and rites. This when it acts in power is the Church's Gospel; and when it acts as truth it is the Church's dogma.'[37]

b—THE WORD OF GOD

We have come to an understanding of Forsyth's use of dogma. We have also seen, from his analysis of the development of the dogmatic idea in the Church's history, the historic justification and value of the dogmatic element. We are now able to place this in the

96

framework of a broader concept of Forsyth: the 'Word of God.' By so doing, we shall summarize Part I of this chapter and at the same time provide a transition to the next two parts, i.e. Dogma and Scripture, and Dogma and the Church.

In the preface to his book *The Church and the Sacraments*, Forsyth defines his use of the phrase 'Word of God.'

> 'It may be expressly noted in advance that the Word does not mean the Bible, but the whole medium of communication between God's soul and man's. As this was gathered to a head in Christ, Christ is the unique Word of God. And since Christ is gathered to a head in the atoning and redeeming Cross as the incarnation not of love only but of grace, the Word is there in the most pointed way. It is the Word as an act and not simply as an exposition of God, who acts not as a genial Father but as a redeeming Father. But as this crucified Christ comes home to a man it makes him active, and it makes him vocal. So he preaches God's Gospel Christ. The Word that was preached from God to him he preaches to the world. The Word works faith, and faith works the word. We repeat with interest what God says to us. The Word is, therefore, God's new creating act on us, and then it is the act of our word through which God new creates. Since it comes from God it is pre-eminently a deed, as all the Creator's words are; as it goes out from man it is pre-eminently a word, through which God's deed works in a sacramental way. As it comes from God the Word is the Son; as it comes from Christ through his Church it is the Spirit, the Gospel.'[38]

For Forsyth, the 'Word of God' is not a book, but it is God speaking in word and deed to man. And as this speaking is gathered up, consummated in Jesus Christ, it is Christ who is the Word of God. It is in Jesus Christ, from the very foundation of the world, that God deals graciously with his creation.

To say that Jesus Christ the Son is the Word of God

97

to man, is not, however, to exclude man's speaking from taking place within the Word of God. For in Jesus Christ, man is reconciled to God. And from within this communion with God, man is given the privilege of speaking about God. First the Apostles were granted the insight to proclaim the God-given *kerygma*, the dogma of the Cross. And today, upon hearing this apostolic preaching and finding the living Christ present therein, men are given gracious permission to tell themselves and others about God in Christ. This human testimony is a speaking within Christ, within the Word of God. And God deigns to use this speaking to make himself present ever anew among men. Thus it is that man's speaking is graciously included within the 'Word of God.'

It is important to note the role of the apostolic *kerygma* in this connexion. It is the first and normative preaching of Christ. It forms the historical continuity which Christ uses to be present in his Cross among men. We must not misunderstand Forsyth as speaking in some mechanical manner. He is not suggesting that, simply by repeating the words of the *kerygma*, man evokes God's presence: 'The Bible loses the age if Christians . . . repeat it more than they understand it, if they do not prolong it.'[39] And how can man prolong the *kerygma*? By the grace of God. God in his free grace, stoops to use man's speech. True witness can only take place in the Spirit. 'Human speech becomes the divine Word only as our words are moved, filled, and ruled by the grace of God.'[40] And the great reality of the Church's speaking is that God *does* so move, fill, and rule its speech.

So it is that the whole Trinity participates in the Word of God; and only in this full trinitarian sense does the *kerygma* or the dogma of the Cross find its proper setting. Only as a part of the total act of revelation, including both God's speaking to man and in man's speaking, can man have the right, the courage, the assurance and the demand to be dogmatic, that is, to bear witness to the final act of God in Jesus Christ.

When we understand the 'Word of God' as Forsyth outlines it above, there is required a reformulation of our understanding of the relationship between the Word of God and the Scripture. Scripture is not, but mediates the Word of God. How is this to be understood? Not only the Scripture but also the Church is called to be the living bearer of God's Word. How does this relationship manifest itself in the life and work of the Church? To these basic questions we must now turn our attention.

PART II

Dogma, the Scripture and Preaching

Forsyth deals with the position of Scripture in revelation in two ways. He speaks of the relation between dogma and the whole of Scripture and he also presents his understanding of apostolic inspiration. In this part of the chapter we will consider these in the above-named order. We shall also find it necessary to include a consideration of preaching in this part for reasons which will become clear as our presentation progresses.

a—THE SCRIPTURE AS CALLED INTO BEING BY DOGMA

This section has the task of giving us the background against which we must discuss the authority of the Bible, its function, and the questions that surround an idea of Biblical authority. Here we are concerned to understand Forsyth's assertion that the dogma or the *kerygma* precedes the Bible; it did so historically and it takes precedence in value as well. Or, put perhaps more aptly, the Bible exists to serve the dogma, that is, the preaching of the Cross precedes and calls forth the Bible for its aid.

Let us turn first to the historical fact that the *kerygma* preceded the New Testament. Forsyth says:

> 'The Christians had a Gospel and not a propaganda, not a programme, not a movement—merely a mighty Gospel. They had no book but the Old Testament, no system of doctrine, no institution. All these were to be made. What they had was called the *Kerygma*, with all its foolishness (1 Cor. i.21, where we hear the scandal of the Cross, the absurdity of what was preached, not of preaching as an institution). *The Gospel was an experienced fact, a free and living word long before it was a fixed and written word.* This is the manner of revelation.'[41]

The first apostolic response to the crucified and risen Lord was that of preaching and not of writing. And when writing did come, by the Apostles and their disciples, it came in the service of the preached gospel.[42] Forsyth uses the analogy of a tuning fork to make this clear:

> 'So that we might, perhaps, put it in this way: God smote upon the world in Christ's act of redemption; it sounded in the apostles' word of reconciliation; and it reverberated and goes on doing so, in the Bible.'[43]

Event and *kerygma* form the fact of the Cross which called into being the New Testament, through which the fact is handed on.

Forsyth is not simply pointing out what any careful reading of the Acts of the Apostles and the Pauline epistles would make obvious. He is making the point that '. . . this is the manner of revelation.' He wishes to make clear that a fundamental principle is involved. The primary and basic response to the event of the Cross is the *kerygma* and not the entire Old and New Testaments, not the Bible. 'It was the Word, the Gospel that made the New Testament. It was the preached

24845

Word that completed the revelation—not the written Word.'[44] Forsyth can even go so far as to say that the New Testament itself is but an expanded form of preaching:

> 'The New Testament (the Gospels even), is a direct transcript, not of Christ, but of the preaching about Christ, of the effect produced by Christ on the first generation, a transcript of the faith that worshipped him. It is a direct record not of Christ's biography but of Christ's Gospel, that is to say of Christ neither as delineated, nor as reconstructed, nor as analysed, but *as preached*.'[45]

It would be a grave mistake to feel that Forsyth, in placing the Bible below the *kerygmatic* preaching of the Apostles, is in any sense belittling the Scripture. Later we shall have to deal with 'preaching' in detail, but at this point it is important to see that Forsyth's view of preaching is a most high one. Forsyth makes this explicit: 'Let us rise above the idea that the preached Word of God is a mere message warmly told. It is a creative sacrament by the medium of a consecrated personality.'[46] In preaching, which is the personal response to the Living Christ, Christ becomes present as the Crucified One. It is to this end that Forsyth subordinates the Bible. And it is for this reason that he finds the central and authoritative point in the Bible to be the *kerygma*, the apostolic preaching of the Cross. It is apostolic preaching that is the norm of all preaching and the Bible is there to transmit and to aid in the understanding of this God-given preaching of the Cross.

It is in this context that Forsyth understands the 'power' and 'sufficiency' of the Scripture: Scripture is sufficient for the effective preaching of Christ.

> 'Our fathers had much to say about the *efficacy and sufficiency of Scripture*. And this was what they meant, its power to be a sacrament of the Word and pass the Church

Lincoln Christian College

on from faith to faith; its power to be a producing source of the faith that produced it, to prolong the Word in which it arose, and speed the message to which it is hands and feet.'[47]

It is for this specific purpose of proclaiming ever afresh the apostolic Word of the Cross, that is, in order that we might make our proclamation, that the Bible is both sufficient and efficacious. 'The Word of God is in the Bible on its way to the soul,'[48] and not there statically, as an end in itself.[49] Revelation, which includes God's gracious self-communication and man's faithful, vocal response, *is* an end in itself. Communion between God and man *is* the eschatologically accomplished goal of God's holy love and, as such, is superior to the means which God uses to actualize his salvation.

'Everything else, Church or Bible, is authoritative for us in the proportion in which it is sacramental of this final and absolute authority, of the Creator as Redeemer.'[50]

We close this discussion with two statements by Forsyth which illustrate the thesis of this section: the Bible stands in the service of *kerygma* as the *kerygma* serves the Living Word, the crucified and resurrected Lord.

'If the Gospel of Christ's grace is the one authority set up among men, the seat of that authority is the Bible, and the witness is the faithful Church. But, as it is the God that sanctifies the temple and not the gold, so it is the authority that hallows its own seat and not the seat's pattern or structure. The King is King by something else than the art found in his throne. And the Gospel is supreme, not because it comes by a perfect, infallible Book or Church, but because it is the historic advent of the Saviour God to the Church's experience and faith.'[51]

'It is not our wonderful body that goes with us into eternity, it is our more precious soul. So it is not the

Bible, it is the Gospel. We shall not read the *Bible* any more when we pass from this world (so far as one may meddle with such forecasts); but the *Gospel* we shall read for ever and ever; and it will deepen upon our gaze as life unto life or death unto death.'[52]

b—APOSTOLIC INSPIRATION, BIBLICAL AUTHORITY AND PREACHING

In this section we must be very careful to do justice to the complexity and significance of Forsyth's thought. When he deals with Scripture he is aware that he is dealing with a central factor in revelation. Here he wishes to be precise, clear, comprehensive, and faithful to the true nature and significance of Scripture. How easy it is at this point to err, to move in the direction of rationalistic orthodoxy or of liberalism! Forsyth has stated that, precisely in the interpretation of Scripture, lies the basic problem for modern theological thought.[53] Modern Biblical criticism has effectively and helpfully destroyed the possibility of misunderstanding the Bible in the orthodox manner of plenary, verbal, infallible inspiration. Liberalism has equally shown that without an authoritative Scripture, theology cannot but become anthropocentric. But what is the nature of a God-given Scripture? It is Forsyth's answer to this question which we seek to make clear in this section.

Before turning to our presentation, a word as to the nature of this material is necessary. It might be possible to see, in the following reasoning of Forsyth, an effort on his part to prove or to externally ground the authority of Scripture. That this is not the case will become clear in the last part of this section and in Chapter III, where we will deal fully with Forsyth's understanding of our personal participation in revelation. What we have in this section is *a posteriori* reasoning. It is Forsyth's effort to think through and to express what *faith* knows to be true with regard to Scripture. He is here offering the testimonies, the evidences of faith, which finds its foundation in God's self-revelation and no-where else. In short, he does not seek a ground of authority outside faith but is seeking to give proper expression to the authority which faith knows. This, however, does not call for less, but for more adequate, more penetrating and strictly faithful thinking on the part of theologians, so that what faith knows to be true of the Scripture does not become blurred and even contradicted by our thought. It is in this sense of rigorous thought that we should understand Forsyth's thinking in this section.

To present Forsyth's position, we shall order our material in two sections: 1. Apostolic inspiration and 2. Apostolic inspiration, the Bible, and preaching.

1. Apostolic Inspiration

Here we must become specific with regard to Forsyth's assertion that God, through the deed of the Cross, evoked or gave the apostolic interpretation of the Cross, the *kerygma*. We must deal with Forsyth's understanding of apostolic inspiration and the authority of their *kerygma*.

First, as we have seen above, there is the necessity of a God-given interpretation of the Cross. The deed is only fully itself in that it communicates its significance to man.

'The mere crucifixion of Jesus was no revelation. Many people saw it to whom it meant nothing more than *any* execution. It does not reach us as a religious thing, as revelation, till it receives a certain interpretation. And not any interpretation . . . but the interpretation which God saw in it, . . . what he did in it. . . . Therefore besides God's act we must have God's version of his act. God must be his own interpreter. He must explain himself and his action. We have seen that none can act for God,

104

none reveal him, but only himself in Christ. . . . None but himself can reveal his own revelation. "God only knows the love of God," when it comes to this.'[54]

Together with this necessity of God to interpret his act, we have the frank assertion by Forsyth that such an interpretation was actually given by God, to and through the apostolic preaching.

'As we have God by the miracle of Christ, so we have Christ by the miracle of the apostolic inspiration. (Mat. xi. 27; xvi.17). If the manifested deed is miraculous so is the inspired. The apostles' understanding of the Cross is miraculous, like the Cross itself. It is there by the direct and specific action of the same Spirit as that by which Christ offered himself to God, though the action took another form.'[55]

Apostolic inspiration needs to be considered from two sides, from the side of its author and from the side of its recipients. We shall begin with the author of inspiration. It is God and his Word which is important here, not the Apostles themselves. 'The gift of the Spirit to the Apostles was not simply to confirm personal faith but to equip them efficiently for their apostolic, preaching, witnessing work.'[56]

(a) *Christ as Speaking through the Apostles*—Forsyth often stresses that it is the Risen Christ that is speaking through the Apostles. This was in direct contradiction to the conclusion some scholars were drawing from the relative silence of the synoptic Christ with regard to his Cross.

'It is very properly asked concerning the synoptic Christ, Why did he not explain himself? And the answer is that he did, as soon as the whole work was done, and the whole fact accomplished which had to be explained. He interpreted himself in his Apostles, in the New Testament.'[57]

It was after the resurrection that Christ spoke of

himself and thereby changed the disciples into
Apostles.

> 'God's Word of the gospel created the Apostolate—the
> word of the Cross and its salvation. Before that they had
> only been apostles designate, they were only disciples,
> students. But that Cross made them ministers; that gave
> them their ordination, unction, and freedom; they were
> neophites no more; they forsook no more, they betrayed no
> more, when the Resurrection gave them the insight of the
> true Cross.'[58]

At another point Forsyth maintains that only in
Christ and from him do we have any sure knowledge
of God:

> '...our human knowledge of the Father, as distinct from
> surmises, analogies, or deductions about a father—any
> knowledge which is comparable in certainty to Christ's
> own—is derived from Christ, and is entirely dependent
> on his will and nature. If we are sons we are sons only in
> him. There is nothing absolute about *our* sonship.'[59]

Jesus Christ, speaking through the Apostles, offers us
his own certainty of the Father. In the apostolic word
of the Cross, the Father and the Son reveal themselves
to the certainty of faith.

In reference to Christ as the source of the apostolic
word, Forsyth asks us to consider the consequences of
the view of many of the liberal scholars regarding the
kerygma. They were saying that the Apostles (especially
Paul) had misunderstood Christ, that they had
corrupted Jesus' simple, lofty moral teaching into the
apotheosis of man. Forsyth asks us to observe the
implications of such thinking:

> 'What was Jesus about to leave such a blunder possible?
> What a gauche Saviour! What a clumsy teacher! How
> awkward a prophet! How unfinished with the work given
> him to do! Regard it. Suppose the central thing com-
> mitted by the Father to Christ's charge was not the

atoning task; suppose he himself is not central to his own Gospel, yet he departs and leaves a body of disciples who do believe his atonement to be the great work, and his person their God. And these have grown and spread into a Catholic Church, which, amid many distractions and divisions, still founds upon this evangelical rock, and is the greatest product of humanity. Well, I say, if there be this central perversion of him by the body of his disciples and apostles, first and last, then and now, what are we to think of him?'[60]

Forsyth is asking us if it really is conceivable to faith that

'The result of all his training of his disciples, and of whatever he meant by the gift of the Spirit, was such a failure that it left them at the mercy of a perversion which entirely changed his centre of gravity, and distorted his message. What a fiasco for him, and for his work on them, if, as soon as he left them, they put the Cross, Resurrection, Atonement, and Redemption at the centre, where he put something else;'[61]

With such remarks, Forsyth is simply attempting to indicate the radically different understanding of Christ which had emerged under liberal presuppositions. Such a view ignores the entire Biblical setting and makes nonsense of the whole of Church history up to the modern period. Such liberal thinking provides its own negative witness to the authenticity of the *kerygmatic* Christ.

In summary, we can say that Forsyth asserts that it is the living Christ who speaks in the apostolic *kerygma*. Christ, by his careful teaching and preaching, by his enacted parables, by his central act of the Cross and the Resurrection, and by his sending of the Holy Spirit, has successfully given to the Apostles the God-given meaning of the Cross. In the *kerygma* we have the 'mind of Christ.'

(b) *Apostolic Inspiration and the Holy Spirit*—It is usual to say that the Holy Spirit is the author of inspiration. We have seen that Forsyth lays first emphasis on Christ as the Godly Inspirer. This is due to Forsyth's interest in the personal content of the inspiration, and not in the subjective state of the recipient. 'Men were not inspired *for* revelation but *by* it. It is the result of revelation, not its antecedent. The revelation inspires, it is not inspiration which reveals.'[62] It is Christ's personal work which is both the content and the power of apostolic inspiration. This, however, does not mean that the Spirit is not involved. We have just observed that Christ promised and sent the Holy Spirit, that Christ offered himself in the same Spirit that inspired the Apostles. What Forsyth is saying is that there is no separation possible between the Son as the content of the revelation and the Spirit as God working in the Apostles' hearts and minds. It is the things of the Son which the Spirit takes to give to the Apostles.[63]

Forsyth takes quite seriously the dominical promise that the Holy Spirit will lead the Church into all truth. He asks those who feel that the Apostles and the Church have erred in their understanding of the *kerygma* to consider the consequences of their view with regard to the work of the Holy Spirit.

> 'If Christ's atoning death is not the central effect of his person, and the central thing to our faith, if that notion of atonement has overlaid Christ's real gospel, how has the whole Church come totally to misread its creator, and to miss what for *him* was central? There has surely been some gigantic bungling on the Church's part.... And, as it concerns the centre and nature of faith, it must destroy any belief in the guidance of the Church by the Holy Spirit—which, however, is not a very lively faith among those whose challenge here occupies us.'[64]

Forsyth also speaks of Christ teaching or interpreting himself to the disciples through the Holy Spirit.

'He taught Paul in the spirit as truly as he taught the disciples in the flesh.'[65] 'If he lived in Paul submerging Paul (Gal. ii.20) then Paul's word here was a continuation of Christ's work. It is Christ, the Lord the Spirit, giving that account of himself.'[66] 'When we say the revelation is Christ we must take the whole Christ, the whole New Testament Christ, the Christ as his Spirit interpreted him, and not only the Christ as an annalist, a reporter, might record him.'[67]

We can summarize the above by saying that Forsyth felt that God in his Spirit taught the Apostles. This teaching, however, must be understood in the most intimate connexion with Christ's earthly life and ministry. It was the true insight into Christ's life, death, and resurrection which the Spirit imparted. The identification is even closer; it is the Living Christ who is present in the Spirit personally making 'his mind' known to his Apostles.[68]

(c) *Inspiration and the Apostolic Consciousness*—Let us shift our point of reference from God the author of inspiration to the recipients. Forsyth offers us two considerations pertaining to the Apostles' own consciousness that bear on inspiration.

First he bids us take note of the attitude of the Apostles concerning their message. Did they feel that it was tentative and deduced, or was it preached by them with a certainty that reflects God's having 'told' them? Forsyth maintains the latter:

'They claimed to possess absolute certainty about the greatest things of God and the soul, and the central action of Christ and his cross. They shared the self-certainty of Christ. They do not write as if any interpretation of Christ besides their own was thinkable.'[69]

Forsyth directs our attention to I Cor. ii as the most valuable *locus* in the New Testament concerning the

nature of the apostolic inspiration.[70] He understands
this to mean that

'... by the supernatural gift of the Spirit, possessed only
in the Church, Paul had knowledge of the intention of
Christ, Christ's implicit thought, God's meaning in
Christ, the theology of Christ and the Cross.... They
(the Apostles) had what they called "the gift of knowledge" as a *charisma* of the Spirit.'[71]

If the above is an accurate interpretation of the
apostolic consciousness as presented in the New
Testament (few, even today, would venture to deny it)
then it raises, according to Forsyth, a serious question.
'They knew themselves, chosen, gifted, and inspired
in such a way that all subsequent Christianity should
but move within their finality and enfold it. Were they
megalomaniacs?'[72]

'Now was this sense of unique insight and final interpretation a delusion? Was it inflation or inspiration? Was
it ideal obsession or divine visitation?... We may note here
that their belief in their own position and knowledge was
accepted by the Church then, and has been corroborated
by the Church ever since.... It had been provided for by
Christ, who said that in the great crises not they should
speak but the Spirit of God should speak in them.'[73]

To question the God-given apostolic *kerygma* is to
question the very sanity of the Apostles and, as
mentioned before, to deny the guidance of the Holy
Spirit.

Forsyth also calls our attention to the pervasiveness
of the *kerygma*. It was no Paulinism as was being
asserted by some scholars of the New Testament; in
fact, scholarship contemporary with Forsyth had
shown that the *kerygma* was the presupposition for all
of the New Testament.[74] Form criticism, which came
into being after Forsyth's death, would even extend
this assertion to cover the period of oral tradition prior

to the actual writing and editing of the books of the New Testament.[75] The theological peculiarities of Paul, Peter, the author of Hebrews, Luke, etc., begin on the far side of the *kerygma* and not prior to it. All of the New Testament writers are *kerygmatic*, and consciously so. Thus Forsyth feels that we should be clear in our minds that the apostolic Christ is the *kerygmatic* Christ of the whole apostolic Church—'And if we repudiate that we should be clear what we do.'[76]

We can conclude from the considerations in this section entitled 'Apostolic Inspiration' that, for Forsyth, the *kerygma* is the God-given interpretation of his action on the Cross, taught by Christ in the Spirit and so understood and confidently believed by the Apostles and the early Church. To deny this is to call into serious question the whole of the revealing action of Christ, to hypothesize a very unlikely theory which casts reflections on Christ, even as a mere teacher, and on the Apostles as humble disciples and which, in effect, repudiates the guidance of the Holy Spirit.

2. *Apostolic Inspiration, the Bible and Preaching*

Having seen Forsyth's arguments for the reality and divine necessity of apostolic inspiration, for the normative authority of the God-given *kerygma* of the Cross, we must now relate this to the whole of Scripture in a more specific manner. To do this, we must deal with the questions of Biblical infallibility and the extent of Biblical authority. That is, we must seek to understand Forsyth's view of the *kerygma* as the 'soul' of Scripture or, as we would more likely put it today, as the centre of the Bible. In this connexion we will come to understand Forsyth's view of the New Testament as the true successor to the Apostles.

(a) *The Kerygma as the 'Soul of the New Testament'*—Here we enter into a very controversial area. Many who will have agreed with Forsyth up to this point in his thinking about dogma and the Scripture will now find him wanting. Some will feel that he has gone the way of all liberalism and others will wish that he had de-*kerygmatized*. Not only is this area controversial, but of the greatest practicality. We can say much about the apostolic inspiration, but we have *practically* to do with the *kerygma* in Scripture. The apostolic witness must meet us in Scripture or not at all; therefore we have the greatest practical need to see what Forsyth will say about the relation of apostolic *kerygma* and the Biblical writings.

First we must take note of the fact that, in the strictest sense of the word for Forsyth, inspiration cannot be predicated of anything but a person. 'We learned last century that inspiration was something too warm and vital to belong to a book; it could only be the state of a living soul. It was personal inspiration and not book inspiration'[77] Forsyth's words, spoken with reference to the sacraments, could also apply here: 'The real intimate means of grace are sacramental souls and not sacramentarian elements. Conversion, regeneration, is the true transubstantiation.'[78]

In the light of Forsyth's view of inspiration as a personal state, we must understand the connexion he sees between the following two statements in order to thereby understand his view of the authority of Scripture.

'I do not believe in verbal inspiration. I am with the critics, in principle. But the true minister ought to find the words and phrases of the Bible so full of spiritual food and felicity that he has some difficulty in not believing in verbal inspiration. The Bible is the one enchiridion of the preacher still, the one manual of eternal life, the one page that glows as all life grows dark, and the one book whose wealth rebukes us more the older we grow because we knew and loved it so late.'[79]

' "The whole Bible or none," it was said. "Take but a stone away and the edifice subsides." This came of the Bible having been reduced to a fabric instead of an organism. And how many sceptics that course has made! How many Pharisees! How many spiritual tragedies! If I were a secularist I would not touch by assault the doctrine of plenary verbal inspiration and inerrancy. I should let it work freely as one of my best adjutants.'[80]

It becomes clear from Forsyth's words above that he is not concerned to deny that God graciously guides and uses the words of Spirit-filled men to proclaim his saving grace. This would contradict all that Forsyth has said up to this point. Nor is Forsyth indifferent to the words of Scripture themselves, for they contain a wealth that rebukes us for having learned to treasure, study, and prize them so late. What Forsyth is concerned to reject is an understanding of verbal inspiration in a specific sense; in the sense of plenary, infallible, verbal inspiration—that every sentence within Scripture must be accepted as infallible. And further, that such Biblical sentences form an errorless unity of doctrine in all aspects, the removal of any part of which would destroy the value of the whole. Such removal would further open the dam of suspicion and the entire Bible would become valueless for the certainty of faith. It is this understanding of verbal inspiration that Forsyth rejects. In this sense of the word, Forsyth refuses to speak of Biblical inspiration at all. We are not to let our gaze stop at doctrine, or sentences, but we are to seek Christ himself through the scriptural witness.

We have seen above, however, that we can say, indeed we must say, that the *kerygma* is God-given, is taught by Christ in the Spirit and received by the Apostles in sure faith. Nor is Forsyth suggesting the absurdity that the *kerygma*, when it is written down, becomes less essential, less God-given, than when it is preached. The apostolic word of the Cross, preached by the Apostles *or written down* is what God saw, what he did, in the Cross. Forsyth is saying that inspiration is a personal state, a God-inspired state in which man's whole self is sensitized and opened to God and for his gracious presence in the Cross. It was, in the case of the Apostles, not a course in scientific theology in which all views in their minds were corrected and guaranteed infallible. To make this clear Forsyth distinguishes between inspiration and revelation:

> 'The difference between the two is that inspiration is subjective; it is a state, an exalted state of the spiritual and imaginative faculties; whereas revelation is objective; it is the burden or base of truth and superhuman reality which the inspiration holds, as it were, in solution. The same molten state of inspiration holds suspended in it both gold and dross, both passing error and permanent eternal truth.'[81]

In connexion with this, Forsyth speaks of a centre, a vital centre which is revelation and which is the cause and goal of apostolic, or any, inspiration:

> 'Must everything in the New Testament be true? Is everything we find in Jesus revelation? Was his geocentric view of the world, was his view of the authorship of a psalm, was his every precept—were these permanent revelation? Again was everything equally revelation that was believed about Jesus by an apostle? Or was there not rather a proportion and perspective of faith? Do such things not stand at varying distances from the vital centre, and are they not vital accordingly?'[82]

There is a centre to faith, Jesus Christ the Redeemer and Lord, and there is a centre to Scripture, the *kerygma* of the Cross. If this living Centre and this written centre be wrong, then all is mere foolishness. But the same does not apply throughout the Scripture;

not all Biblical statements are on the same level; they do not all stand equally near to this vital, authoritative centre. It is from this centre that all must be evaluated. This is what Forsyth is emphasizing when he draws a careful distinction between apostolic inspiration and revelation. The Apostles could be wrong on many matters but about Christ and his Cross, with regard to the centre, they were speaking a God-given gospel.

This distinction which Forsyth makes is not to be equated with liberalism's imposition of a norm derived apart from revelation, for Forsyth wishes to start from the centre of Scripture itself. Therefore we may not simply dismiss Forsyth as a liberal but we must ask more carefully about his understanding of the centre, the 'soul of Scripture.'

As we have noted, it is the *kerygma* that is the centre of Scripture.

> 'And where is the permanent element . . . not only good for all time but creative? Surely if we ask the writers, the Apostles in particular, their answer is that there is such an element, and that it centres about the person, place, and work of Christ, involving a real incarnation and atonement.'[83]

To understand Forsyth's meaning we must keep in mind that the *kerygmatic* centre of Scripture is not there to teach us doctrine, or simply extend our knowledge, but to be the means of God's presence with us in Christ, of his placing us in living communion with himself. Therefore inspiration is God supplying the adequate means to this purpose of communion and not the means to a comprehensive, infallible theology:

> 'It is inspiration, therefore, which does not guarantee every statement of view, even of an apostle. . . . The Bible's inspiration, and its infallibility, are such as pertain to redemption and not theology, to salvation and not mere history. It is as infallible as a Gospel (God's dealing

115

with us in Christ) requires, not as a system. . . . Christ
did not come to bring a Bible but to bring a Gospel. The
Bible arose afterwards from the Gospel to serve the
Gospel.'[84]

'When the Apostles spoke as they did upon such central
matters as the eternal sonship and due worship of Jesus
Christ they did not speak from themselves; . . . they spoke
as men in whose experience there spoke still more the
Christ who lived in them. . . . though on matters lying
further from the centre, on matters of anthropology
rather than theology (like the connexion between sin and
physical death), they were less authoritative.'[85]

Thus the centre of the Scripture, understood as the
kerygma, means that the heart of Scripture is where the
believer meets the living Christ. It is through the
kerygma that Christ becomes authoritatively, creatively
present to the believer. And in terms of his presence
there, he is present throughout the whole of Scripture;
but throughout Scripture only in the light of his
presence through the *kerygma*. Thus the *kerygmatic*
Christ becomes the norm of the whole Bible.

This *kerygmatic* centre of the Scripture is not
arbitrarily chosen by Forsyth. It corresponds to the
centre of the act of God in Christ, the Cross. It is also
the point at which each believer verifies the authority
of Christ in his own life as we shall see in Chapter III.
Or to state it in another manner: the centre of
Scripture does not lie on the theoretical level but on
the moral level; it lies at that point where Scripture
points to a forgiving, atoning, reigning Christ. And
this is true because final authority exists only on this
level and in this Person. This too will be discussed in
detail later in this and in the next chapter.

It will aid us in understanding the implications of
Forsyth's view of the *kerygma* as the centre of the
Scripture if we observe how this applies to the teaching

of Christ and to that of the Apostles. We turn first to Christ's teaching.

> 'Yes, the very teaching of Christ in his Apostles corrects, sublimates, and eternalizes the words of his own mouth upon earth, which were sometimes said but to the hour or the man, and did not bind the Church for ever. But if ever Christ's teaching in his preaching Apostles is more valuable than his teaching of his learning disciples, it is only because of his own act in the Cross and in the Spirit, which fulfilled and finished all.'[86]

The words and deeds of Jesus of Nazareth must be viewed through the eyes of faith; he must be seen as the crucified and risen Lord. This means that all of Christ's teaching, healing and actions must be interpreted from a *kerygmatic* centre, for he was and is such a Christ. It is important, at this point, to emphasize that Forsyth is not interested in belittling the true significance of Christ's teaching. In fact, the very opposite is true; he wishes it to be seen in its reality and eternal relevance. This, however, is only possible when it is placed in the light of the whole Christ who taught.

> 'An antithesis is discussed between the teaching of Jesus and the work of Christ which is none of my making. Is it necessary to say that the stress I place on the latter is not at the cost of the former, but only against the value given it by some (as others treat the Sacraments) as the thing most precious in the Grand Legacy. None ever spoke like Christ. There are no words so authoritative, so profound, so lovely. But the power, depth, and beauty of such words is ultimately due to their place in the perspective of the supreme and complete Word of Grace; which lifts them, fixes and eternalizes them all in the Cross and what was *done* by the Holy there, when all saying or showing (even his) was in vain.'[87]

To isolate Christ's teaching would be to treat Christ purely as a great rabbi. We note with Forsyth, that none of the Apostles dealt with Christ's teaching in a non-*kerygmatic*, casuistic, scribal manner.

As we saw in an earlier quotation, Forsyth believes that Christ was not exempt from the scientific views concerning man, physical science and scriptural authorship, which views he shared with his contemporaries. Any errors in this dimension should not trouble us, for these matters lay outside of Christ's central concern; they are too far from the vital centre to have much significance for us.

'It is for faith, it is not for science that revelation is final. It is *the soul's* certainty and power that it assures. It is religious finality that Christ claims. . . . It is a qualitative and not a quantitative finality. He declares the whole counsel of God but not every counsel. He does not give us a programme of history or a compendium of doctrine, as the Catholic and old-Protestant theory of a book-revelation is. He gives us a power of God, a certainty of faith, a quality of life, a finality of destiny, in contact with him. . . . The revelation of Christ is final, and was meant to be final, for all that concerns God's decisive will, purpose and act for our salvation. Christ is himself the final expression of that.'[88]

What we have said about Christ applies in larger measure to the Apostles and the other writers of New and Old Testament books. They ceased to be neither men nor sinners in their writing. Everything a person writes as inspired is not to be thought of as revelation. Speaking of their writings as a whole, Forsyth says:

'To take the Bible as a whole, it is the record of a vast and voluminous inspiration, which fused up in its heat a whole mass of human interests, passions, beliefs, ambitions, and errors; but it is not impossible, as every Christian knows, to extract from the mass the pure gold of the historic, superhistoric, and eternal revelation of the holy love and free grace of God in Jesus our Lord.'[89]

'We shall not be judged by what we thought of the Bible,

118

but by the way it made us realize we were known of God. We shall be rich not by the ore but by the gold.'[90]

The authors of the books of the Bible were subject to the scientific opinions of their time and subject to the perversion of sin. Therefore it remains a mystery and a miracle of grace that their witness does point us to the Christ. We should rejoice in the gracious adequacy of their writings and not be anxious and distracted by any contradictions or errors which we think we find therein, for

> 'If the pure and perfect act of God when it entered human history was mixed with human sin in a way that baffles our thought, need we be surprised that the Word of that act, as *it* entered human vehicles and human story (by speech or writing), should also be mixed with foreign and imperfect elements in a perplexing way?'[91]

We can summarize Forsyth's presentation of the *kerygma* as the 'soul' of the New Testament by saying that faith is freed from all anxiety and for an always new and deeper reading of the Bible, precisely when it is led by the Holy Spirit to find its certainty through the apostolic *kerygma* in the crucified Christ—the centre of the Scripture—and to judge all Biblical statements in relation to *his* light.

(b) *The New Testament as the Successor of the Apostles*—That we treat this subject here, under 'Dogma and Scripture' and not under 'Dogma and Church' is indicative of Forsyth's understanding of the relation of Bible and Church. The apostolic word of the Cross comes *to* the Church. It stands as God's gracious gift over and against the Church. The ordained ministry, in so far as it is a ministry of this Word and this *kerygma*, in so far as it is a ministry sacramental to Christ, is God's gift to the Church and stands over and against, as well as within, the community of faithful believers. In this sense it is proper

119

and even necessary, due to the Church's temptation to find its ground within itself, to speak of the New Testament and the ministry of the evangelical word as the true apostolic succession. It is Christ, present in his Spirit, who provides both the ground and the continuity of the Church. Christ is present in and through the faithful proclamation of the Cross in word and sacrament.

It is true that we cannot actually separate the presence of the Lord in his Church (through Scripture and ministry) from the life of the Church itself. We must, however, point out the necessary distinction between Christ and the Church and therefore the sense in which Scripture and the ordained ministry stand as ambassadors of Christ over and against the Church. It is only thus that the Scripture and the ordained ministry are free to serve the Church. It is this distinction that we are concerned to emphasize in this and the following sections.

Seen from the point of view of its function within revelation, the Bible is Christ's and not the Church's. *Christus est Rex et Dominus Scripturae.* The Bible is a part of the divine initiative, the divine self-expression in revelation.

'There are two classes of historical document. There are those that simply report a transaction as a narrative of it might do, either in a book or a newspaper. And there are documents which are documents in the case, which, like treaties, focus the action, form an integral part of the deed itself, and carry not only the consent which made the act, but the signature which sends it forth, and perhaps codicils of authoritative explanation. The New Testament writings (taken of course out of the ban of verbal inspiration, or of an equal inspiration in every part), belong to the second class. They are part of the whole transaction, integral to the great deed. And we do not get the whole Christ or his work without them.'[92]

Herein lies the glory of the Scriptures; '. . . we do not get the whole Christ without them.' In this sense the Bible is a part of the deed of God's calling man into communion with himself. And in this sense, for this purpose and this purpose only, to offer the whole Christ, does it provide the true apostolic voice to the Church at all times.

In this sense also the Bible is a part of the apostolic succession. Forsyth speaks of this succession so:

> '. . . the need arose for filling a place, . . . the place of the Apostles, whose companying with Christ, and their gifts of normative revelation from him, had been quite original, unique, and historically intransmissible. The strict successor of the Apostles is the New Testament, as containing the precipitate of their standard preaching. It is not the ministry that is the successor of the Apostolate, but the ministry *plus* the true apostolic legacy of the Bible— the ministry *of the Word*.'[93]

However, Forsyth is just as concerned to stress that his words above must be understood in the light of the continuing work of the Holy Spirit. The apostolic succession can be expressed adequately only in terms of Bible and ministry in the Holy Spirit:

> 'The Apostolic succession is the Evangelical succession. Its continuity lies not in a due devolution but in a common inspiration, a common ministration of God's grace as mercy.'[94]

From the perspective of revelation, this means that Forsyth has a very definite understanding as to the value and the limits of the Church's ordained ministry. Let us first be aware of its limits and of the danger of vain pretension on the part of the Church through the false glorification of its ordained clergy. Forsyth describes the growth of the Roman, Eastern Orthodox and Anglo-Catholic view of the ordained ministry in these stern words:

'To assure the apostolicity of these formal but saving truths, the figment of the apostolic succession of the episcopate had to be invented, by a process which culminated in Irenaeus; and truth was based upon office where, at the outset, office had stood upon truth. So one lie leads on to another, as in childhood we were often told. An edifice of falsehood rises round a central delusion. A religion of mere position grows out of a religion of proposition. Orthodoxy demands a miraculous clergy for its vouchers. Their unbroken succession guarantees the purity of necessary but unintelligible truth. So now concurring in such truth at such hands, you may go to Christ without fear of offending him—"Lord, I believe in thy Church and incarnation; have mercy on me." '[95]

Here we see clearly the need for limitations which, according to Forsyth, should be placed upon the ministry. The ministry must point to the apostolic Christ and not to itself or to its doctrine. It guarantees nothing. It must and can only be a ministry under Christ and under the Scripture, if it would not usurp Christ's place. An ordained ministry which guarantees its own message has and is '. . . no message to the Church but only its soliloquy, the Church calling to its own soul.'[96]

We note the close connexion which Forsyth points out between a propositional view of revelation and the rise of episcopal apostolic succession. That is, he sees a close connexion between the doctrine of revelation and an understanding of the role and power of the ordained ministry. One implies the other, for the ordained ministry serves the revelation. In Forsyth's view of revelation, the true service of the ordained ministry is to preach the Christ who himself, in his Spirit, guarantees the authority of the apostolic witness. When the ordained ministry does otherwise, it has ceased to be a part of the apostolic succession, a part of the ministry of the Word. It has forgotten that:

'The ministry is but the virtual, not the official, successor of the Apostles, i.e. they are such in virtue of the same word of the Gospel, and not of institutional continuity.'[97]

(c) *Preaching*—This apostolic succession becomes actual in a specific act—the act of preaching. 'The apostolic continuity is in the function, not in the entail; in the Eternal Word proclaimed, not in the unbroken chain prolonged. It is in the message, not in the order of men.'[98] With the apostolic succession understood as centring in the proclamation of the Cross, we must consider what Forsyth understands the nature of preaching to be.

(i) *The Essence of Preaching*—In dealing with preaching, we remain in the realm of revelation proper. 'The Christian preacher is not the successor of the Greek orator, but of the Hebrew prophet. The orator comes with but an inspiration, the prophet comes with a revelation.'[99] Forsyth goes even further; true Christian preaching comes with *the* revelation. In his definition of preaching, Forsyth makes this clear:

'With preaching Christianity stands or falls because it is the declaration of a Gospel. Nay more—far more—it is the Gospel prolonging and declaring itself. . . .
And by the Gospel of this grace I would especially urge that there is meant not a statement, nor a doctrine, nor a scheme, on man's side; nor an offer, a promise, or a book, on God's side. It is an act and a power: it is God's *act* of redemption before it is man's message of it. It is an eternal, perennial act of God in Christ, repeating itself within each declaration of it. Only as a Gospel done by God is it a Gospel spoken by man. . . . The gift of God's grace was, and is, his work of Gospel. And it is this act that is prolonged in the word of the preacher, and not merely proclaimed. The great, the fundamental, sacrament is the Sacrament of the Word.'[100]

123

Preaching is truly Christian preaching only when it is sacramental to Christ, only when it is an act of man which is at the same time God's act. It is the Cross, the crucified and risen Christ, declaring himself to man. The authority of proclamation is God's authority. It is the Risen Christ who claims man, by pointing to his Cross. 'Therefore, the pulpit has an authority. . . . Yet the authority is not that of the preacher's person; . . . not the authority even of his truth. . . . It is not statements . . . it is a Gospel, it is an urgent God.'[101] 'The real presence of Christ crucified is what makes preaching.'[102]

As Christ's presence is what constitutes preaching, so the purpose of preaching is Christ's purpose— communion. 'God is not really opened to me till he opens me to him. All this is only possible if revelation and preaching be much more than declaration. Revelation must be an act.'[103] 'The preacher's word, when he preaches the Gospel and not only delivers a sermon, is an effective deed, charged with blessing or with judgement.'[104] 'Impressive preaching is not the ideal Christian type, which is regenerative. . . . Churches are made by conversion, rather than by mere impression.'[105]

In summary, we can say that, according to Forsyth, the essence of preaching is Christ himself, urgently acting through the words of the preacher for the purpose of calling men and women into the reconciliation of his Cross.[106]

However we cannot stop with our description of the essence of preaching at this point. We must go on to speak more explicitly of the congregation as hearers. Hearing as well as speaking belongs to the essence of preaching.

> 'Every great true sermon is a great true sacrament, the sacrament of the word, in which the people participate as

really as the preacher. . . . Every true hearer is not a hearer only, but a doer of the word. . . . To hear as the Church should hear is really to preach. . . . On every such occasion those who hear in faith are not simply present, do not simply listen, they assist in the service.'[107]

Preaching, since it is a means of God's self-revelation, necessarily includes men as hearers. It involves both the gracious Word and the gift of faithful hearing— both God's Word and man's response. Forsyth's description of revelation as actualized communion, which we outlined in the first chapter, is determinative for his understanding of preaching.

(ii) *Preaching and the Scriptures*—What we have outlined above concerning Forsyth's understanding of the connexion between God's act on the Cross, the apostolic *kerygma*, and the Scriptures, finds expression in the relation of preaching to Scripture. Forsyth's term 'objective preaching' points up this connexion.

'Now the grand value of the Bible is just the other thing —its objectivity. The first thing is not how I feel, but it is, How does God feel, and what has God said or done for my soul? When we get to real close quarters with that our feeling and response will look after itself. Do not tell people how they ought to feel towards Christ. That is useless. It is just what they ought that they cannot do. Preach a Christ that will make them feel as they ought. That is objective preaching.'[108] 'We must speak to the Church not from experience alone, but still more from the Word.'[109]

Objective preaching is to preach Christ, the total Christ of the Scripture. This does not mean, for Forsyth, that we are to simply repeat the same sermon time and time again, nor that every sermon must deal explicitly with the atonement, but rather that the crucified, resurrected Christ must be the presupposition of all preaching. No expository sermon (and Forsyth suggests that we preach expository

125

sermons[110]) is really preaching if the atoning Christ is not presupposed by the exposition.

'To preach Christ is indeed fundamentally to preach his atonement; but it is not incessantly to preach about it. We must always preach it, but we need not always preach about it. . . . But today it may be more needful in certain positions to preach the Christ of the Cross than the Cross of Christ. There is a strategy in the holy war. . . . To preach only the atonement, the death apart from the life, or only the person of Christ, the life apart from the death, or only the teaching of Christ, his words apart from his life, may be all equally one-sided, and extreme to falsity. . . . Preach the total Christ therefore in the perspective of evangelical faith, but with immediate stress on that aspect most required by the conscience of the hour.'[111]

Another way in which Forsyth stresses the Biblical basis of all preaching lies in his assertion that only Biblical preaching is really contemporary.

'The only preaching which is up to date for every time is the preaching of this eternity, which is opened to us in the Bible alone—the eternal of holy love, grace and redemption, the eternal and immutable morality of saving grace for our indelible sin.'[112] 'We must all preach *to* our age, but woe to us if it is our age we preach, and only hold up the mirror to the time.'[113]

Biblical preaching is contemporary precisely because it centres in that eternal act of God on the Cross. We have seen Forsyth's understanding of the Cross as God's eternal act in our first chapter; here we see this eschatology reflected in his understanding of preaching.

Before we leave this theme of preaching and the Scripture, it is important to note Forsyth's opinion about the use of Biblical criticism in the pulpit:

'. . . it is the preacher's duty, in most cases, to touch questions of Bible criticism only in so far as they clear the ground for a real and positive Gospel. The structure of the Bible may be discussed in the pulpit only in so far as it affects the history of revelation, . . . the preacher is not an academic; he is an evangelist. The minister's conscience is not scientific but pastoral.'[114]

Forsyth is not suggesting a double standard of truth. He is not suggesting that the preacher should suppress his views about the structure of Scripture; that is not his point. As we shall see later in this chapter, Forsyth was not anxious in the face of Biblical criticism. What he is saying is that the purpose of preaching is not to teach about the way the Bible took literary shape. The only possible reason a preacher could have to discuss such matters would be if they helped him to present the total Christ more adequately. The minister is conscience-bound to preach Christ for the salvation and sanctification of his congregation. He is not to teach them anything unless it serve this supreme purpose. It is not the fear of Biblical criticism but a complete misunderstanding of preaching and the pastoral ministry which Forsyth is fighting.

(iii) *Preaching and the Church*—Above we have stressed that preaching is God's speaking to the Church. This is indeed the most important, the objective reality about preaching. But it is important not to overlook the fact that preaching is at the same time an action of the Church. In the speaking of one of its members, and in the hearing of the others, the Church is acting. Preaching takes place in the setting of common worship, of congregational worship. The Church's preaching at such times is itself a confession by the Church of its faith.

'Preaching then is the Church confessing its faith. And it is as surely a part of the service as the reciting of a creed could be. It is another aspect of the same response to the Word given. It is less organized, but no less collective than

127

the great creeds. And in the Churches where there are no formal creeds it takes their place.'[115]

Lest there be some misunderstanding of Forsyth on this point, we must add that, for the Church to confess its faith by the act of preaching does not imply in any sense that the preacher is simply reflecting the Church's self-consciousness:

> 'What is done in preaching to the Church, therefore, is not to set out its own consciousness. . . . It is the Spirit speaking to the Churches. . . . No preacher (I have said) is only the representative of the Church's consciousness.'[116]

The preacher is not called to preach the Church but to preach Christ.

There is a negative side to the relation of preaching and the Church. We might put it thus: If the act of preaching is an act of the Church confessing its faith, it is at the same time a confession of sin, an act of the Church done by sinful men in a sinful communion. We can best see this when we think of the temptations which the Church puts before the preacher. And the preacher shares in this tempting for he is a sinful member of the Church. He is tempted to be impressive, creative, successful at the cost of his message. He is tempted to preach what the Church wants to hear, to erect a verbal golden calf. He is often put on a pedestal and is tempted to vanity. Or he can fall into the temptation of despair, seeing no joyful reception of the message he preaches. In either case the preacher is tempted by the Church and by himself as a member of the Church, to take matters into his own hands and to so change the message with which he is charged as to bring about 'good' results, when in reality he is to preach the

> '. . . old Gospel! It is not needful that the preacher should be original as a genius is, but only as a true believer is. . . . It is enough if he be a living voice; he is

not a creative word. He is not the light; he but bears witness to it.'[117]

It is precisely the reality of the temptation to seek to be the light that constitutes the confession of sin which preaching must be.

It is for this reason that Forsyth speaks of prayer in connexion with preaching. Preaching is also a prayer; it is ringed by prayer and throughout the week it is prepared for in prayer and borne up by prayer. Just as temptation is overcome in prayer, so must the very act of preaching be done in God's sight. It must be a prayer. Forsyth indicates the connexion between the temptation by the Church and preaching as prayer in the following manner:

'If a man seems *spiritual*, easy, and interesting, they do not ask if he is effective where the preacher's effectiveness begins—with God, if he is accessible to God, and so, effective as an apostle. The ministry of the Word and prayer go together.'[118]

Perhaps the greatest temptation which the Church puts before a preacher is simply not to ask if his preaching is a prayer, a communion with God, a message from God. And therefore Forsyth stresses the fact that *the ministry of the Word and prayer go together*. These words point to the fact that preaching is an act of the Church which gains all of its meaning from God's gracious presence with the Church through this act. 'The ministry of the Word and prayer go together.' These words serve us well as a summary of Forsyth's understanding of the whole of preaching.

(*d*) *Inspiration, Preaching and Authority* In this section we are concerned to deal with a specific misunderstanding which might arise from Forsyth's view of authority in relation to inspiration and preaching. It is possible for this misunderstanding to arise if we conceive of

129

Forsyth as teaching that, because we first know the Apostles as the inspired messengers of God, bearing to us his Word of the Cross, we should therefore *pro forma* trust their message. This same misunderstanding could be carried over into Forsyth's understanding of preaching. We could assume that, because preachers preach a God-given *kerygma*, a Biblical message, they are to be trusted, believed, accepted as authoritative. But this misunderstanding is the very inverse of Forsyth's position. We do not find preaching or the Scriptures authoritative because we first, in some independent fashion, ascertain that they are inspired. Rather we know them to be inspired and to speak authoritatively because God the Holy Spirit speaks to us through these deeds. Through these acts the one Act becomes visible. God, his crucial Word, is the authority which creates faith.

Inspiration is to be understood as the means which God used to express his Word in and through the Apostles and New Testament writers. Illumination is, similarly, the means which God uses to speak to us through their *kerygma* and through the preaching growing out of his Word.[119] These means are not externally provable; they are the hidden work of the Holy Spirit of the Cross. They serve him in his task of pointing to Christ, who came, and comes and will come. He, the Lamb of God, is authoritative for faith!

'When we trust an Apostle, for instance, it is not for foregone infallibility we trust . . . Nor is it his veracity, nor his competency as a reporter of dictated truth. But we trust his truth as an integral expression of his personal experience and reality in a select historic position, his truth as an organ of the Spirit.'[120]

'It thus becomes necessary to go into the deep things of God as they are revealed to us by the Holy Spirit, through his inspired Apostles, in Christ and his Cross.'[121]

We have given no positive discussion of authority and faith at this point. It is a very complex problem and will receive full treatment in the next chapter. Here we have simply attempted to remove any understanding of inspiration which would make it a formal authority, for Forsyth did not so understand it.

Throughout the second part of this chapter our concern has been to present Forsyth's view of the relation of Dogma and Scripture. We found that it was necessary to discuss preaching as well, since it shares a place alongside Scripture as a means of God's speaking to his Church. The following quotation from Forsyth will serve to sum up our findings and at the same time to point us toward the final part of this chapter.

> 'In positive revelation we have to do with two things. The one fact has two constituents. We have, first, the history or the manifestation, and we have, second, the inspiration or the interpretation of the history. We have, first, God entering the world, and we have, second, this entry of God entering man. We have the fact, and we have the word of the fact. The fact we have in Christ; but the word of it, the meaning of it, we have in believers and apostles moved by Christ. And especially in the Apostles, whose insight becomes itself a fact, in turn, working upon believers from faith to faith. So that we have three things— first the incarnate fact, then the word or interpretation of it by Apostles, and, thereby, the fact again, but the fact enshrined in the soul of the believing Church.'[122]

PART III

Dogma and the Church

As we indicated above, it is important for an understanding of Forsyth to give separate attention to the relationship between dogma and Scripture and to that between dogma and Church. Only in this way, according to Forsyth, can we avoid the basic error of equating the Church and its activities of worship, theologizing and Biblical interpretation with its own foundation—Jesus Christ. Therefore in this part of the chapter we deal with the relation between the Cross as the Word of God and the Church. Our presentation includes two sections: a. The Cross as calling forth the Church and b. The Cross as the norm of Church theology. We shall also present in an excursus, Forsyth's view of Biblical interpretation. Here we are not concerned to discuss the Church's personal or existential participation in the Dogma, that will require the entire next chapter. The emphasis at this point is on the Cross as the Word of God who founds the Church and who is the Lord of the necessary activities of theology and exegesis which the Church carries out.

a—THE CROSS AS CALLING FORTH THE CHURCH

'The Church was not created by the inward light. It was not created by the Spirit of God alone. It was created by the Holy Spirit through an apostolic Word of Jesus Christ crucified; it was created by the redeeming Lord as the Spirit. As a matter of fact, this was so. And its principle is given in its creation.'[123]

Forsyth maintains that we must go back to the *Cross*, if we would rightly understand the Church and its activities. For 'the Church's one foundation is not simply Jesus Christ, but him as crucified and atoning.'[124] It is this 'dogmatic' Jesus Christ who in his Spirit is the foundation and Lord of the Church. The Church is in him and therefore derives its principle, its character from him.

Forsyth supports this by pointing out that it was through the apostolic preaching of the Cross that Christ worked mightily to call his people into existence.

'In so far as the Church is a creature, it is the creature of the preached Gospel of God's grace forgiving, redeeming, and creating us anew by Christ's Cross. The Church was created by the preaching of that solitary Gospel, and fortified by the sacraments of it, which are, indeed, but other ways of receiving, confessing, and preaching it. The Church is the social and practical response to that grace.'[125]

When we go on to ask precisely what are the characteristics of the Church due to its being called into being by the Cross, we find that Forsyth offers us three: the Church is the trustee of Scripture; it is a society; and it is the organ of the Holy Spirit for the regeneration and sanctification of its members.

Precisely because of its being called into being by the Cross, the Church knows itself to be under the Word of the Cross. 'No Church produced the Bible. Both the Bible and the Church are products of the Gospel. . . . Hence no Church has the control of the Bible, but only a stewardship of it.'[126] Forsyth thereby stresses Christ's continual reforming Lordship over the Church as exercised through the Bible:

'The Bible has more to do for the Church than ever the Church has done or can do for the Bible. And the Bible never does so much for the Church as it does when it puts us in a position to judge, condemn, and reform the whole Church by its light. It is only that light that can reform the Church. It is not the light of nature, the common man, the worldly parliament. Set the Church free from these things, to be acted on by its own Bible.'[127]

The Church, because it comes from the Cross, is a society. The Cross is God's act calling men into communion with himself and therefore with one another. The Church is latent in the Cross itself as God's actualization of community.[128]

'The power that makes the Church a community of

133

men is the same power that makes communion between man and God; and that again is the same power which makes the eternal bond of communion between Father and Son—the Holy Spirit. So solemn as that is the Church —no less unearthly than that—resting on the Word of a Reconciliation which binds in one the powers of eternity itself.'[129]

Called into being by the Cross, the Church is the organ of the Holy Spirit of the Cross for God's purpose of salvation.

'We believe *in* his grace, but only *through* his Church. . . . The Church is the historic medium, but the Spirit is the historic mediator, whose organ the Church is. The very meaning of the Holy Spirit in history is a mediated immediacy of our relation to historic fact.'[130]

These few remarks do not present Forsyth's doctrine of the Church even in outline, but simply serve to point out the nature of the relationship between the revealing act of the Cross and the Church. For a full treatment of the doctrine of the Church, which would take us beyond the limits of this study, the reader should turn to Forsyth's book, *The Church and the Sacraments*. Having described the Church as the community of which Christ is the foundation, we now turn to an examination of the relation of the Cross to the theological-exegetical work of the Church.

b—THE CROSS AS THE NORM OF THE
CHURCH'S THEOLOGY

Here we shall have to relate Forsyth's definition of dogma to the broader areas of creed and the work of individual theologians. These areas need definition first and then their interrelatedness needs to be indicated. With this accomplished, we will then discuss the nature and task of theology in the Church as Forsyth understands it.

1. Dogma, Creed and Theology

First, through a statement by Forsyth, we shall outline these three areas and state their relationship one to another. Then we shall return to each specific area to make any clarifying and amplifying remarks that seem necessary.

'Let us put the relation of dogma and doctrine in this way. The order of development in the spiritual interior of the Church is, first, faith as personal trust; then the knowledge latent in faith, of its fact, of the content which lifts it above mere subjective religion; then the brief common confession of such creative and intelligent faith; and then its expansion in the noble heat of conflict into theology and doctrine. There is for faith a theology which is latent in the Gospel and a theology which is more and more explicit.

'There is a theology without which it cannot be stated or confessed, but remains mere mystic religiosity for individuals; and there is a theology into which it must expand as part of its growth and wealth in a Church. The former we may call *primary theology*, and the latter *secondary*. . . . The former is verifiable by personal experience, and is the Church's *dogma*, "I believe that God was in Christ forgiving and reconciling the world through the Cross." The latter is experience which has passed into the Church's reflection; it is its *doctrine*, . . . The one exists for the Church's foundation and standing, touches the rock, and has to do with grace, atonement, faith and love in the Holy Ghost. It is God's direct gift in Christ. . . . The other has to do with the Church's *grasp*—not its firm footing but its wide grasp—and especially its grasp of the mentality of each age. . . .

'But now to pass to theology more strictly taken, as distinct from either dogma or doctrine. Before the Church can make the corporate confession of the doctrine or teaching into which its dogma expands there must be long periods of theological culture and freedom. Theology is tentative doctrine; doctrine is selected theology. The doctrine of the Church is a corporate property, but

135

theology is an individual or sectional pursuit. . . . Doctrine is tentative compared with dogma, and theology is tentative compared with doctrine. . . . But the chief object of theology is not to provide matter for the individual pulpit, nor scope for the individual mind, but to prepare material for the doctrine by which the collective Church preaches its dogma to the intelligent world. . . .'[131]

We are familiar with Forsyth's understanding of dogma from our discussion about it earlier in the chapter. Here he adds nothing new to what we have said but simply applies it and underlines the foundational character of the dogma or *kerygma* when he refers to it as the Church's footing. It is important in this connection to note again that Forsyth does not equate dogma or *kerygma* with revelation. The reader will recall the distinction and intimate connexion which Forsyth makes between Dogma and dogma, between Jesus Christ and the apostolic word of the Cross. At present we are concerned with the theological movement from dogma to creed through theology. Waiting to discuss the personal experience or 'verification' of the dogma until the next chapter, we turn now to Forsyth's understanding of doctrine.

Forsyth refers to this area variously as 'doctrine,' as 'creed' or 'confession,' as 'secondary theology' or as 'the Church's grasp.' We have moved from that which supports the Church to the Church's reflection upon its *kerygmatic* footing. We are, therefore, in a somewhat tentative realm. But we are in an area which has the stability of the Church's approval or of its common Confession. It is important that we examine this area rather closely for, according to Forsyth, it is the primary task of theology to provide the material to make possible (humanly speaking) the Church's confession. Forsyth also underlines the significance of this area by pointing out that a formal Confession is one of the ways in which the Church preaches its dogma to the world. Involved here is also the whole question of confessions (denominations) and Church unity.

We turn first to Forsyth's understanding of Church Confession itself and then follow his application of this to interdenominational unity as an illustration of his view of doctrine. Forsyth's remarks about Church Confession can best be presented in two groupings: first, the necessity for Church Confession and second, the authority of such Confession.

The necessity for the Church to confess is basically that of its being thankfully obedient to its Lord. The Church must confess Christ because it knows him as the Saviour of the world and he wishes, as such a Saviour, to be confessed before men.

> 'A Church, as soon as it is a believing Church, must above all else be a confessing Church, i.e. it must be more concerned to show forth the Lordship of Christ and his Gospel in its every special action and enterprise, than to hum with energy. . . .'[132]

Another way of approaching this same necessity is from the fact that the Church's faith derives from an historic, living Christ and not from mystic feeling or rational idea. Therefore the Church, simply in speaking of its foundation, confesses Christ; in speaking of itself it must tell his story, and his significance for all men.

> 'The Church is founded on faith, else it has no foundation at all; and on faith not as a subjective frame, but as our collective relation to a given object of holy Love, an object which gives itself in grace, and in that act creates the faith. . . . But, faith being an objective and living relation, some living statement of it is not only possible but necessary if it is to be conveyed to others or confessed at all. . . . And the Church's first duty is to confess in some form this common faith which gave it being. But if that be an act of worship (as all true confession really is) it can only mean the confession of the object and

137

matter of faith. . . . The Church says but "hear me"; it does not say "look at me." For then the Church would be preaching itself; and we preach not ourselves, nor our experience, nor our faith, but Christ crucified.'[133]

And this confessing 'Christ crucified' means for Forsyth to preach the atoning Christ. Not simply the events of *heilsgeschichte* must be listed, but their *kerygmatic* meaning must be confessed.[134] There is a specific knowledge of God in Christ, which in its concreteness and givenness is the foundation and necessity of confession. For Christianity

'. . . theology is intrinsic. . . . What we adore (as in the Trinity) is not a mystery, it is a revelation. It is not the mystery that is the object of religion but the light; nor is faith but a flash, it is a knowledge. We do not "worship we know not what." And a worship that knows what it worships is not religious merely, it is theological religion.'[135]

The second aspect of the necessity for the Church to confess (now we think primarily of those moments when it must actually formulate a written confession of some sort), lies in the particular situation in which it finds itself in the world. The world, the age, both inside and outside of the Church, often presents the Church with the need to say a common word about its Saviour, and to say it in such a manner as to answer the challenge of the hour.

'The first thing we have to recognize in the creeds of the past is that, however lamentable may have been the proceedings of certain councils, the existence of the creeds was due to a moral necessity, rising at a crisis out of the nature of the Gospel as it faced the world.'[136]

It is in response to such challenges that the different Confessions have come into being. Indeed, the Church exists only in such confessional bodies. 'It organizes itself by its very nature into particular intelligent and social forms. It lives only as confessions and Churches.'[137] The major Protestant bodies and post-Tridentine Roman Catholicism, for example, exist as Confessional bodies which were called into existence by the encounter between the Gospel and the moral crises of the sixteenth century.

If confessions are formulated to meet particular crises, the question arises as to the abiding authority of such acts of confession. Forsyth's basic answer is that such acts of Confession are descriptive and not proscriptive. To appreciate his view, it will help to first stress the positive side of their real, if not final, authority.

We have already seen above that Forsyth would agree with the view which maintains that the Church at times can, indeed must say, 'It seemeth good to us and the Holy Spirit so to confess Christ.' If we lose this trust in the Holy Spirit as leading the Church in common confession, 'If we do not really believe in the present guiding Holy Spirit of a living Word and Gospel in our midst—then we are not churches.'[138] While such guidance in no way implies infallibility and irreformability, it does imply that such confessions must be heard with the profoundest respect by the individual believer, for we are dealing here with God's faithful promise to strengthen and guide his Church.

Also the individual member must pay close attention to such common acts of the Church since he dare not make his personal knowledge an absolute norm under which the whole of the Church's knowledge of the riches of Christ is to be measured. Forsyth can speak of the Church as possessing authority in the 'second degree': 'If the first authority be God in his salvation renewing the soul, the distilled elixir and ordered experience of ages of that salvation must be an authority in the second degree.'[139] And again:

'Let us never in the name of a personal Christianity so reject the authority of the Church as to do despite to the great communion and conviction of saints. . . . If the final authority is God in Gospel, the Church shares in that authority as the expert of the Gospel and the soul. . . . To own a Church authority duly, to own it as real though not absolute . . . is to enlarge oneself . . . The Gospel revelation contemplated a Church; therefore only a Church could grasp the whole compass of the revelation. . . . We have no right to repudiate elements in that tradition merely because they are as yet beyond us, so long as they do not contradict the evangelical principle of the revelation itself.'[140]

Keeping both of these factors in mind, i.e. the guidance of the Holy Spirit and the broad experience of the Church, we must go on to say that Church Confessions are not absolute. They are '. . . not inerrant and final.'[141] They are, first of all, not final because finality lies in the Cross of Christ on which the Church stands and not in the Church's effort to confess that Christ at any particular point in time. Christ is final and, although he comes finally in and through the Church's confession, he alone is final. Finality does not belong to the theological work of believing man. 'If doctrine is the scientific expansion of dogma, and if, in science, there is no finality, then doctrine must go on being edited, revised, and enlarged by the theological activity which it sets free in various minds.'[142]

Another way in which Forsyth expresses the lack of finality of Confessions is to say that they are expressions of the Church's unity at a point in time but not the centre of such unity.

'True enough, the creeds, once in being, in course of time became perverted in their use. From declarations of the Gospel whereby the Church delivered its soul in terms prescribed to it at a particular crisis by the mentality of the age, they became tests and palladia in themselves for all time—as if the creed were the centre of the Church's unity instead of the expression of it. That is confessional fanaticism. . . . None of the products of the Church, whether creed or episcopate, can be the centre source or condition of the Church's life, however imperative and valuable at a juncture.'[143]

'The bane is not the fixing of the tradition, but letting it rust into its place, and become permanent in the first form. It is not fixed tradition that is fatal but frozen.'[144]

To seek finality in Creeds or Confessions, is simply to misunderstand their function. They are expressions of the Church's common faith in the face of a particular situation. Forsyth does not thereby imply that Confessions have no abiding significance at all. They must be continually listened to, for the Church could well find that this particular witness must be made again with but minor changes to suit an old foe in slightly new garb. What he does emphatically reject is the assigning of absolute authority to a Confession. The authority of an existing Confession must always be a new authority given to it by the present work of the Holy Spirit. Or to put it differently: the unity of the Church can ever anew find an existing Creed or Confession useful for its common confession; but only by finding itself 'useful' in this manner can an existing creed possess real authority. The binding must remain the work of the Holy Spirit and not the accomplished fact of the Church's theologians.

Excursus: CONFESSION, DOGMA AND CHURCH UNITY

In the light of what we have just heard concerning the Confessions, Forsyth makes a radical suggestion. He proposes that Church unity no longer be conceived of on the secondary level of written or formal Church Confessions but rather that it be conceived of on the

141

primary level of dogma.[145] Such a distinction would affirm that all Christians are one while allowing for sincere differences on the level of Confession. Forsyth does not mean that there is no longer a need for the Church to confess in a formal way. It could well be that doctrine (or Confessions) along Baptist, Lutheran, or Reformed lines would continue. Forsyth was not primarily concerned to merge such bodies into organic union.[146] But it would be clear that such denominations did not de-church one another. As long as a man or a denomination confessed the atoning Christ, then there could be no question of breaking fellowship and mutual aid.

Forsyth felt that Rome, on the one hand, had badly obscured the Gospel but on the basis of her continued confession of God's revelation in Jesus Christ she could still be reformed. On the other hand, those who had denied the Christ of the New Testament *kerygma* and replaced him with man's religious feelings or rational concepts or ideas, had in effect left the Church; they could not be reformed but only converted. In the face of Rome's pretensions and of the widespread anthropocentric religiosity which was challenging the Church, Forsyth felt that it was of pressing necessity for Protestants to confess their common faith in the Christ of the Gospel. Thereby they would point to the Cross as the true, gracious centre of Church unity.

This pointing to the Cross, this being unified around the central Dogma, is a reflection of Forsyth's understanding of dogma and finality. Earlier in this chapter, we mentioned that the reduction from dogmas to Jesus Christ's living presence in the dogma or *kerygma* of the Cross would be of prime significance to Forsyth's understanding of Church unity. Here we see its application.

In his writing about this problem, Forsyth dealt in some detail with the various aspects of church unity, i.e. ministry, organization, etc., but in the last analysis he felt that the problem of Church unity did not really lie in Church structure. 'The Church is not an organization but an organism. It was born one. The unity is not a matter of structure but of life, not of fabric but of faith.'[147] Church unity lies in Christ who gives the Church its life.[148]

In this short excursus we have touched only upon the most essential elements. The reader who is interested in seeing how Forsyth's view works out in more detail is directed to his major work on the Church, *The Church and the Sacraments* and to his smaller book *Congregationalism and Reunion*. We can best conclude this excursus with Forsyth's own condensed presentation of his view.

> 'I look forward to see the whole Church confessing but one Article, stating at once the source of her life, the principle of her action, and the warrant of her freedom. . . .
>
> 'First (in preamble), she would recognize, by virtue of the revelation which gave her being, that the central question of practical religion for men as we actually find them is one of the conscience—How shall Humanity stand before its righteous Judge? . . .
>
> 'And second (in substance) that the holy grace, on which everything turns, is not mere graciousness . . . but is consummate, final, and effectual only as the self-donation of God to guilty man, . . . in the justifying, reconciling Cross of Jesus Christ the eternal Son, our risen Lord who in that act creates his Church by his eternal Spirit.'[149]

* * *

Finishing the above excursus we have concluded our remarks with reference to Confession; now we turn our attention to that preparatory stage of Church confession which Forsyth designates by the titles, 'theology,' 'tertiary theology,' or 'the Church's reach.' We can consider this level of individual theology by examining Forsyth's remarks about theology in general. While these remarks apply to the whole theological work of the Church, they apply most directly to the work of the individual member of the Church who feels called to serve the Church in this particular task.

2. *The Nature and Task of Theology*

We shall consider theology in three aspects; the authorities, the task, and the nature of theology.

There can be no doubt as to the primary authority for theology in Forsyth's view. Christ, as present through the *kerygma*, is the final and primary theological norm. Thus it is that theology must be undertaken in prayer, in personal communion with the norm of theology.

> 'If it be true that the whole Trinity is in the gospel of our salvation, it is also true that all theology lies hidden in the prayer which is our chief answer to the gospel. And the bane of so much theology, old and new, is that it has been denuded of prayer and prepared in a vacuum.'[150]

Church theology; it takes place among the company of Theology is an act of faith, or worship, and as such it is the faithful, not in a vacuum apart from Christ or his people.

In the preceding section we have noted that there is a secondary authority for theology—the Confessions or Creeds of the Church. We must also refer to a tertiary authority which lies in the theological work of individual Church theologians throughout the history of the Church. This particular authority for theology was dear to Forsyth and he often stressed its value. At the time when he was writing many of his contemporaries were contemptuous of the great theologians who had gone before them. They felt no need to sit at the feet of the fathers and brothers of the

Church's theological history, preferring to begin afresh as if nothing of value had ever been said or written. There are many things wrong with this attitude; we shall follow Forsyth as he points out the necessity for reading and appreciating the work of other theologians.

It is important (and often overlooked) that we must start by appreciating the mature theological work of the New Testament writers. We must not forget, however, the distinction which Forsyth draws between the final *kerygma* of the Biblical writers and the important, though non-absolute, realm of their theological views.

> 'We cannot as a Church reproduce today, and offer to the world, the inchoate Christianity of Judaist disciples. They had a historic right where they were as catechumens, as disciples; but they became apostles; and it does not follow that their rudimentary stages have the same right on this side of the Pentecostal watershed of revelation as on that. Those who teach at that level . . . refuse light which did not then shine.'[151]

What applies to the New Testament writers applies in principle to the whole of the history of theological work.

> 'The past is not devoured but lives on, and comes to itself in the future. The new arrivals do not consume their predecessors, and do not ignore them; they interpret them and carry them forwards. . . .
>
> 'The amateur, or the self-taught, therefore is at a great disadvantage. . . . He does not come in where his great co-workers left off. He must start *ab ovo*. . . . He wastes himself criticizing what has long been dropped, and slaying the long-time slain. . . . The Bible is enough for our saving faith, but it is not enough for our scientific theology.'[152]

As a member of the Church, it is sheer folly for the theologian to ignore the careful reflection done by other theologians. Such ignorance is simply irresponsible and, at times, ludicrous. In addition to the

145

practical reason for listening to other theologians, Forsyth points to another:

> 'Their theology was like the wounds of Christ, graven on their heart and on the palms of their hands. To denounce and ridicule here is sheer heartlessness. The call is for interpretation. The need of the hour in respect of past theologians ... is informed and sympathetic reinterpretation. We must ask what their profound and solemn minds aimed at, and what they strove by their system to guarantee; though we may modify their way of securing it.'[153]

We stand in the same brotherhood, the same Church with the older theologians. They bore the marks of Christ; our basic purpose is theirs, to confess Christ. Can it be anything but a lack of love, a stepping outside of the fellowship of saints to ridicule their efforts? Forsyth asks ironically of those who scorn the older theologians:

> 'Would it not take all the earnestness out of our individualism if we were sure that most who come after us would treat us and our effort with the neglect and contempt, with the perversion *in malam partem* that many of us expend on the experience of the past?'[154]

Having discussed the authorities of theology which Forsyth accepted, we turn to his understanding of the task of theology. We have seen the stable framework in which the theologian does his work. Christ, Scripture, Church tradition and Christian fellowship offer the theologian his foundation and supports. So grounded and supported, Forsyth feels free to define the task of theology as an aid to the Church in confessing Christ to the age. It must take seriously the contemporary form in which the one basic question is posed: How can man stand before his righteous Judge? Forsyth uses Luther as an example of his understanding of the task of theology:

146

'Luther, for instance, did not just tumble into his contemporary world with a vehement iteration of New Testament themes. He condensed in his own person the moral problems special to that age and to the generations before it. . . . The questions that Luther answered with his gospel were not first century questions any more than twentieth. They were medieval questions. . . .

'It is the like thing we must do today.'[155]

Forsyth describes what he felt the central task of theology to be in his own day in the following manner:

'And now the great struggle of our time in this region must be to recover for the Bible Word the positive and final authority it has parted with . . . To the Bible as the Reformers read it we can never, indeed, return. And the Bible of the illuminationist is at best an edification, it is not a revelation. Means must be found of placing the Gospel, which is the Bible's core and life, in the place which the infallible Book once held; and of securing it in authority over the popular subjectivism by which the churches must fade into spiritual egoism, religious sentiment, rational anarchy, and moral impotence. A theology of the great fact must replace a theology of the mere spirit of Christ. That is the task of modern evangelicalism, to rescue from the Bible its positive and final gospel.'[156]

Forsyth has stated that the task of theology in material terms remains ever the same. It is to serve the Church in confessing the Gospel of forgiveness to guilty man. It is to answer constantly the question of guilty man with the affirmation of grace: You shall stand before the Holy God in the communion of the Cross! But the formal aspect of theology's task is a changing one. The form of the sinful rejection of grace and of the Church's confession changes. Forsyth understood the formal task of theology before him to be the confession of the authoritative revelation of God in the Cross as witnessed to in the Scripture. To do this required a rethinking of the role of Scripture in revelation. Scripture was at the centre of the matter, for the denial of God's grace had taken the form of a relativizing of the Biblical *kerygma*. Rome claimed to be the sole interpreter of Scripture and had proceeded to obscure the clear witness of the *kerygma*. Rationalistic orthodoxy had obscured the *kerygma* by replacing a historical, personal centre in Scripture with an embracive theological system. Liberalism had relativized the message of grace by immanentist presuppositions, seeing in the Bible man's religious product, but no clear message from God. In its own way, each of these movements contemporary with Forsyth had obscured the fact that *Christus est Dominus et Rex Scripturae* and thereby had obscured the Word of the Cross. Man could neither hear the answer of grace nor fully formulate the question of guilt until the Church confessed the authoritative revelation of the Cross and the place of Scripture within it. This Forsyth saw as the formal task before him and all of his writings serve to aid the Church in this confession.

We must now turn to the more general question of the nature of theology. In this connexion Forsyth poses such questions as: Is theology a science? If so, in what sense a science? Is theology free? Is it possible and desirable to have a theological system? In what sense does theology differ from theosophy? What is the role of paradox in theology? How is a modern positive theology to be distinguished from contemporary liberal theology?

We shall consider first the question of the scientific nature of theology. If by science we mean an Aristotelian view of science in which theology receives its axioms from the first philosophy, from metaphysics, then Forsyth would not agree in calling theology a science.

'It (a science of faith) does not mean a science of thought attached to faith, like Greek metaphysics. It does not mean a metaphysic of being, or a philosophy of jurisprudence, imported into the Christian faith by the circumstances of its history and growth.'[157]

Nor does Forsyth consider the deductive or syllogistic method of proof, central to Aristotelian science, to be the primary method of theological reasoning.

'The prime interest of the Church is not theological in the ordinary sense (where theology is an inferential discipline with "Greek demonstration"); it is dogmatic (where the theology is simple, fundamental, revealed, and creative with "the demonstration of the spirit and of power").'[158]

With these remarks Forsyth rejects what he understands to be Roman Catholic speculative theology. Such theology is over intellectualized, receives its axioms from a human source, and is too far removed from its living centre. It is too little *kerygmatic* to serve the task of theology which is to help the Church confess Christ crucified and risen.

Forsyth also rejects an understanding of theology which makes it receive its dominant principles from psychology.

'Nor on the other hand does it (a science of faith) mean a science of the subjective religious acts, a psychology of religion. Far less does it mean that the psychology of religion shall provide the dogmas or "broad general truths of religion," to whose test every belief of faith must submit, as the modern way is. . . . It is a science wherein faith is not so much the observed object as the observing subject. It is faith thinking and not only faith thought of.'[159]

Having seen Forsyth's rejection of the two chief ways in which theology was conceived of as a science by his contemporaries, it will be of help if we cite a present-day definition of science and then see in what ways Forsyth might agree and disagree with it. We shall then be better able to summarize Forsyth's view of theology as an independent, practical science. The following view of theology as a science is offered by a contemporary Roman Catholic theologian as suitable to the modern consciousness:

'By "science" in the objective sense is understood today a system of methodically worked-out knowledge about a unitary object. Theology possesses a unitary object, uses a methodical process adapted to the object, and unites its results in a closed system.'[160]

Passing over any objections that Forsyth might have to the word 'possesses,'[161] we are certain that he would agree that theology as a science derives its individuality or autonomy from the study of a unitary Object and that its method must be suitable to the uniqueness of this Object which it studies. He would further agree that such knowledge deriving from the methodological study should be understood in its interrelatedness and presented as a reflection of its unified Object. But that this knowledge is to be presented in a closed system would incur the hearty disagreement of Forsyth.

Theology is a science but it is not a closed system. In fact, even to continue to think in terms of system, not to mention a closed system, is to reintroduce the old Aristotelian view of science in a different form.

'There is not infallible system. System is not the manner of the soul's relation to God. Revelation has ceased to be primarily a thing of proposition and statement, a scheme of intellectual truth, a piece of knowledge in the noetic sense of that word. It has therefore dropped the ambition of intellectual unity as a postulate, and it courts it only in a scientific way as a product and an approximation.'[162]

Since the theologian does not begin with an idea but

with a person who stands over and against him, a closed system is entirely out of place; we must rather speak of knowledge derived from this personal object and related in whatever unity is appropriate. The unity lies in God and his revelation. It is not an idea, but the unity of his person.

The word 'closed' is also out of place. The theologian works with a knowledge of God which is open, that is, though final it is not complete or perfect. It must be judged where it is sinful; it must grow; and it must be expressed by the theologian in reference to the times in which he lives. He must, in humble prayer, be continually open to the Object of his study, praying that he does not turn from his living Object to the worship of an idea or a system. As Forsyth prefers to put it:

'... a theology of Christian truth is a living thing and not a closed system, a living reflex of a corporate soul fructified by the germ of experienced grace.... The Spirit is the living steward of the Holy Word. And to that gospel of grace, as we are continually sent forth from it, so we must continually return, to adjust our compass and take our course.'[163]

We have seen the sense in which Forsyth would affirm that theology is scientific: theology is the study of a unitary Object, in a manner suitable to the Object, deriving knowledge from that Object, to be organized in terms of the data which is given. Forsyth would add one more item to the above. He would call theology a *practical* science. It has its place in the Church and exists to serve the Church.

'Divinity belongs to the practical sciences which cannot be pursued in a social vacuum, and which have a vast effect on the long large course of public life. And it has therefore features of its own which are other than those of pure research, and which ought not to be determined by

151

that interest alone, or even perhaps in chief. Divinity belongs to the practical sciences, which do not resent, as research does, the prescription of a particular end or even system. In the case of Divinity, that end is given in its historic beginning, in the nature of the revelation which provides the facts and secures the end.'[164]

This practical nature of theology has caused some to question whether theology is sufficiently free to be a science. It has as its Object a dogmatic revelation and it requires faith and not presuppositionless inquiry on the part of its practitioner.

To such objections Forsyth points out that all science recognizes a dogmatic authority:

'"But," it will be persisted, . . . "A free science owns no authority." Except, of course, the authority of the facts it founds on; to say nothing of the axiom that we can trust our faculties. "Oh yes, of course, that is different." But is it different? Is it not the very point?'[165]

Forsyth is convinced that this applies to theology in particular for '. . . religion is an obedience before it is a liberty; and its first requisite is an authority; and for authority the first need is a real objective . . .'[166]

And the peculiar nature of theology's object shows the necessity of faith as a presupposition of theology. If it is true that all science must stand under the authority of its object and that the Object of theology is the living God in his revelation in Jesus Christ, and if faith is man's participation in such revelation, then it follows that faith constitutes the contact which the theologian has with his Object. Without faith, theology would simply cease to exist. A faithless theology is as unscientific as it is impossible. Faith is the God-given, the gracious freedom of the theologian for his Object.[167]

Being free for its Object, theology is free from other objects or laws deriving from the study of other objects. That is, theology is an autonomous science. For example, since the object of theology is a Subject, God in his Word, the theologian does not fear to use paradox. Theology must always '. . . be conditioned neither by the logic of a rational principle, nor the intuitions of a sympathetic heart, but by the central nature of the objective revelation of grace. . . . '[168] And the nature of grace is in itself the paradoxical relation of the sinner in communion with a Holy God.

> 'However it may be with the writer, the preacher must not be afraid of paradox. . . . a string of paradoxes, ingeniously invented, is one thing. It is smart, metallic, offensive. . . . The haunting moral paradox of the Cross is another thing. . . . Nonsense is just the word a cultivated Roman would have used for such speech. The offence of the Cross, the scandal of it, the blazing indiscretion and audacious paradox of it, has not ceased.'[169]

The freedom of theology from other objects applies also to the 'faith' in which theology must be practised. Forsyth points out that theology is not a science of faith in the sense of having faith as its object. Its proper Object is God in his revelation, though this includes as one of theology's dependent themes, an investigation of the faith which is man's response to God's self-manifestation. But even here faith is studied in relation to God, its giver. At no point is theology content to be but a type of religious psychological phenomenology. Theology is in this sense free from faith as its object, though theology must be practised *in* faith.

Being free by grace, theology is also free from an absolute binding relation to the secondary and tertiary authorities which we mentioned earlier. To be free for God means being free from Confessionalism or from a particular theological school. In this sense Forsyth sees a positive role for heterodoxy within the Church and distinguishes heterodoxy from heresy.

153

Heresy denies the *kerygmatic* Christ; there can be no room in the Church for it. Heterodoxy remains rooted in the evangelical Christ; it may represent tomorrow's creed.[170]

Is theology a free science? Forsyth answers that theology is a free science precisely when it stands under the gracious authority of its Object. It takes place in the Church, in the gift of faith. And it is free from other objects and other authorities by the continual freeing action of its Object. Only as such a free science is theology in a position to serve the Church and through the Church the generation of its day.

We can best summarize Forsyth's remarks concerning the nature of the Church's theology by presenting the distinction which he sees between positive theology and theological liberalism. Forsyth describes theological liberalism in the following manner:

'. . . by liberalism I mean the theology that begins with some rational canon of life or nature to which Christianity has to be cut down or enlarged (as the case may be).'[171]

'. . . the liberal theology starts from certain rational, metaphysical, or ethical principles existing in human thought, which determines by science, and not by obedience, whether any revelation, even Christ's, is divine.'[172]

Or in terms of Christology Forsyth says:

'For positive theology Christ is the object of faith; for liberal he is but its first and greatest subject, the agent of a faith directed elsewhere than on him. It is really an infinite difference. For only one side can be true.'[173]

What Forsyth saw to be most characteristic of liberal theology was its inability to take a God-given historical revelation seriously. Even in its search for the historical, non-dogmatic Jesus, its basic interest was in an immanentist teaching or an aesthetic appreciation of Jesus' personality.[174] The historical Jesus who, as the dogmatic Christ, was himself the source and norm of what should be thought of him, remained out of sight for liberalism. Once scientific theology makes this basic error, it must move in one of two directions; it must become either theosophy or rationalism. Both of these possibilities Forsyth felt were actualized in the liberalism of his day.

'If we discard that historic base, and still pursue the scientific interest, the matter of religion may be treated in two ways. Either it is taken in hand by a Rationalism in which it is trimmed down to the laws indigenous to formal thought; or it is given over to a Theosophy in which the matter itself is provided by an intuitive knowledge somewhat intractable to logical control. So that while Rationalism ceases to be Christian, Theosophy ceases to be scientific. There is no doubt that the latter—an intuitive idealism—is the favourite resort of the hour.'[175]

Having seen Forsyth's understanding of liberal theology, we now consider in what ways a positive, modern theology differs from it. We consider the term 'positive' first. Forsyth explains that positive means the '. . . *effectual primacy of the given.*'[176] 'Given' in this sense has a double significance: Forsyth refers to revelation as involving a given, historical fact and also that revelation is a gift of grace—it is given to man. In an historic act in Jesus Christ, God gives himself to sinful man. This is the foundation of positive theology.

'Positive' is also explained by Forsyth in the following manner:

'A positive theology is an evangelical theology. Positivity in this connexion has a chief reference to what I have often to describe as the primacy of the will. It is moral; but moral in a far higher sense than a mere imperative—moral as being not diffused in an idea or organized in thought, but concentrated in a personal act, in redemption. The love manifested by Christ in his life was positive in the

155

sense that it was not merely affectional but rational and moral. That is to say, its great features were first that it understood the total situation (i.e. between God and man) ... and second that it condensed into one definite practical purpose—it was saving and moral. . . . Positive means moral in the great evangelical sense. That is to say, in the first place, it means that the supreme form of God's love was a real act, central in history and critical for eternity. . . . In the second place, God's gift was an eternal life, something beyond natural goodness. . . . For what is morality, when we are at the height to which we have now come? . . . It is the soul co-operating with the holy energy of God and fulfilling its redeemed destiny.'[177]

In this second explanation of 'positive,' Forsyth points to the act of the Cross as the moral act of God in which he gives himself to man and in which man's destiny is fulfilled. Here again it is the historic act of grace which is the meaning of positive. A positive theology, according to Forsyth, is one which has historic grace for its Foundation, its Object, and its Norm.

The term 'modern' means primarily that theology is always an act of the present. Theology exists to serve the Church in its task of confessing to the contemporary world and of overcoming its present temptations in the world. And 'modern' also points to the fact that theology is as a science human, a *theologia viatorum*. It is a pilgrimage, never finished and always in need of forgiveness and of improvement.[178] In this sense 'modern' means the effort to improve upon prior theology and to make use of whatever new insights are available to the theologian. It is important to add that the ability to become aware of new insights, to purge sinful distortions, and to use new things in the culture, comes from the old foundation which is itself ever new. It does not mean seeking a new foundation from within contemporary culture, which would be a return to liberalism.

'Theology, on the whole, has been constantly modern-
ized. But it all proceeds on the basis of a reality above logic
and beyond criticism, the reality of experienced redemption in the Cross, of faith's knowledge, and the Church's
communion with Christ. . . . The Church's dogmatic
faith (Christ present in faith) is the great corrective of the
Church's dogmatic thought.'[179]

Christ himself, present with the Church, remains the
Norm and the modernizer of the Church's theology.
We might best put it this way: for theology to be
modern it must be positive; it must have the living
Christ as its Norm. Only such a theology will be free
to serve the Church in its contemporary task of witness
and obedience.

The following statement will serve us as a summary
of our discussion of the authorities, task and nature of
theology, according to Forsyth.

'But Theology, on the other hand, is the statement,
simple or scientific, of a living revelation given at a historic
point, creating its own society, and persisting in a continuous social experience. It is not the science of the Christian experience, which would be no more than a Christian
psychology, or a phenomenology of the Christian spirit.
But it is the science of such a historic and self-communi-
cated God as is given only in the region of our experience
in receiving him, and especially in the region of a Church's
collective experience. It is super-historic in the field of
history, and super-egoist in the field of our own experience.'[180]

To conclude this chapter on Dogma as the Word
of the Cross, we turn to an excursus which presents
some reflections by Forsyth on Biblical interpretation.
It is desirable to include this excursus for a number of
reasons. As we have observed, Forsyth's understanding of the task of theology required a reconsideration of the function of Scripture in revelation.
We have also examined the results of Forsyth's

157

reconsideration of the role and nature of Scripture. Both of these discussions will become more specific and alive if we can see how they are worked out in terms of Biblical interpretation. Also we have often had occasion to remark that, according to Forsyth, the living *kerygmatic* Christ, present in the Holy Spirit, is the Norm of theology. In the context of Biblical interpretation, this too becomes concrete.

Excursus : BIBLICAL INTERPRETATION

In this excursus we shall present in outline some of Forsyth's statements which indicate the nature of Biblical interpretation and illustrate it in practice. The epistemological presuppositions which lie behind these statements will be discussed in the next chapter in some detail.

In dealing with the question of Biblical interpretation, as in all documentary interpretation, we have to do with four factors, or with three elements and their interrelatedness. We have the reader, the document to be read, that which is to be communicated, and the *continuum* binding all three together in which communication takes place.[181] In reference to Forsyth's remarks concerning Biblical interpretation, we shall therefore consider the reader, the Bible, and the living Christ as present in the Holy Spirit.

(a) *The Reader*—We have used the term 'Biblical' interpretation. Does this mean that Forsyth would maintain that a special interpretative method is necessary when reading the Bible? To this contemporary question we can only reply Yes and No.

Forsyth would say that since the Bible was called forth by God and intends to communicate him, it requires a unique response from the reader. In this connexion Forsyth feels that faith on the part of the reader is a requirement of Biblical interpretation. But

158

on the other hand we must say that this does not really imply a requisite for the Bible alone, because faith is man's proper relation to God and therefore all books can and should be read in the light of Christ.[182] There is no book written which did not come into being under God's providence and upon which Christ could not shed interpretive light. If, therefore, we agree that in Biblical interpretation we meet the conditions proper to all interpretation, then we would say No; Forsyth does not offer a special type of interpretation which is to be used only with reference to Holy Scripture.

Let us look in more detail at the requirements which Forsyth places upon the reader of Scripture. If we speak of the expert, he would quite naturally require the special 'tools' of the trade—historical, philological, and textual. Speaking of the non-specialist, Forsyth mentions the importance of simply trying to understand the Bible, of reading it, of letting the facts appear, of beginning with the Bible itself and not with theories about the Bible.[183] He makes the further request that the reader not read individualistically. He must read as part of a body which is concerned with the meaning of this book and he should seek help from and give help to others so concerned. He must also read as a member of the human race with a long past, a past for which he shares the responsibility and in which he stands organically. He is to read as man as well as individual man.[184]

However, Forsyth places the major emphasis on the requirement of faith for the proper interpretation of the Bible. He feels that it would be '. . . vain to try to establish the Bible's real value by historical canons without realizing the experience of its grace.'[185] In dealing with various portions and questions in Holy Scripture, Forsyth finds it essential that 'We should bring to the question, as a real element of criticism, our experience of his salvation—just as to the evidence

159

of the Resurrection we bring the experience of dealing with the Risen.'[186] For with such experience '. . . a man is bound to approach the critical evidence of Christ's Resurrection in a different frame of mind from the merely scientific man who has no such experience.'[187]

We might sum up the subjective requirements for proper Biblical interpretation by saying that for all readers, expert and non-expert, faith is the prime necessity and the ground of any ability to deal fairly with the Biblical material. For the expert exegete and expositor, technical knowledge is also required[188] but expert knowledge without faith is completely inadequate. For communication takes place only within some *continuum* and faith is the human participation in the only adequate *continuum* between God and man. The nature of this *continuum* will become clear as we consider the last two factors, Christ and the Holy Spirit.

(b) *The Bible*—The second factor which we mentioned above is the Bible. In essence all of Forsyth's remarks with regard to the Bible are aimed at stressing its unusual unity. He wishes us to appreciate this unity, but in the proper manner. He refers to the Bible as having an organic unity and therefore requiring an organic usage. What does Forsyth mean by the organic unity of Scripture?

This we can best understand if we mention first some of the differences which meet the reader in Scripture. There is first of all the basic division of the Bible into the Old and New Testaments. Throughout the Bible there are different literary types, i.e. narrative, poetic, etc. In the New Testament there is the division of gospels and epistles. There is the difference often pointed out between the preaching of Paul and that of Jesus. The variety of authors and the time span covered in the material, all lend to the diversity which meets the Bible reader. That such literature is all gathered in one book, in one authoritative canon[189] indicates that there is some sort of unity. Some principle of selection has been exercised; some kind of cohesiveness has manifested itself. This unity can be described in various ways. In orthodoxy the unity supposedly lay in the doctrinal coherence, in the theological system of Biblical doctrine which united the Bible. This is rejected by Forsyth not only as being unjustified in the light of careful exegesis, but primarily as being based upon a view of revelation that is rationalistic and detrimental to the Church. The unity has also been described by asserting that this is a generic collection of the literature of a people. The unity therefore lies in the life and interests of this historic people. Aside from merely repeating the obvious, this does not really point to a unity within Scripture itself; it is content to point to the people in which it arose and simply avoids the reality of the unity in the Bible.

Forsyth describes his understanding of Biblical unity as follows:

> 'The unity of the Bible is organic, total, vital, evangelical; it is not merely harmonious, balanced, statuesque. It is not the form of symmetry but the spirit of reconciliation.'[190]

> 'The library is a unity in virtue of this historic message and purpose. It is not nationalist. It is not a history of Israel, but it is a history of redemption. It is not the history of an idea, but of a long divine act. Its unity is a dramatic unity of action, rather than an aesthetic unity of structure. It is a living evolving unity.'[191]

According to Forsyth, the unity of the Bible lies in the one purpose of God, reconciliation, and in his historical actualization of his purpose. It is the unity of one 'long divine act' beginning with Abraham and culminating in Jesus Christ. The unity precedes the parts. Thus, in viewing Scripture, one does not try to combine different units but rather one sees the whole in the light of the Cross, and only then looks at the smaller units. Forsyth puts it this way: '*If we are to take the Bible as Christ did we may not feel compelled to take the whole Bible, but we must take the Bible as a whole.*'[192]

Another way of describing this organic unity is to refer to it as a *kerygmatic* unity which finds its centre, its soul, in the *kerygmatic* Christ. This we noted earlier in the chapter. And in such a view, it is the *kerygmatic* Christ who is the Norm of all Scripture. We will not feel compelled to place all parts of Scripture on the same level, rather they will find their significance in their relation to him. Such is the organic or *kerygmatic* unity of the Scripture as Forsyth understands it.

Before we see how Forsyth's view of Biblical unity applies to the diversities in Scripture which we mentioned at the beginning of the excursus, let us consider two principles of Biblical interpretation which Forsyth derives from his understanding of the nature of Biblical unity. He speaks of an organic and of an historic usage of Scripture.

By organic usage Forsyth refers to the necessity for a passage to be interpreted in terms of God's whole act of reconciliation. The reader must ask, 'How does this passage reflect God's purpose?' Also, Forsyth feels that passages should be read in the light of other Biblical statements about the same theme. All of Paul's statements concerning righteousness, for example, should be read together and compared with the statements of other Biblical writers on this theme.[193] But this should not lead to a non-historical harmonizing of the material. Having rejected a view of Biblical harmony which centres in a system of revealed doctrine, Forsyth expects a more personal correlation of the statements of the different Biblical writers. This is due to the fact that they are all witnessing to the same, the one *kerygmatic* Christ. And they are being read by a Church organically united in God's long act of redemption fulfilled in him.

Forsyth also refers to an historic sense as important for the interpretation of Scripture. What does he mean by this? As we saw earlier, he does not mean dogmatic historicism. He means that the historical forms of life change and that only in Christ do we have in history that which is equally normative for all points in history. Expressed in relation to Biblical interpretation, this means that interpretation is not simply the establishment of the historic doctrine and practice of the early Church which is to be held up as the norm for the Church now. Rather Biblical interpretation must let each passage point to the *kerygmatic* Christ in order that *he* might speak to the *present* historical situation in which the Church finds itself. Forsyth states it as follows:

'... the normative in the New Testament is not a pattern. It is there in a historic context, not on a desert island.... Neither Church history nor Church piety is a continuous fall from the first century, where each age feels itself at the bottom, and must start scrambling up. Rather the whole of history converges and ascends through the present. And we must interpret the originality and normality of Christ and the New Testament consistently with that. We have to solve our own problems as the whole past presents them. We have to draw from an eternity which is brought to our door by the whole course of history up to now.... We have to interrogate eternity through the unity of history, past and present.'[194]

As an illustration of Forsyth's meaning at this point, we might consider the question of infant baptism. He would say that it would be a most non-historic usage of Scripture to attempt to establish what was the early

Church practice in this matter and then simply to maintain that this must be normative for all periods of the Church's history. Rather the question of infant baptism must be decided in the light of the centre of Scripture, the *kerygmatic* Christ. It must be a dogmatic-historic decision. Only such an approach is adequate to the finality of Christ and to the historic conditions of any given time. Historical criticism serves the Church's interpretation of Scripture by making clear the witness of the early Church to the *kerygmatic* Christ in all its historic actuality, but not by prescribing a normative pattern or theological system for the Church.

Now let us apply Forsyth's view of the *kerygmatic* unity of Scripture and the principles deriving from this view, to the differences which we noted in the Bible.

Forsyth points out that *kerygmatic* interpretation must allow for the different literary types within Scripture if they are to bear their proper witness to Christ: 'The literal and scientific mind of the West has thrust its dogmatic categories upon the fine blossoms of Oriental piety, and they have been withered by the touch.'[195] With reference to the relationship existing between the epistles and the gospels, Forsyth points out that the epistles are older and more normative. The gospels are in reality but an expansion of the epistles:

> 'The gospels were not meant for a finished portrait of Christ, or a complete manual of his truth. They were but supplementary in their origin. It is unhistoric to treat them as sole and complete. They were written for people who had already received the gospel, or had the epistles, in order to fill out their knowledge of Christ.'[196]

Forsyth admits of no basic tension or difference between the witness of the synoptic gospels and the rest of the New Testament writings; they all centre their witness on the Cross and resurrection of Christ.

'If you look at the Gospels you will see that from the Transfiguration onward this matter of the Cross is the great centre of concern; it is where the centre of gravity lies.'[197] Similarly, the distinction between the preaching of Paul and that of Jesus is not to be exaggerated: 'We must not sharply contrast Paul and Christ. We cannot, as I have said. *All we possess is the evangelical Christ common to Paul, the other apostles, and the first Church.*'[198] The Old and New Testaments also find their unity in Christ. Christ himself read the Old Testament in a non-critical (in the sense of Biblical criticism) way and read there of God's great purpose of grace culminating in himself: 'He used his Bible as an organ of revelation, not of information, for religion and not science. . . . He prized it wholly as the revelation of God's gracious dealings with men. He cared for events only as they yielded his Father's grace.'[199] Therefore, for the Christian interpreter of Scripture too:

'The key of the New Testament is in the Old Testament. The Old Testament explains the New Testament, as the New Testament interprets the Old. We cannot understand the Old Testament without the New; and we cannot account for the New Testament without the Old, which it fulfils.'[200]

We have, with these remarks about the unity of the Bible, already pointed to the third factor which we must consider—Jesus Christ.

(c) *Jesus Christ as present in the Holy Spirit*—The Bible exists to tell men about Jesus Christ, to point to him as the fulfilment of God's redemptive-revelation. According to Forsyth, it is this pointing to him that forms the unity of the Bible. But what is to be communicated is not simply information about Jesus Christ: it is Jesus Christ himself whom the Bible seeks to communicate. The Bible seeks to serve that faith which can come to

Christ in prayer. The Bible is there to be sacramental to Christ's presence. It is Christ himself who is the third factor in Biblical interpretation. Reader, Bible, and the Risen Christ are the elements which must find their interrelatedness in a *continuum*.

Forsyth would reject man's reason as providing the *continuum* between these elements for this would lead to a type of rationalism, based on some form of natural theology.[201] Nor would he accept the on-going life of the Church, understood as the *Christus prolongatus*, as the *continuum*. This is the view of Rome which confuses, as does the rationalist-humanist view, the human and the divine. The *continuum* which Forsyth accepts is the gift of the Spirit. It is he who, as the presence of Christ through the *kerygma*, calls man into faith, into the communion of the Cross. We might say that it is Christ present in the Spirit, who is both that which is to be communicated and the *continuum* in which communication takes place. Forsyth expresses this as follows:

> 'And from within the historic figure there issues upon us, to make us Christians, the immortal reality itself as a living power, a present Lord, a really present God. And we know then our Redeemer has found us. . . . He becomes his own witness in us.'[202]

So it is that the hermeneutic circle is closed by Christ in the Spirit: it is the Holy Spirit who is the '. . . supreme religious expositor of Scripture.'[203]

Here again we see why it is that faith is as much a 'tool' of Biblical interpretation, being man's participation in the *continuum* of communication, as are the tools of scientific scholarship.

In connexion with Biblical interpretation, it is important to consider Forsyth's understanding of the value and limitation of higher criticism, literary and historical. The limitation of higher criticism arises

166

from the fact that it does not deal with the whole of the Biblical witness. Higher criticism, in its very methodology, operates with the probabilities of historical occurrence, with the reconstruction of what most probably took place. But, in and of itself, it cannot deal with the supra-historical or raise the question of the significance of the occurrence of those events which it does examine.

> 'The difficulty only begins with facts which are more than merely historical, whose value lies not in their occurrence, but in their nature, meaning, and effect. It is not the crucifixion that matters but the Cross. So it is not reanimation but resurrection.'[204]

The critic is tempted not to see the limitations of his methodology. He is tempted to feel that he can remain within his discipline and still raise the question of the valid significance of the events which he believes have occurred. Such an attempt on the part of the higher critics displays a twofold error. It indicates that the critic has ruled out of consideration the supra-historical within history. Since his methods have no way of dealing with God in historical action, the critic simply denies that God is within history, except in a general, immanentist sense. The second error is that the critic himself then establishes some meaningful significance, some pattern of value in the events. He can only do this on the basis of some philosophical or religious conviction. And when this is not faith in the *kerygmatic* Christ, it would certainly distort Biblical interpretation.

The most flagrant example of such 'overstepping of the boundaries' by higher critics with which Forsyth had to live and against which he fought was the reconstruction of the 'historical Jesus,' the 'non-dogmatic' Jesus, Jesus as he 'really was.' Not believing, with Forsyth, that 'it is the whole Biblical Christ that

167

is the truly and deeply historic Christ'[205] some critics sought to penetrate behind the synoptic gospels and, on the basis of what was humanly possible and morally of value, to free Jesus from the bizarre distortions of the early Pauline Church. In reference to these efforts of the higher critics who were, in effect, finding a different centre to Scripture on the basis of an idealistic-ethical *continuum*, Forsyth has these words to say:

> 'The school I name takes, indeed, too much on itself when it dissolves into syncretistic myth the version of Christ that has made the Church, and goes behind even the Jesus of the Gospels to reduce him to the limits of a spiritualized rationalism.'[206]

> 'Its treatment has gone far beyond the secondary elements of faith; it has plucked the source of Christianity out of its native heaven and made it natural to earth. But in doing so it has surely proclaimed another religion and dissolved the apostolic Church.'[207]

Such misuse of higher criticism, even though it was so prevalent and dangerous during his time, did not blind Forsyth to the positive value which this tool has for the Church's task of Biblical interpretation. Indeed Forsyth looked upon higher criticism as a gift and instrument of the Holy Spirit. Speaking of higher criticism he said:

> 'The great function of criticism is positive. . . . And criticism is but Greek for judgement, and judgement is but the Latin for righteousness. So criticism is the agent of right and truth. Judgement is not a dreadful thing, but a glorious . . . a mighty hope. That at least is the Bible view of it. It was looked forward to. And such is the purpose and promise of the form of judgement called criticism.'[208]

The value which Forsyth saw in higher criticism was twofold. By its careful reconstruction it was to bear witness to the historical base of faith.[209] Faith's affirmation is that God was active in certain historical events, giving them a specific significance. It is one of higher criticism's tasks to witness to this faith by confidently and actively investigating this historic base. The second task which Forsyth saw for higher criticism we have already mentioned in our discussion of the 'historic sense.' It is to help the Church to hear in all clarity the contingent reality of the early Church's witness to the *kerygmatic* Christ. Our understanding of their witness to Christ is enriched as we know more of the historical conditions in which they made their confession.

Forsyth provides us with a summary of his attitude to higher criticism in the following statement:

'Criticism, therefore, is not to be discouraged but to be criticized. It grows to its work as compound interest, so to say, by the criticism of criticism. One school criticizes the other, correcting but continuing its tradition. . . . The higher criticizes the lower, and all is criticized by the highest, by the central revelation and gospel of grace.'[210]

We end this excursus by simply quoting at length an example of Forsyth's interpretation of Scripture, in which the above discussion of Biblical interpretation may be seen in practical application.

'Take the parable of Dives and Lazarus. Regard it for a moment as if the whole Bible were squeezed into that tractable size. Treat it as the Bible in small—as a bibelot. What have you here? You have the medium and the matter, the husk and the kernel, the setting and the gold, the scenery and the soul. You have the large pictorial element, the vehicle, and within it the truth or idea. You have scenery sketched in from notions current at that time about the world beyond death, and you have the truth which Christ used these to teach. You have a background taken over ready-made from inferior artists, and you have the foreground carefully painted by the Lord himself. The day is gone when we could find in the drapery of the parable a topography of the future state, guaranteed accurate by the authority of Christ. He tells us nothing of such posthumous geography or procedure. He gives us no book of the dead. He did not come either to correct or to sanction the popular ideas on such things. . . .

'But beyond all the scenery he had two ideas in the front of this parable that he did mean to stamp and to wing—possibly there may be two parables fused up in our story with an idea to each. First, he did want to press the truth, which so often engaged him, of heaven's *bouleversement* of earth, God's subversion of the social verdict. He often taught that the kingdom of heaven was in standing irony to the social order, that grace upset the current criteria of social worth (as in the case of the prodigal and his brother), and that it meant the revaluation of the moral values of the natural order, and often their inversion—the first last and the last first. And, secondly, he wished to send home the principle that, in spite of that, grace had a moral basis, that it was not freakish, and was not magical, and was not sensational, that the soul's fate was settled by a moral revelation rather than a miraculous. "If they hear not Moses and the prophets neither will they believe if one rise from the dead." It is the moral appeal that is the marrow of the Gospel, not the prodigious, not the portentous, not the thaumaturgic, not the astounding; it is the spiritual, the redemptive, not the sensational. The saving revelation is addressed to the guilty conscience not to the domestic affections, and not to the sense of wonder. . . . Its genius is faith and not imagination, not mere sensibility; and what it would produce in us is not an impression but a confession.

'Such is the Gospel in this parable. . . . and such is the place of the Gospel in the Bible. It is blended for educational purposes, with much that has no voucher, no perpetuity. Much is scaffolding that is taken down for the house to appear. The Bible has its earthly house which must be dissolved for the sake of God's building, heavenly and eternal. . . . We shall not be judged by what we thought of the Bible, but by the way it made us realize we were known of God. We shall be rich not by the ore but by the gold.'[211]

* * *

In the first chapter we dealt with the historical act of the Cross as the fulfilment of God's revelation in history. In this chapter we have dealt with the Christ of the Cross as the Word of God, who stands as the ground and norm of the Scripture and the Church. In both chapters we have found ourselves anticipating the theme of Chapter III, i.e. personal participation in the event of the Cross. This has been inevitable because the historic Cross is the re-establishment of personal communion between God and man. The Word of the Cross is the Living Lord present with his people through the Spirit-led interpreting of Scripture and the faithful confessing and preaching of Christ.

CHAPTER III

Personal Participation in the Fact of the Cross

IN this chapter we are concerned with the believer's personal, cognitive participation in the fact (event and word) of the Cross. We are to investigate the act of faith as personal participation in revelation. Forsyth's movement of thought will not allow us at this point simply to deal with the believer. We must first consider the work of the Holy Spirit of the Cross in the believer. Only then can we deal with the work of man in the Holy Spirit. In Part I of the chapter we shall examine the act of faith with its theological foundation receiving the accent and in Part II the act of faith with the anthropological response in the foreground.

PART I

The Twofold Work of the Holy Spirit in Man's Participation in the Fact of the Cross

a—THE HOLY SPIRIT OF THE CROSS—THE UNITY OF THE WORD AND THE SPIRIT

We have seen in our discussions of the sacrifice of the Cross, of eschatology, of the relation between the Cross (Dogma) and the *kerygma*, and in the excursus on Biblical interpretation, that Forsyth sees a most intimate or polar connection between the Cross and the work of the Spirit. Forsyth's use of the title 'the Holy Spirit of the Cross' underlines this fact.

Christ, the Word of God, is for Forsyth the source and the content of the Spirit's work. Christ sends the Spirit and the Spirit comes to witness to Christ in the hearts of men. There can be no thought of separating the Word and the Spirit, much less an exaltation of personal experience in the Spirit over the Word. 'It is that Gospel of moral redemption that is the one gift of grace and the one source of the Spirit; which Spirit was not a second and superior gift.'[1]

Just as the romanticism around Forsyth was laying stress on the Spirit, so rationalistic orthodoxy tended to stress the Word to the exclusion of the Spirit. In reply to the romantics Forsyth writes:

> 'And the historic Word was not Christ as the mystic Logos of spiritual humanity, sparkling in every soul (which was the Quaker line), but Christ as the saving action and grace of God for a new humanity at an eternal and creative point in history for our reconciliation and regeneration.'[2]

On the other hand, in opposition to the excesses of doctrinaire orthodoxy, Forsyth emphasizes the necessary work of the Spirit. No pure *fides historica* was adequate to revelation as interpersonal communion with the living God in Jesus Christ. Against any such historical positivism he writes:

> 'The Spirit when he had set the Word down in history did not abdicate for it and its rich posthumous effects. He is always there, personally with and over it. . . . He is immanent always to the Word (for this Word is a perpetual act); he . . . carries it home from within for the individual soul.[3]

b—THE HOLY SPIRIT OF THE CROSS—THE PRESENCE OF THE LIVING CHRIST

Having seen Forsyth's concern for this polar unity between the Word and the Spirit, we can turn to a consideration of the Spirit's twofold work of actualizing the presence of Christ on the one hand and, on the other, his work of opening the heart of man to receive Christ. Christ present in the Spirit, and man open in the Spirit—such is the Spirit's work.

'The ministry of the Spirit was not to supersede the historic salvation, and yet it was to do more than merely transmit it. It was to be at once its continuity, its amplification, and its individualization—all three.... The Holy Spirit is associated in the most close and exclusive way with the act of the Son, the action of the Word, and the existence of a Church of new souls. It is given by Christ as his greatest gift; therefore it was the fruit of his greatest act and consummation. It has its source in the Cross, and its first action in the Resurrection and its Word. Its prime action therefore is in its nature miraculous; it is ... first to regenerate, by organizing men into Christ's new creation. So that it is not one of Christ's gifts, as the Gospel is not, but the complete and effective gift of Christ himself.... So that, also, we cannot continue to speak of the Spirit as *it*, but must go on to speak of *him*, as he enters more deeply the personal life.

The Holy Spirit is thus inseparable from this work of Christ and from the word of it in the apostolic preaching which is crystallized in the Bible.'[4]

The Spirit's work in revelation is beautifully summed up by Forsyth: 'The action of the Spirit is immediate to the soul yet not unmediated by the Word.'[5]

Let us turn to the first task which Forsyth sees in the work of the Spirit; he is to make present the living, historic Christ. There can be no doubt, according to Forsyth, that it is the historic Christ with whom the Christian enters into communion in the Spirit:

'We believe in the Holy Ghost. We have in Christ as the Spirit the sanctifier of our single lives, the reader of our hearts, the helper of our most private straits, the inspirer of our most deep and sacred confessions. We must have

175

one to wring from us "*My* Lord and *my* God." We need not only the risen Christ, but the returned Christ. . . .

'That is the Christ we need, and, thank God for his unspeakable gift, that is the Christ we have.'[6]

To faith it is a fact that Christ is truly present in the Spirit. The Spirit does actually present the crucified and risen One to the believer. Forsyth's task is to give some account of or to exposit this reality. How is it accomplished that the *kerygma*, the preaching of the early Apostles, inspired as it was, is the means for personal communion with Christ?"[7] Here the problem presents itself in terms of temporal distance and of contingent event. In answer to this question, Forsyth speaks of the Spirit's work in terms of eternity and time.

'That is the work of the Spirit—to make us realize the simultaneity of eternity in time. If we look back, faith, by the Spirit, abolishes time, and finds the fontal Christ of long ago to be the fundamental power of today. He rose upon history in a remote age, and he rises in history now from its profoundest depths. So, looking forward, the same faith, by the same Spirit, realizes his final goal of the Kingdom to be the deepest of all forces in history . . . The soul's future goal is its present ground.'[8]

Forsyth's answer to the problem in terms of eternity and time is essentially teleological. It is similar to his position given in our discussion of the Kingdom as working itself out in history. There we heard of Christ in his victory on the Cross as being that pure eternity which is equally related to every point in time. So it is that the Spirit points us to a Christ present and victorious, reigning over every moment of time, calling us into communion with God in himself, which is but the actuality of the Kingdom in history. In other words, the Spirit-worked faith in the Cross is itself the teleological destruction of the time-gap, for all time stands under the sign of the Cross.

Forsyth also dealt with this aspect of the Spirit's

work in a different manner. He approached it in terms of a distinction between history as chronological, datable happenings and history as existence-shaping power; that is, the difference between history as *Historie* and as *Geschichte*. He defines the difference as follows:

> 'We are far removed from the facts of *Historie*, it may be, and we can hold them at arm's length and peer at them with a disinterested knowledge; but we are woven into the tissue of *Geschichte*. It has made us. We cannot be disinterested here. . . . It is the evolving organism of mankind taken as a moral and spiritual unity.'[9]

Forsyth is saying that the single events of history have mediated or have been sacramental to a living force which has given us our very being and has formed our very existence. We stand in organic connexion with our past, with all past in so far as it has contributed to the shaping of our existence. As we saw in our discussion of the Kingdom of God in Chapter I, Forsyth understands that history (in both senses of the word), is constituted by the relationship between God and his creation. Therefore, the *Geschichte* which is sacramentally mediated through the *Historie* ultimately proceeds from, is determined by, and leads to the sovereign grace of God. (This, however, is to anticipate Forsyth's conclusion.) He continues the above line of thought as follows:

> 'Having distinguished thus we may interpret Lessing's phrase to mean that detailed facts of *Historie* will not prove the eternal truths of *Geschichte*. We answer, they may not prove, but as a matter of experience they convey. . . . In a word, such events do not prove the truths; they convey them. They are not proofs, but sacraments or sources. The death of Christ does not prove anything. It conveys the grace of God, and it is the source of a new life.'[10]

Forsyth has asserted the fact that human existence

is shaped by the forces that act through the events of history. Thereby he has moved out of the realm of logical proofs (as Lessing originally posed his question), into the realm of historical influence in which all men share. At this point Forsyth leaves the general discussion of *Historie* and *Geschichte* and makes a special application. This transition from logic to *Geschichte* allows Forsyth to maintain that '. . . it sounds too much like an *a priori* judgement to which the historic fact must be squeezed down . . . (to maintain that) historic Christianity cannot be the absolute religion because no single point of history can be absolute.'[11] Who could say beforehand that no point of history could be the source of that power within history which would transform human existence as God will have it? Indeed, speaking *a posteriori*, the Christian must confess that in Jesus Christ this very thing has happened. A specific time in history has become absolutely decisive for his and mankind's existence. We have to do with the event of the Cross which conveys the grace of God. As Forsyth states it:

> 'The historic Christ *has* founded an absolute faith. . . . As a matter of historic fact, the divine person of Christ, as construed by the apostolic Word or preaching of Christ, did become the Christian foundation, the object of the Church's faith, and its source.'[12]

Forsyth therefore stresses the sheer factuality, not only of powers in history, but of the *absolute* determinative historic fact and power, known to Christians in history.

The Cross mediates the grace of God. And since grace is the redeeming act of God calling man into personal communion with himself, this historic centre is more than impersonal power or influence; it is the presence of the living Christ in the Spirit. Forsyth closes his discussion with these words:

Apart from the Holy Ghost, with his individualizing and time-destroying action, there is no means of making the past present in the Christian sense. Only the Lord the Spirit, by the Word of the Gospel, makes the person of Christ so near as to be the ever-present revelation and ever-creative redemption by God. . . . The historic fact of revelation that we are taught becomes the Word of revelation that we hear. Such is the Christian experience.

'It is not to be denied that in this there is something without parallel or analogy, something inexplicable and dogmatic, essentially different from our contact with every other piece of history. The relation is not evidential, nor is it merely continuous. It is sacramental. Nay more, it is a creative relation, acting in a creative evolution. There is an element of miracle in it, and therefore of freedom . . . The Spirit stands, like the great angel, with one foot on the old fact and one on our new soul. And fact and soul are united in his consciousness, which we share.'[13]

Leaving aside for the present Forsyth's interesting statement that we share in God's self-consciousness (this will be dealt with in the third part of this chapter), we find Forsyth declaring that in a way not paralleled by other events of history, as *sui generis*, the *kerygmatic* history of Jesus Christ serves as the means of a personal relationship between man and the living Lord. The original distinction of *Historie* and *Geschichte* proved helpful to move out of strictly logical categories, that is, to provide us with a phenomenological approach nearer to historical reality. But this distinction is not adequate to the whole of what takes place in the relationship between Christ in the Spirit and the believer. Here we have no merely posthumous immanent influence (e.g. the influence of Plato's philosophy), no matter how powerful it might be; rather we have an interpersonal communion, a communion with living *personae* on both sides. Here we have to do with the relationship of the resurrected, living Lord, present in the Holy Spirit to his believers.[14]

Such is what we might call the 'objective' work of the Holy Spirit as the presence of the living Christ with the believer within time. Because we are speaking of a personal relationship between Christ and believer, we must go on to consider the work of the Holy Spirit which opens the *human subject* to this relationship. Man finds, in this being-in-communion with God in Christ by the Spirit, that he is a new being, a new creation. Man's own existence is made new and determined by this relationship. Therefore we are led into the consideration of the work of the Holy Spirit opening man to Christ.

c—THE HOLY SPIRIT OF THE CROSS AND THE NEW CREATION

In this section of the study, we shall examine a number of the ways in which Forsyth has described or presented the work of the Holy Spirit in renewing man. In turning to consider man as a new creation, we imply by the term 'new' that there is a necessity for renewing work on the part of the Holy Spirit. The creation, and man as the representative head of this creation, stands not simply apart from communion with God in Christ. It stands in active rebellion against all communion with God except such as is idolatrously controlled by man himself. It is precisely due to the seriousness of this rebellion that there must come into being a new heaven and a new earth. Even now in this aeon, a New Humanity, a rebirth of man, a regeneration has taken place for, as was presented in the first two chapters, the Cross is the event of reconciliation in which communion *has been* and *is* re-established between a holy God and sinful man. It is for this reason that regeneration is the basic theme of the following discussion.

1. The Holy Spirit and the New Man

'Christ had to make the soul which should respond to him and understand him. He had to create the very capacity for response. And that is where we are compelled to recognize the doctrine of the Holy Spirit as well as the doctrine of the Saviour. We are always told that faith is the gift of God and the work of the Holy Spirit. The reason why we are told that, and must be told it, lies in the direction I have indicated. The death of Christ had not simply to touch like heroism, but it had to redeem us into power of feeling its own worth.'[15]

Regeneration is basically the work of the Spirit opening the sinner to Christ. It is not the awakening of man's slumbering potentialities, not the impression of the old man, not even the satisfaction of the needs which he considers important. It is new life, not just more life; it is new birth and not just the awakening and impressing of the old man.[16] It is God meeting his own holy demands and thereby the true needs of man and not what man himself might decide is needful. It is because of man's slavery to sin that Christ had to be the *Redemptor* as well as the *Consummator*[17] and that, in the Spirit of the Cross, man is a regenerate as well as a disciple.

'In the New Testament the Holy Spirit, the Lord the Spirit, is an objective power, working, before all sanctification, a new creation, and effecting it from the focal point of the Cross and Resurrection, and the thing done there once for all. It is not the spirit of discipleship but of regeneration by that Word.'[18]

Forsyth points out the connexion of the individual's regeneration with that of the race's regeneration:

'This rebirth of the race is not a thing yet to be done but a thing already done . . . ; "God hath regenerated us in the resurrection of Christ from the dead" (I Peter i.3); and it is prolonged in the Christian experience of many centuries.'[19]

Even in such a personal work as regeneration, Forsyth allows no individualism and no introspection. We are all sharing in a common work of the Spirit with the race, and we share in it by looking to the Cross where that regeneration was accomplished and not within ourselves. This in no way excludes experience in faith for the Spirit '. . . turns the living gospel Word into living and personal experience.'[20] But, as we shall see later, it means that Christian experience is concentrated upon Christ and not upon the self.

Forsyth also expresses regeneration in terms of a new world in Christ: 'The last theodicy is our regeneration, which makes credible the new birth of the world whereof the soul is an organic part.'[21] It is only the believer who can justify God because he knows God's world-wide new creation through his own personal regeneration. Which is to say that regeneration is a participation in God's self-justification.

We can best summarize Forsyth's understanding of regeneration by saying that it is the Spirit's gift of faith to the sinner. It is that opening of man's heart to the risen Christ which is sheer grace and the out-working of the Cross. And it is that gift of participation in the Cross which carries with it a sure confidence of that rebirth of all creation which was accomplished there.

Forsyth can also describe this 'opening' work of the Spirit, this giving of faith to man, by the term 're-pentance.' We recall from our discussion of the regenerative aspect of Christ's work on the Cross in Chapter I, that man's repentance is evoked by Christ's sacrifice. Here too man is not in the realm of his own potentiality. 'Repentance is never regarded in Christianity as a thing possible by itself, or a condition effectual by itself without God, but only as that part or action of the complete work of Christ which takes effect through us.'[22] By the last phrase Forsyth means that only as the sinner sees the judgement of God which has fallen on Christ ('. . . the exhaustion of judgement and not its remission'[23]) is the sinner enabled to repent and not simply fear or rebel. Only so is the sinner able to bring forth the '. . . penitence which is forgivably sensible both of the goodness and the severity of God.'[24] Forsyth conceives of such repentance as being in polar relationship with the Cross of Christ united in the Holy Spirit.

'And the two polar experiences, joined in one spiritual and organic act of mystic union, form the complete type of Christian faith. The repentance is ours alone; the penalty is not, the judgement is not. The penal judgement or consequence or curse of sin did fall on Christ, the penitential did not. The sting of guilt was never his, the cry on the Cross was no wail of conscience. But the awful atmosphere of guilt *was* his. He entered it, and died of it. Our chastisement was on him, but God never chastised him. The penalty was his, the repentance remains ours. His expiation does not dispense with ours, but evokes and enables it. Our saving repentance is not due to our terror of the judgement to fall on us, but to our horror of the judgement we brought on him. The due recognition of the wounded law was his, but the sense of having inflicted the wound is ours alone. Yet not possibly ours till we are acted on by what was his. The truth of penalty is penitence.'[25]

Forsyth can lay such radical stress on the saving significance of our repentance precisely because he understands it as a thing impossible in itself but the Spirit-worked consequence of Christ's confession. And, due to the fact that such repentance is the faithful recognition on our part of God's righteousness (his holy love), it is at the same time a sharing in the communion of the Cross and a hallowing of his Name. Such is the significance of the Spirit's opening work in man, as seen in relation to man's repentance.

It is clear that we can also describe this single activity or work of the Spirit in man as justification by

183

faith. Here faith (the gift of the Spirit proceeding from the Cross), is the response of man to Christ whereby he enters the communion with Christ accomplished and grounded in the Cross.

> 'The mystery and the power of Christianity is faith—understood not merely as a religious sympathy or affection, but as direct, personal communion with Christ, based on forgiveness of sins direct from him to the conscience.'[26]

And so understood as man's personal participation in communion with Christ, faith is salvation.

> 'Faith *is* salvation; it is not rewarded with salvation. To be forgiven much is to love much, which is to live much and live anew. The new life is the faith which constantly takes home forgiveness, regeneration, reconciliation, and all they imply for the heart.'[27]

Forsyth makes no effort to arrange these descriptions of the work of the Spirit in man into an *Ordo Salutis*; rather, as mentioned above, he sees them as different ways of describing the one work of the Spirit which is the opening of the heart of man to the living Christ.

There is a further work of the Spirit which cannot be separated from this unitary work of the Spirit but must be distinguished from it[28] as a foundation is distinguished from that which is built upon it, or more personally, as the specific activities of friends must be distinguished from the basic commitment and trust which constitute friendship. We refer to the work of the Spirit which he does as man's sanctifier.

Sanctification is growth and advance in grace. Forsyth points to this aspect of the New Man in the following statement:

> 'And is there any religion that can do it but the religion of Jesus Christ? Is there any other influence you know

that can so change a man's moral centre of gravity as to turn him from an eager getter to a cheerful giver? The permanent condition of reconstruction is redemption.'[29]

But, if under sanctification we stress the growth, the change which the Spirit brings about in the person's life under Christ, we must never separate this from its foundation in grace. Our sanctification is never able to bear the weight of justification; it is only known in faith and is worked by the Spirit through faith. The permanent condition of sanctification is justification. Forsyth makes this clear in this description of Christian perfection:

> 'Let no mistake linger, then, in your minds. Christian perfection is the perfection not of conduct, character, or creed, but of faith. It is not a matter of our behaviour before God the Judge, but of our relation to God the Saviour. Whatever lays the first stress on behaviour or achievement; on orthodoxy, theological, moral, or social; on conformity to a system, a church, a moral type, or a code of conduct; on mere sinlessness, blamelessness, propriety, piety, or sanctity of an unearthly type—that is a departure from the Gospel idea of perfection; which is completeness of trust, and the definite self-assignment of faith amid much imperfection. . . .
>
> 'Your faith (that is, your soul) may be perfected when everything else is very crude and fragmentary. Your attainments even in grace may be very poor, but your faith may be perfect. You may utterly trust him who saves to the uttermost. You may perfectly trust your perfect Lord, and charge him with the responsibility both for your sin and your sanctification.'[30]

As a final consideration of the work of the Spirit in the New Man, we must discuss one of Forsyth's views about prayer. In prayer, according to Forsyth, the goal of revelation is anticipated. Here too the work of the Spirit is central for 'When we speak to God it is really the God who lives in us speaking through us to himself. His Spirit returns to him who gave it; and returns not void, but bearing our souls with him.'[31]

It will be of help to us to note two aspects of prayer which account for Forsyth's considering it as the centre of the Christian's life. First, prayer is for the Christian an end in itself. 'Prayer is often represented as the great means of the Christian life. But it is no mere means, it is the great end of that life.'[32] It is the expression of man's sharing in the communion restored in Jesus Christ. 'Prayer is for the religious life what original research is for science—by it we get direct contact with reality.'[33] Forsyth emphasizes this centrality of prayer by showing its negative implications: As prayer is the height of our communion with God in Christ, so the depth of sin is lack of prayer. 'The worst sin is prayerlessness. . . . Not to want to pray, then, is the sin behind sin. And it ends in not being able to pray. That is its punishment.'[34]

We can sum up this first aspect by saying that prayer is life; it is communion with the Risen Lord; it is life in the Spirit, a foretaste of heaven. It is not only an end in itself but *the* end in which the believer eschatologically shares.

Secondly, prayer is of great importance as the means whereby God works mightily in and through us.

> 'There is no such engine for the growth and command of the moral soul, single or social, as prayer. Here, above all, he who will do shall know. It is the great organ of Christian knowledge and growth.'[35]

> 'Prayer alone prevents our receiving God's grace in vain. Which means that it establishes the soul of a man or a people, creates the moral personality day by day, spreads outward the new heart through society, and goes to make a new ethos in mankind.'[36]

The element of living growth or sanctification in Spirit-led prayer is there precisely because prayer is interpersonal. It is an act of Will encountering will. We have here no auto-suggestion, no aid to stoic resignation. The obedience and humility which emerge from a life of prayer are not fatalistic acquiescence.[37] There is a real self-limitation on the part of God whereby he takes our prayers seriously and responds to them.

'As we pray, the discipline for the prayerless is altered to that for the prayerful. We attain the thing God did not mean to give us unless he had been affected by our prayer. We change the conduct, if not the will, of God to us, the *Verhalten* if not the *Verhältniss*.'[38]

These words of Forsyth will serve to conclude the few remarks which we have presented regarding prayer as the work of the Spirit in the life of the New Man:

'*Magna ars est conversari cum Deo* ... We must learn that art by practice, and by keeping the best society in that kind. Associate much with the great masters in this kind; especially with the Bible; and chiefly with Christ. Cultivate his Holy Spirit. He is the grand master of God's art and mystery in communing with man. And there is no other teacher, at least, of man's art of communion with God.'[39]

With this short discussion of prayer we conclude our section on the work of the Spirit in the life of the New Man. We have not been exhaustive in presenting the work of the Spirit, but rather have dealt with only those aspects of his working which provide a background to an understanding of man's knowing in the communion of grace. We shall again see these different aspects of the unitary work of the Spirit as they appear in our discussion of man as a knowing subject in the communion of the Cross. This discussion was presented separately and first in order to underline Forsyth's conviction that our participation in the

Cross must be described primarily in terms of *God's* will to communion, that is, in terms of the Holy Spirit and not in terms of man's thinking, feeling, or willing except as these take place within grace.

Before we turn to consider man's act of faith in the Spirit, it will be helpful to consider, as general background material, the cosmic dimensions of the New Creation in Christ and the relationship which Forsyth sees existing between the first and second creations, between nature and grace. This material will then find its reflection in the last part of the chapter with regard to man's cognitive participation in the Cross.

2. *The New Creation and the First Creation*

Forsyth rejects a radical idealization of the New Creation which would separate the physical and spiritual aspects of the creation. He states:

'The solution in the Gospel is wrought once for all because it was on a world scale, an eternal scale, because he, and he alone of all men, was on such a scale. . . . He was to command not only the race but the universe, and save not only the soul but the whole groaning and travailing creation. That is one reason for believing in miracles, and especially the miracle of the Resurrection. He is King, Subjugator, and Commander both of nature and the soul. . . . Christ's miracles are parts, and even functions, of his moral conquest and control of the whole world.'[40]

It is therefore important for us to keep in mind that, when Forsyth refers to the moral dimension of grace, he includes the totality of creation, the physical as well as the spiritual. Creation itself is a part of God's plan, the work of his Word, and therefore must be seen in the light of his purpose. Forsyth indicates this moral or purposive nature of the first creation as follows:

'For the world is not so much the abode of God as the act of God; and man's function in the world is not so much to settle immanently into it, even into its growth, as to overcome it, subdue it, and find himself for a transcendently active God in it. In either case the movement is a vast act, and the goal is a personal communion of acts.'[41]

Therefore the very act of creation, its preservation and man's role within creation must be described in terms of God's purpose.

God's holy love stands behind and in charge of the whole of both the first and the new creations. To read into Forsyth a separation between the spiritual and physical spheres of creation would be a fundamental error and spiritualizing of his view of creation. According to Forsyth, both the first and the new creations include the whole cosmos.

Having seen that Forsyth's use of moral includes the whole of creation, we ask what relationship he sees to exist between the first and the new creations? This he describes in the following manner:

> '. . . the first creation with its providential course was made for the second, and only comes home in it, though by the way of creation and not evolution, of redemption and not mere development. Conversely the second creation has all along been reacting on the first and moulding it. Nature, if not the mother, is the matrix of grace. Salvation is the ground plan of creation, and the *primum mobile* of Nature itself. And it is from the second creation and its new birth that the last powers and initiations proceed which subdue the prepared ways of the first to its control, as the goal is rest after strife. The whole creation creaks and groans for the manifestation of the crucified Son of God, and the bringing forth of his judgement unto victory.'[42]

There are here two things of significance. We must note the care with which Forsyth distinguishes between grace and nature. And we must note the care with which he connects them. Forsyth is insistent that there is no identification between nature and grace and no continuity from nature to grace. We cannot climb from the world of nature to God. Such a view would be most perverse, for it would reduce Christ to but the apotheosis of man and the Spirit's work to but the impressing of the old man. It would place religion in the stead of faith and speak of obedience apart from forgiveness.[43] Here Forsyth is unequivocal: There is no path from the first creation to the new creation.

Having said that, we must also note carefully that Forsyth does feel that we can reverse the statement. There *is* a path from the new creation to the first creation; the '. . . key to the first creation is the second'[44]; by grace we come to understand nature. Christ is the *Consummator* in being the *Redemptor*. 'The second was the first tragically "arrived." . . . (However) the first does not glide into the second; there is a crisis of entirely new departure.'[45] It is the same God who made and remade the creation. But in the remaking he did not call out of nothing but he renewed a moral wreck and, as the Redeemer, he revealed himself more deeply to his re-created people.[46] The discontinuity lies in the type of creation he was called upon to create, the continuity in the Creator. Or to put it differently, God, who was not surprised by evil, would never have created once if he had not known that he could re-create in the face of any moral degradation and evil power.

From this Forsyth concludes that 'Grace is Nature's destiny. We are born to be saved.'[47] There is a continuity from grace which embraces nature. It is not that of development but of a God-given destiny, not of growth but of a gift from the one who has always been the *Redemptor-Consummator*. So Forsyth understands the distinction between grace and nature and the continuity from grace to nature. When man participates in the New Creation in Christ, he is at the same time participating in the fulfilment of the first creation

190

which arrives in the crisis of the Cross. Grace is the 'ground-plan of creation' and the key to nature.

In this first part of the chapter we have considered the regenerating work of the Holy Spirit of the Cross in so far as it relates to and provides the background for our discussion of man's knowing participation in the fact of the Cross. The knowing of man must first be described as the action of the Holy Spirit in man. However, this does not exhaust the theme: it is man's heart which is opened to Christ. It is man who believes and who trusts, who hopes and who is certain of his Lord and the destiny of the world in him. Therefore we are called to follow Forsyth's exposition of *man's* active knowing within the work of God's Spirit. This is the task of the final part of this chapter.

PART II

Man as a Knowing Subject in the Communion of the Cross

The importance which Forsyth felt the topic now under discussion to possess is indicated by the frequency with which he deals with it through his writings. It is also significant that his largest, most systematic work, *The Principle of Authority*, is an exposition of this topic. Such concern arises from Forsyth's understanding of revelation as a God-effected interpersonal communion in Christ; man must knowingly participate in such a communion or revelation is not actualized.[48]

We shall present Forsyth's reflections in the following manner: A. Man knows because he is known—God the Knower; B. Authority and certainty in man's knowledge of the Cross; C. Man's knowledge as experiential participation in the Cross; D. Man's knowledge of the Cross as a miracle of grace; and E.

The Church's knowledge of the Cross and its task in the world.

All through this part of the chapter we shall find that the themes will interpenetrate one another. The reason for this is that man's knowing has as its centre the Cross, God's act in Jesus Christ. It is there that we are known; it is there that Christ is revealed as Lord; it is the atoning Christ of whom we are certain; it is his forgiveness which we are allowed to experience and trust. We are dealing with man's knowledge of the final act of God on the Cross and the different themes of this part of the chapter are simply different aspects of this one act. This, of course, parallels what was said earlier regarding the unity of the work of the Spirit in man. Now we shall be viewing this unity of the Spirit's work from the perspective of man's act of faith.

a—MAN KNOWS BECAUSE HE IS KNOWN—GOD THE KNOWER

According to Forsyth, that which is most basic, most certain in man's knowledge within the communion of the Cross is the knowledge that he is known by God.[49] To be known by God is to be chosen, loved, created, elected by him. The uniqueness of religious, or better, of Christian knowing is this being rooted in the divine knowing or loving election of God.

'It is not mere contact with a great, and even immeasurable, moral personality. For such a person might be ignorant of us and our contact, neutral to us, heroic in his moral dignity but not divine in his care. Nor is it simply that we know one who knows things; but we know that he knows us, that we know religiously only as we are thus known by him. It is a knowledge in which he does not simply take cognizance of us, but knows us, in a special sense, with such a creative intimacy as love alone provides. In religion the fundamental movement of the knowledge

192

is in the reverse direction from that of science. In science we move to the object of knowledge; in religion it moves to us. We know him, as we love him, because he first knew and loved us.'[50]

In the above quotation we see that God's knowing is the primary knowing. And it is primary in a specific sense. It is primary as the foundation of the communion in which man's knowing takes place as a secondary or responsive movement. Forsyth feels it to be important to accentuate the fact that our knowing of God and of ourselves begins in and rests on God in order that it be clear that the centre of gravity of our knowing lies outside ourselves.

'Our knowledge of ourselves rests on God's knowledge of us. We are most certain of our thought when we know that God is thinking us and through us. . . . The root certainty is not, "I think," it is, "I am thought"; not, "I know," but, "I am known." If we know that, we need not fret at the limitations of our ignorance. . . .

'Our thought will prosper, and our science, as we realize that it is not the first thing but the second.'[51]

It is not, therefore, the extent or quality of our own knowing that forms our foundation; it is God, the 'Searcher of hearts' who knows us by his 'Eternal Choice.'[52]

The place in history where we know that we are known by God is the Cross.

'In Christ there is a spot where we are known far more than we know. There is a place where God not only speaks but comes, and not only vouches but gives, and gives not only himself to the soul, but, by a vast crisis, the soul to itself and the world to his Son. Our error and uncertainty go back at last for their power to our guilt, and they pass away in the gifts of the grace that destroys it. The grace that magnifies the guilt in the act of mastering it takes away the doubt. Trust gives us the security denied to sight.'[53]

193

God's revelation of himself in Jesus Christ gives the basic form to man's knowledge of God. He deals with our guilt as one who eternally, lovingly knows us. Consequently, our most fundamental knowledge of ourselves is that we are forgiven—that we are known. It is in the forgiving, loving knowledge of God that we find our security and rest. This placing of the heart of the matter in God's faithfulness, frees us from anxiously examining our knowledge of God to see if it will bear the weight of our self-certainty. Here, as in good works, all begins with and grows from the certainty and the wonder of grace.[54]

There is a second factor that needs to be mentioned as part of Forsyth's stress on God's knowing as the foundation of man's. It is this: in discussing man's knowledge of God and of himself within the communion of the Cross, we are dealing with a knowing that arises between Subject and subject. Speaking of eternal life, Forsyth describes such knowledge of God as follows:

> 'It is to know God as holy love. But it is not to know him as an object, not to know him as science knows, not to know him in a cognition, which sees a thing at the other end of our observation or of our thought. It is to know him by an inner appropriation. It is by an interpenetration. We know what begins by knowing us. We know because we are known. It is the kind of knowledge which does not *give* power but *is* power, where our self is not just enhanced but lost, and only in that way found in its fullness. . . . Eternal life is much more than contact; it is living communion with spiritual and eternal reality. And on that reality's initiative. Real love is not that we loved God but he us.'[55]

Therefore to forget that we have to do with knowledge in the form of interpersonal communion when we talk about our knowledge of God and of ourselves is a drastic error.

'The common vice, therefore, of all these imperfect forms of religion is that they treat God as an *object* of knowledge more or less theoretic, instead of treating him as the *subject* of a knowledge, which is inceptive and creative, as searching, as it is infinite, and as particular as it is universal.'[56]

Such de-personalizing of our knowing of God and of ourselves stems from pride and leads to idolatry. Man refuses to acknowledge that he is able to know God only in terms of God's self-manifestation and because God has graciously redeemed and reconciled man in his Son, that is, only because God has opened man's heart.[57] Such de-personalizing ignores both God's personal mystery and man's sin. This idolatry can be termed the sin of man's epistemological *self*-confidence and it leads inevitably to a conclusion or an idea instead of to God in personal intercommunion.

In contrast to such subject-object types of knowing, Forsyth bids us think in terms of a knowing within communion, of a knowing that finds its foundation in the gracious knowing of God, who knows us through the Cross. It is within this interpersonal frame of reference that man's knowing must be considered.

The next theme has already been indicated in our remarks regarding God as the Knower, for it has to do with man's certainty of being known by God and the authority of God's knowledge of man.

b—AUTHORITY AND CERTAINTY IN MAN'S
    KNOWLEDGE OF THE CROSS

Before concentrating upon the 'evangelical experience' in which man personally takes home God's self-disclosure and from which man's knowledge of himself arises, it is important to examine some general or formal characteristics of man's knowledge of God and of himself within revelation. Their rootage

195

in the 'evangelical experience' will become clear in the next sections. Further, this will allow us to consider some very fundamental theological themes as Forsyth understands them, for he treats them as aspects of man's knowing in revelation. These themes cluster about authority and certainty.

Revelation is authoritative or it is no revelation. 'The principle of authority is ultimately the whole religious question, . . .'[58] Many around Forsyth did not seem to grasp the need for authority and were unaware how pressing the problem had become.

> 'The question of the ultimate authority for mankind is the greatest of all the questions which meet the West, since the Catholic Church lost its place in the sixteenth century, and since criticism no longer allows the Bible to occupy that place. Yet the gospel of the future must come with the note of authority. Every challenge of authority but develops the need of it . . . the Church can never part with the tone of authority, nor with the claim that, however it may be defined, the authority of its message is supreme. . . . it preaches the absolute right over us of the Christ who bought us—the active supremacy in conscience of our moral redemption.'[59]

We see again that Forsyth was in full agreement with those movements of his time which asserted that neither an institutional church nor a canonical Scripture possessed ultimate authority for man. However, this must not be construed to mean that man can live apart from an ultimate authority or that the Church was thereby bereft of an authoritative message. Jesus Christ is the ultimate authority for mankind.

But in what sense is Christ the final authority? Forsyth states:

> 'Authority, we keep finding, is only a religious idea. In science it does not exist, and in politics it is but relative.

In any ultimate sense it concerns but the soul. There only is it absolute; everywhere else it is but relative. And it rules through the soul, by the response of the moral personality. It is a personal relation and a moral, the relation of two wills and consciences. It is the authority of an absolute, holy Person. And in religion nothing is authoritative except in so far as it shares the authority of God himself, and holds of the holy. . . . But the holy is the absolute conscience. So this divine authority is exerted upon a conscience. But on a conscience which, as soon as it realizes the holy, realizes itself in the same act as sinful and lost. . . . It is therefore, further, the authority of a Saviour. . . . It is the new-creative action of the perfectly holy conscience of God on the helplessly guilty conscience of man. It is life from the dead. . . .

'The last certainty is only ours as a personal experience of an eternal salvation. And so it is there also that we realize our absolute Authority, whose we are, and not our own at all, being bought with an infinite price.'[60]

This is a very rich quotation and contains much that we will be examining shortly. At this point we wish to observe that the authority of Christ is the authority of the Holy God, personally encountering man in the conscience. It is a practical Lordship based on the Cross; the final authority for guilty man is a Redeemer.[61] Further we note that this authority is deeper than, or in a different dimension from, the relative authority of the scientific statements of the Church's creeds and the individual work of its theologians.[62] Here we have to do with the final authority of sovereign grace.

Another way in which Forsyth points to this authority in man's knowledge of God is in his description of faith or eternal life as obedience. Authority calls for obedience, the obedience of faith.

'Eternal life is absolute obedience, an attitude to One who has a right over us high above all his response

to us, one to be trusted and obeyed even amid any dere-
liction by him and refusal of his response. He is our God,
not because he loved and pitied, but because in his love and
pity he redeemed us. God is for us and our release only that
we may be for him and his service. He is for us, to help,
save and bless, only that we may be for him, to worship
him in the communion of the Spirit and serve him in the
majesty of his purpose for ever. First we glorify him, then
we enjoy him for ever.'[63]

Grace bestows and claims. It is God hallowing his
own Holy Name. Redemption' is not merely redemption from sin and Satan, nor only the price paid
by Christ in our place, but it is a regeneration to
communion with God, to a life of service and sanctification. Faith is the obedient recognition of the right
of God to be our Redeemer and our Lord.

But lest we misunderstand the life of faith as a
slavish obedience, a heteronomous recognition of
authority, Forsyth tells us that faith is freedom; it is
theonomous.

> 'Faith is not a thing but a freedom. It is a soul in a
> certain relation, a certain state, a certain free act. It is a
> moral soul coming to itself. It is a coming therefore to the
> freedom which is the unique badge of soul, coming to the
> higher freedom from which the lower was made. If it was a
> divine thing to create man free, a free will, it is a divine
> thing to emancipate that first freedom—to redeem. . . .
> 'Redemption is re-creating a free soul through its freedom.
> It is converting its freedom, and not its substance. It does
> not change its natural psychology. . . . Its condition is a
> positive authority. The old man becomes a new man only
> by receiving a new master. The new creation is a new
> obedience; and the new Creator is one whose perfect
> service is perfect liberty, and who enables the soul in this
> submission to find itself and its destiny.'[64]

Man was made for God; he is free to be himself only
when he is free to be for God. God's authority does not

198

limit man's freedom but rather calls it into being. And in redemption he reconstitutes it. Only as man is freed from bondage to sin, to himself, to false lords many, can man be truly free. Thus faith as man's participation in grace is both the profoundest act of obedience and at the same time of the fullest freedom. We are restored to our destiny as sons not slaves, indeed we have even been called friends of God. In this context we can understand how strange the desire to rebel from God's authority for the sake of 'free thought' must sound to the believer. For he knows that truly free thought is part of the gift of grace and is ever hampered by sinful autonomy. Apart from the overruling of grace no man escapes in the slightest from being bound by the '. . . prejudices and passions of the common natural man, or by that "collective suggestion" '[65] of his environment. Only a free man in Christ is capable of free thought, and even then only to the extent that the old man is subdued in him. Forsyth summarizes the connexion between authority and freedom most perfectly as follows: 'But God's sovereignty is redemption. He is never so sovereign as there. He is never so absolute as in making freedom.'[66]

We have seen that revelation comes with the mark of authority, and that it calls forth free obedience in man. However, there is another way to describe the response of man in revelation. God's knowing of man calls forth certainty in man's knowing of God and of himself. Forsyth uses some striking analogies to describe this certainty. But before we take note of them it is important to realize that this certainty is in itself a form of obedience.

'The truth may be a shock to some stalwart ideas, and some prickly rights of private judgement, but certainty is really obedience. Without that note it is but a mode of

14—TTOPTF

self-assertion, in which we are more sure of ourselves than of each other or of anything.'[67]

'What such people miss in their egoistic heat and hurry of private judgement is this, that certainty means certainty *of something*, which we do not arrive at but which arrives at us. If I am certain, it does not really mean that I am certain of being certain. In religion, at least, I am certain of something beyond my certainty and creating it. . . . The more we fix our attention on the object of our certitude, the more we humbly realize that it is a something *given*. Its source is not in us. It is of grace.'[68]

Thus we see that conviction or faith is not self-generated but is truly a response, obedience to the given. And of course the given in this context is grace. Indeed Forsyth is so concerned to stress that faith is a response and no self-produced certainty that he feels it necessary to reject the *schema* of man's need and God's action, preferring to stress the given by reversing the phrase and speaking of God's action and man's need.[69] 'God's grace is not certain just because it satisfies our need, but because it has pleased him to reveal it in an historic, authoritative fact which creates the chief need it fills.'[70] Man's sense of need is too egocentric, too distorted to provide an independent norm for the recognition of revelation. To base our certainty on the fulfilment of our need would be to have a self-based certainty. It would not be a certainty which is obedience to the given—to grace.

How then does Forsyth describe this certainty which characterizes faith? Perhaps the most striking description which he uses is that of our sharing in God's own knowledge of himself. It is a function of God's Spirit in us.

'And our certainty is, by the Holy Spirit, a most incredible thing—it is a function of the certainty which God always has of himself. It is a certainty of experience truly, but it is more than experience; it is a reflection of his own self-certainty. It is his own self-certainty immanent in us by faith. He never doubts himself, and he lives in us. The things of God are only known by the Spirit of God, whether in him or in us.'[71]

For faith there can be no question of a hidden God, or a hidden decree. Faith is a response to God in his gracious self-giving. To be sure it is a reflection only, for we are men and not God, but a reflection which is trustworthy, borne by the Spirit of God to our spirits. God makes himself known as he is, as he knows himself to be—holy, trustworthy. And our certainty is based on this communicated knowledge which God has of himself. Here is grace indeed, that man is given such intimate communion with God in Christ. And such is the communion which God bestows through the Spirit of the Cross, the Spirit who searches the deep things of God.

Another way which Forsyth describes faith's certainty is to point out that it is a moral, a personal certainty. This is the correlate of the fact that God's authority is moral.

> 'It is the certainty of reconciliation, and its experience of communion. It turns upon God's initiative of grace and reconciliation. And Christian faith is faith in the Justifier, the Reconciler, the Sanctifier, and not merely in God the Father. It is the soul intimately certain as to the world's saving, redeeming, forgiving, regenerating God in Christ.'[72]

This same point is made when Forsyth distinguishes between theosophy and theology. He points out the difference between true certainty which is of the morally given, and a pseudo-certainty based upon an intuition of thought.

> 'In a theosophy (like Hegel's system) what we use is the intuition of thought by thought, in theology it is the

intuition of a person by faith. In the one we have an ideal monism, thought discovering itself everywhere; in the other we have a moral dualism, in which a person finds another person by way of salvation and not mere discovery. In the one case it is the intuition of truth in a mind, in the other the intuition of personality in a community.'[73]

These considerations point us to an examination of the moral event which is faith, or as Forsyth often refers to it, the 'evangelical experience.' It has become evident that to fully grasp his whole concept of authority and certainty in man's knowledge of God we must come to understand the role of the conscience in this experience. For God makes himself known through the Cross and thus deals with man as a moral person and not as an intellectual substance.[74]

But before we leave the treatment of certainty to seek its roots in the 'evangelical experience,' we take note quite briefly of how Forsyth understands the opposite of certainty, that is, doubt.

> 'The Protestant position is that we contribute nothing; that our salvation is wholly and solely of God's grace, with which we are placed in direct contact, and are sure at first hand; that it is quite undeserved by us, and on God's side absolutely free. In which case the lack of certainty is lack of faith, lack of direct personal contact, lack of communion, and, by so much more, lack of Christianity, which is entirely the communion and trust of a saving and forgiving God.'[75]

It would seem that Forsyth asserts that doubt is far from inherent in the finitude of creation but is rather a mark of faithlessness, a form of sin. To doubt is not to be courageously honest in the face of the Gospel, but to maintain man's sinful autonomy.

Now let us turn to the 'evangelical experience.'

c—MAN'S KNOWLEDGE AS EXPERIMENTIAL PARTICIPATION IN THE CROSS

The task before us in this section of the chapter is to come to an understanding of Forsyth's use of the term 'experience' with reference to man's participation in the Cross and to see what relation it has to the authority and certainty of revelation which we have just been considering. We must discover what Forsyth means by the phrase 'evangelical experience' and examine some aspects of its uniqueness. We must consider the seat of this experience and its content and then go on to discuss the role of man's will and intellect in relation to his participation in the Cross.

1. *The Evangelical Experience*

There is one experience which, for the Christian, is both absolutely fundamental and totally unique; it is that of participating in the reconciliation with God wrought by Jesus Christ. This experience is a unique encounter with Christ in which an awareness of the self as restored to communion with God is coterminous with an awareness of Christ as the *Redeemer* and *Lord*. The following two statements of Forsyth illustrate the experience of Christ as Redeemer and Lord and of ourselves as reconciled sinners.

'We are to think about Christ whatever is required to explain the most certain thing in the soul's experience—namely, that he has given it the new life of God and mercy, and saved it from the old life of guilt, self, and the world. ... who not only opens communications but restores to such as we are real and complete communion with God, one who does not pass us on but keeps us in himself.'[76]

Speaking with reference to man's soul Forsyth states:

'And he came not as its servant (its Jesus) nor as its ideal (its Christ), but as its *Lord* and very God. What we

203

really get in our conversion is not only a Saviour but a Sovereign.'[77]

According to Forsyth, this experience is existential involvement or total personal participation. 'You must let that come home to *you*, to your own peculiar case.'[78] 'All Christology must rest on a moral salvation, spiritually and personally realized.'[79] '. . . authority has no other root *for us* than in our experience of his unique and divine function in forgiveness.'[80]

We can summarize by saying that the 'evangelical experience' according to Forsyth, is the personal awareness of Christ as Redeemer and Lord and of one's self as redeemed and ruled by God in Jesus Christ. Now we must consider the various ways in which this experience is *sui generis*, entirely different from what we usually mean by the word 'experience.'

2. *Some Aspects of the Uniqueness of the Evangelical Experience*

This experience differs from the manner in which we experience things around us. With Christ we are directly addressed.

'Our experience of Christ is thus quite different from our experience of an objective world. Our moral sense of an agent, and that agent a Redeemer, is a different thing from the inference or postulate of an objective world behind sense to account for our impressions. That may be a cause but this is a Creator. When the objective announces itself as a heart and will, which not only chooses, or influences, me, but saves me, then the response of my active will, of myself as a person, is a different thing from the commonsense that instinctively places an object behind passive sensation.'[81]

The directness, the objective confrontation of Christ's presence is contrasted with the more passive inductive manner with which we experience the objective world.

204

The presence of Christ breaks through the wall of our subjectivity and commonsense postulation, creating us anew. The *Ding an sich* becomes phenomenal, declaring himself to be our Lord and Saviour.

Forsyth also points out that an evangelical experience is distinct from any other experience in that it is a moral experience. It is of fundamental significance that Christ is present in the believer's experience as the Redeemer, the One who has borne his sin and forgiven his guilt, and as the Lord who commands his total commitment and obedience. It is this which makes the evangelical experience an experience in the moral dimension. To experience Christ on the aesthetic level, the ethical level, or the intellectual level, is not the evangelical experience of faith. Forsyth puts it negatively as follows:

'. . . if any conscience, recognizing the centrality of moral issues, can place itself before the absolutely holy Power, with whom it has finally to do, and yet feel no sense of hopeless guilt, there is no more that men or books can do. It is temperamental defect or moral hardening, and it must be left to another influence, another experience, and another light.'[82]

We have seen that Christ in the evangelical experience encounters man in his guilty conscience. It is as the Holy Lord and Redeemer of man that the *kerygmatic* Christ is present. This means, according to Forsyth, that faith knows the conscience in man to be the seat of its experience of Christ.

3. The Conscience as the Seat of Man's Evangelical Experience

Forsyth describes man's self-consciousness in the following manner:

'Man is more than a consciousness, he is a conscience. He is not only aware of himself, he is critical of himself.

There is in the soul a bar, a tribunal; our thoughts and actions are ranged before it; judgement is passed there upon what we have been and done. Every one who believes in morality believes in the conscience as the power we have of passing moral judgement upon ourselves. . . . What a strange thing we are—two, yet one! Two that cannot agree—one that cannot be severed. Our enemy is of our essence, taken from under our very heart. We are one by being two. We are unhappy both because we are two and quarrel, and because we are one and cannot part. Neither of us can go out of the other's hearing.'[83]

Forsyth here directs our attention to the general phenomenon in man of the conscience which is man passing judgement upon himself as guilty. Man is self-conscious as a guilty conscience. There is, in reality, this dualism in man that must be dealt with if theological reflection is to be adequate to life as man experiences it. Forsyth emphasizes this dualism because he feels that the monism of theoretical thought simply does not and cannot do justice to the phenomenon of the guilty conscience in man.[84]

Forsyth makes a second observation about the conscience understood as man passing judgement on himself. He refers to man's dependency upon and his openness for the norms which he must use to judge.

'What speaks in conscience? What is the word to it? If conscience is its own Word, then there is no revelation to it, and ultimately no revelation at all, and ethic swallows up religion. But conscience is not a legislator, it is a judge. It does not give laws either for action or belief. it receives them; it recognizes the authority, it owns it. It does not give religion a constitution, it can but own the value and authority of a constitution to faith by revelation from without.'[85]

It is true that man is self-conscious as a conscience, but this remains a formal description. Man, as an historic person, exercises his self-judgement with

206

reference to some material norms; some content fills his conscience. This deep, mysterious dependency in man lies at the heart of his created nature.

Thus, from the conscience, we learn of the duality of reality and of the tragedy of man. The duality is reflected in man in that he stands before a lord. He judges himself in reference to some lord. He is not the law-giver but a judge in the lower court. Man is a creature listening to a Word from beyond himself. And secondly this duality is a tragedy because man must ever judge himself as guilty. No matter how distorted the content of his conscience may be, he lives in the tragedy of guilt. He is not able to live according to the light to which he is committed. Thus man, even in sinful rebellion and distortion, and quite unconsciously, reflects the true duality of God and creation which has become the tragic duality of God and sin. It is to man in his predicament of guilt that Christ comes as the Word of God to his conscience.

4. The Content of the Evangelical Experience—Christ in the Conscience

Christ in the conscience: here lies the heart of the evangelical experience as Forsyth understands it. When Christ is experienced by man in his conscience as Reconciler and Lord, we have to do with a *new* conscience. It is not the natural conscience that recognizes Christ as its Lord or trusts him as its Saviour. But the certainty of faith is not of the new conscience *per se*; it is of the Christ and his work; the attention is on Christ. These two points need to be examined in detail.

It belongs to the uniqueness of the evangelical experience of Christ that man must be regenerated into the ability to receive him. This is, of course, known only *a posteriori*. In knowing Christ, one is aware that a discontinuity lies between the old self and the new. This new conscience exists in the fact that it has a new Lord. The newly-found forgiveness, comfort, and power in the new conscience come from the new Lord. The material and formal changes in the conscience are the same, that is, the new conscience is nothing else than the *relation* to Christ as Lord and Redeemer.

Here again we are confronted with the intimate connexion between the work of the Spirit and the work of Christ. It is only in the Cross that man receives a new conscience and it is only in the new conscience that man participates in the Cross. It is only as man's conscience receives Christ that it is renewed by the Holy Spirit of the Cross.

'The final moral conviction cannot be brought about by the conscience alone, but by God's Spirit in the conscience. . . . That is what gives the great accent of reality. It does not mean being true to our convictions; it means that our convictions be true to the conviction and conversion of the conscience by the Holy Spirit, true to the central moral reality of the Cross, true to the new world set up by God's condemnation of the old world there.'[86]

'Wherefore, the great question is what the *contents* of the conscience were, or are; not how the man held to his conscience, but how his conscience held to reality, revelation, and truth. Luther's merit was not the heroism of his conscience, but the rediscovery of a new conscience beyond the natural, and beyond the institutional. . . . He found a conscience within the conscience. He found anew the evangelical conscience.'[87]

It is Christ in the Spirit who re-creates man's conscience so that it can receive him. The uniqueness lies in Christ.

What about the second point? Does not the term 'experience' point us to ourselves? Is Forsyth suggest-

ing a religious introspection? No, this is not the case
at all, for he states:

> 'The first content of my religious experience is not
> myself as feeling so or so—e.g. dependent (Schleiermacher)
> —not myself in a certain frame, but God in a certain act, as
> giving, as giving himself, as thus grasping, saving, new
> creating me.'[88]

Surely Johnson is correct when he writes regarding
Forsyth's aim:

> 'Forsyth attempted a final break with the tyranny of
> experience that had gripped Protestant theology at the
> turn of the century, and did so in the name of "the
> evangelical experience." He posited a clear-cut differen-
> tiation between the human seal and the divine source of
> authority, designating the former "experience," and the
> latter "the experienced"; and then insisted that the
> primacy of concern must be shifted to the latter.'[89]

We must be clear as to the issue which Forsyth sees
regarding the experience of Christ. On the one hand
man must personally, subjectively participate in
revelation; he must experience it. On the other hand,
the experience *per se* cannot become central, over-
shadowing him who is experienced; this would be
subjectivity, psychologism. Forsyth phrases the issue
as follows:

> 'A real authority, we have seen, is indeed *within* experi-
> ence, but it is not the authority *of* experience, it is an
> authority *for* experience, it is an authority experienced.
> All certainty is necessarily subjective so far as concerns the
> area where it emerges and the terms in which it comes
> home. The court is subjective, but the bench is not.
> Reality must, of course, be real for me. . . . But it makes
> much difference whether it have its *source* in my conscious-
> ness as well as its *sphere*.'[90]

The fact that Christ is *extra nos* is not to be swallowed
up in his *pro me* relationship to the believer. Rather,

the evangelical experience is the perfect unity of both of these moments. Forsyth seeks in several ways to make it clear that faith centres in an objective Christ and not in the subjectivity of the believer.[91] First we turn to his arguments for the objectivity of the experienced Christ.

Forsyth points out that faith has as its object the historic person Jesus Christ.[92] He, the crucified One, is the Object of faith. Or Forsyth refers to this historical aspect in another manner by saying that it is the Word that calls forth faith.[93] Word and Spirit are, as in the Reformers, not to be considered apart. Rather, all concentration is on the Son for it is to the Son that the Spirit witnesses. So it is that Christ's historical life, ministry, death, and resurrection and the witness of Scripture, all serve to emphasize the fact that faith has an objective reference in One who comes into our world and personal experience.

Secondly, Forsyth suggests a number of ways in which faith, due to the nature of its object, knows of a God and his Word which transcend a personal experience of Christ.[94] In Christ, faith trusts in a world salvation, in the victory of God over all evil which assures the coming of a new heaven and a new earth. We cannot directly experience a world salvation but we do know a world Saviour.[95] This same transcendence is indicated when Forsyth points out that experience lies within time and space, and yet, in Christ, eternity enters our experience, thereby pointing to a Christ larger than our experience. In him we trust but do not experience our own eternity.[96] In this connexion belongs Forsyth's statement that the Holy can be immanent in our experience only as the Transcendent. When we experience the Holy in Christ, we are related to the transcendent mystery of God which far transcends our experience of him.[97]

Finally, Forsyth points out that faith is not individualistic, though it is personal. Christ is the One whom the historic Church has known from the beginning. In him we can speak of a common faith. The One whom we experience has called a cloud of witnesses about him of whom we are but one of many. Therefore Christ, in the common faith of the Church, witnesses to himself as transcending our individual experience of him.[98]

Having seen that Christ stands in objective polar relation to the believer in the evangelical experience, we need to note Forsyth's concern to point out that Christ is the *centre* of the evangelical experience.

Firstly, faith knows Christ as its King, its Lord. He is not faith's possession but the possessor. He, in his Confession of God's holiness on the Cross, has purchased crown rights over man. There is an 'oughtness' to faith because it centres in God and his action in Christ. Faith is Christo-centric and Theo-centric. It is for this reason that faith knows to glorify God; it knows that, in being gracious to man, God is hallowing his own holy name.[99]

Secondly, the certainty of faith is in the Christ of the Cross. It is in the One who has finally wrought salvation in the Cross. The source of all grace and of all certainty lies in him who has acted eternally, for all time. God is the primary Knower who calls into being man's knowledge of him through the Cross. It is for this reason that Forsyth states:

> 'If our Christian experience tell us anything, it is not about ourselves in the first place, nor about our creed, but about Christ. . . . That is why we must preach Christ, and not about Christ; why we must set the actual constraining Christ before people, and not coax or bully people into decision. If we put the veritable Christ before them, he will rouse the faith before they know where they are.'[100]

When the believer is in difficulty, in doubt, it is to the Christ of the victorious Cross that he must turn for help.[101] For the source of faith, as well as its objective ground, is Jesus Christ present in the Spirit.

In the above ways Forsyth has attempted to indicate the objective ground which faith knows itself to have in Jesus Christ and that: 'The height of faith is to lose sight of itself in Christ.'[102] The following two statements emphasize and summarize this for us:

'Surely the more inward it is the more is it external. . . . The more inward we go the more external the authority becomes, just because it becomes more of an authority, and more unmistakably, irresistibly so. . . . It is a cure for our subjectivism that we need, a cure for our egotism. And that is to be found in nothing physically external, nothing institutionally so, but only in an objective, moral and spiritual, congenial yet antithetic, in an objective to the ego, yea to the race, which objective alone gives morality any meaning. Our suzerain must indeed sit in the court of the soul, but he must be objective there.'[103]

'We are to be much more sure of God's grace in our faith than of our faith in God's grace. Faith is not getting up a certain degree of receptivity and so inviting, facilitating, or even deserving God's grace. It is answering grace's prevenience.'[104]

Now we are in a position to relate explicitly the evangelical experience of Christ in the conscience with what we have noted above regarding authority and certainty, and to consider in this connexion the significance of the primacy of the will in man's participation in revelation.

5. *The Evangelical Experience and the Primacy of the Will in Man*

In this section we are concerned to note the conclusions which Forsyth draws from the nature of the evangelical experience with its authority and certainty and to see how this results in a 'primacy of the will' in man.

First the relationship of authority, conscience and certainty needs to be clear to us:

'The Christian Gospel is an authority for the will, in the will's sphere of history; it is not for the intellect—except in so far as the intellect depends on the will. It is an authority which is felt primarily as living moral majesty, not as truth—as Christ was felt, not as the Scribes. That is, it is morally realized, not mentally; personally, not officially; ethically, and not aesthetically, not contemplatively. It is for conscience, not for thought, in the first place, nor for imagination. It so settles the whole moral man that in the region of truth there is entire flexibility and freedom. We have the liberty in that region which rests on final confidence and security in the moral region.'[105]

The final authority is moral; it settles the man by determining his moral region; it involves the whole man by speaking to his conscience and will. This is the basic thesis which Forsyth is asserting. He can express the same thing in terms of authority as personal:

'As revelation is God disposing of his personality to us in grace, faith ... can only answer by disposing of our personality to him. We do not respond according to an irresistible law of our nature (i.e. logical proof) but according to a free choice of our will.'[106]

How does this relate to what we have said above regarding revelation as authoritative and faith as a certainty? We can best answer this by referring back to some material from Chapter II. There we noted that creed or doctrine and the work of individual theologians remain somewhat tentative, that is, of a secondary and tertiary authority. Only God's own speaking is finally authoritative. 'Every statement

213

about God is challengeable till God states himself, in his own way, by his own Son, his own Spirit, his own Word, his own Church, to our soul, which he re-makes in the process.'[107] With the evangelical ex-perience before us, we are now in a better position to see why, according to Forsyth, the creeds and theology must remain tentative, and precisely how it is that God states himself to man's soul.

Creed and doctrine are tentative because they are extended theoretical descriptions of a more basic moral certainty, of a more interpersonal finality. In the scientific realm there is no personal finality but only an approximation addressed to a given historical situation. On the other hand in the moral realm, Forsyth asserts the finality of the Dogma or the *kerygmatic* Christ. *He* is God's final, authoritative Word to man addressed to guilty man's moral centre, the conscience. In the conscience man knows with certainty of his forgiveness and of his being possessed by a new Lord.[108] In other words, the absoluteness of the *kerygma* or its authoritativeness lies m the fact that it is the God-given means through which Christ presents himself as having dealt with, and as now commanding man's conscience. His Lordship over the total man, indeed over creation, is revealed absolutely in his act upon the Cross through which he dealt with the conscience of God and of the race. Faith in Christ is the personal certainty of this reconciliation and this Lordship. Thus it is that man's '. . . final confidence and security (is) in the moral region.'

What we have said concerning authority, certainty and conscience implies, according to Forsyth, the centrality of the will or conscience in man.[109] It is primarily as a moral creature, a creature centred in the will, that man participates in revelation. For this reason it is essential that we know precisely what the centrality of the will implies for Forsyth, and, most importantly, that we understand what Forsyth sees as the relation between intellect and the will. We shall present in an excursus the relevant aspects of Forsyth's view of man's psychology and then, in the next section, discuss the role of the intellect in faith. This will allow us to complete our presentation of man's experiential participation in revelation, for he participates as an intelligent will.

Excursus : THE PRIMACY OF THE WILL IN MAN; FORSYTH'S ANTHROPOLOGY DERIVED FROM THE CROSS

Throughout this study we have used 'moral' and 'personal' as equivalent terms. This implies that Forsyth has a most specific view of man. According to Forsyth, man's personality centres in the will, around and in which the ethical, aesthetic, and intellectual activities of man are unified.

Due to Greek influence, it has been customary in the West to interpret man's personality as centring in the mind and not in the will or feelings. It is not customary to visualize man as intelligent will as does Forsyth.[110] Since we are all inclined to be influenced by our culture in the direction of intellectualism, it is necessary that we first briefly list the ways in which Forsyth finds a mind-centred or intellectualistic view of man to be inadequate for faith.

Perhaps Forsyth's most fundamental objection to an intellectualistic view of man is that it is inherently subjectivistic. It fails to reach the objective truth on which it claims to be based. Rationalism, just as much as romantic intuitionalism, remains locked up within the thinking, human subject. When this is seen in the context of man's participation in revelation, it means that 'we do not escape to a real object who approaches and seizes us, loves and saves.'[111] There is no breaking-in by God into the creaturely realm, no divine speaking in which man can hear something beside his

215

own immanent thoughts. When the mind is seen as central, God is replaced by the rational idea of God as it fits into a general *schema* which man projects. All is seen ordered and evaluated from the subject's mind; it is subjectivism.

Another weakness which Forsyth sees is closely related to his first objection. He points to the fact that thought, when interpreted in the context of an intellectualistic view of man, is impersonal. It is the movement of logical necessity. Man is pictured as the observer of reality who observes the ideas in necessary connexion. In reference to man's knowledge of God, such a view is irreligious. It fails on two accounts: first it posits for man a neutral position whereby he observes God. But man never stands in such a neutral position with reference to his Creator. Secondly, it is ideas that man observes but God is personal Spirit in interpersonal relation with man. This type of thinking can never emerge into the personal realm. It tends to relate man to a divine book or to a theological system of truths, to a world view or a philosophy of history, but not to God in his personal self-manifestation in Jesus Christ.[112]

Related to the inability of intellectualism to be truly personal, is its inability to deal with evil and guilt. In one way or another, evil and guilt are transformed into an impersonal aspect of the development of the good or else they are declared to be non-existent or unreal. It follows therefore that in the face of evil, intellectualism has no convincing word to say about teleology or eschatology.[113]

If intellectualism is not adequate to the actuality and mystery of evil, neither can it accept the paradoxical. To admit that which transcends reason in such a fashion as to lead man to polar statements which cannot be logically united is impossible for intellectualism. It is built upon a confidence in the sufficiency and efficacy of logical reason to unite man to a rational reality. Intellectualism, for example, cannot think of the paradox of the incarnation, the God-man, without either deifying man or drawing God completely into the world process. It cannot conceive of a self-caused God, of a Cross where God justifies himself, nor can it find room for truly inter-personal prayer before an omniscient, omnipotent God. Forsyth points out that such paradoxical realities of faith are not solved by a theory but by practical solution in life. Therefore the paradoxes of faith, as well, serve to point out that man's connexion with reality lies in a deeper dimension than the intellect.[114]

Lastly, Forsyth finds it of significance that there is no finality in intellectualism. On the one hand, there is the necessary movement from axioms to deduced conclusions, but the axioms must be assumed to be self-evident. Deduction is always in the form of: if A be true and if B be true, then C follows. On the other hand, a scientific induction from phenomena can never lead but to high probability. In neither case can intellectualism explain the certainty of faith. Such certainty also points to a deeper view of man than intellectualism can provide.[115]

For the above-mentioned reasons Forsyth asserts that faith, in its anthropology, must take note of the limits of the intellect:

'Is it not part of our intellectual duty to know the limits of our intellect? . . . Criticize your competency as well as your ancestors and your superiors. . . . It is a poor artillery that knows more of the target than of the gun.'[116]

Keeping these remarks of Forsyth regarding the limits of the intellect in mind, let us recall the basic importance which he believes the evangelical experience of the Cross to have for a view of man:

217

'The great authority over us is miraculous before it is rational, and external more than intrinsic to our soul. It is not foreign, but it is other. It is mastering to the soul before it is perfecting, the soul's conquest rather than its fruition. It is rational so far as this, that it is the authority of a spiritual *nature* kindred to our own. On each side there is a person with a rational constitution. But it is not the rationality of its nature that makes the person or makes the authority. . . . It is the freedom of its conscious *will*. The action of authority on us is not the action of a truth or an ideal of the reason, but of a will, which is free as we are free, but whose free grace is a mystery greater than any freedom of ours to sin. There is no greater miracle than our freedom, except the authority which is its source and salvation. That grace is a standing miracle, in command of all the rationality of the world.'[117]

The authority of revelation is personal. Jesus Christ is man's Lord and Redeemer. But Christ is an authority in the conscience as he who forgives man, reconciles man and God and commands man's obedience. We must so understand the nature of man and the role of reason in man as to do justice to and to clarify his relationship to this *kerygmatic* Christ. For Forsyth, that view of man which is most adequate to the evangelical experience is voluntaristic. The will or conscience is the centre of man.

In such a view, Forsyth in no sense isolates the will; nor does he conceive of man as a bundle of faculties. In fact, Forsyth is most cautious when he uses such terms as 'will' or 'faculty.' He prefers to speak of the whole man's being involved in all of his activities.

'Let us here remember, first, that psychology has outgrown the "faculty" stage. We are not faggots of faculties. No "faculty" can exist by itself without the rest, or simply be roped up with them. They are all organized in the unitary action of the whole personality. It is the one indivisible personality that acts in each. . . . Belief rests

218

not merely on evidence but on the will to believe. And conversely moral action is impossible without due knowledge. Each "faculty" implies the rest because it is the action of the whole person.

'For religion especially this principle is of great importance. Faith is not a faculty.'[118]

It is clear that, for Forsyth, 'Voluntarism means only the primacy of the will, not its monopoly. A will, acting without reason, on other than intelligent principles, is not a will but a mere instinct or impulse.'[119] Forsyth is no irrationalist[120] and no compartmentalist, but rather he wishes us to picture man as a unified personality in whom the various functions of the personality find their synthesis and centre in the will.

What does the primacy of the will or man as intelligent will mean in terms of man's thinking or knowing? We can answer this by following Forsyth's discussion of how thought is rooted in and serves the will, or better, the will-centred personality. Then we can follow his discussion as to how man comes to certainty in order to see the interconnexion of will and intellect in this act.

We turn our attention first to Forsyth's understanding of the function or place of thought and how it reflects the primacy of the will. He offers us two approaches to this relationship.

Forsyth points out that we are inexact when we speak of 'thought.' It would be much better if we simply referred to 'man thinking.'

'There never did exist a thought separable from the subject thinker, the object thought, and the experience that unites them. There is no form of thought in consciousness which did not arise from the activity of living men in the world.'[121]

This is of the greatest significance, for, by keeping the thinking man before our eyes, we are not likely to forget that thinking is a function of the personality, an activity of the whole man in his specific existence.

Forsyth continues by pointing out that in the life of the whole man, thinking is not an end in itself but is rather done by the man to serve his personal life commitment. Man's basic attitude to life is wilful, assertive and purposive.

> 'But thought is not an end in itself, and therefore not the nature of reality. It is only an instrument serving the purposes of that activity which we call life.'[122]

> '. . . truth is not a matter of systems but of values. It is not a matter of congruity (which is its scientific sense), but of reality (which is its moral sense). . . . It is not truth as cold fact that concerns us, but truth as living experience; and as experience which *promotes* the soul, involves its destiny, and does not simply *exercise* it.'[123]

> 'Knowledge always follows life-interest in the long run. We prosecute the knowledge of what we are interested in, of what appeals to life, feeling, force, concern.'[124]

In this first approach, Forsyth presents man primarily as a wilful agent in life and not a passive spectator. Man is busily engaged in the activity of living, of wilfully pursuing his interests, his commitments. And thinking takes place within this context and, 'in the long run,' for practical purposes. The intellect's function is to inform the assertive will.

Forsyth presents the function of thought in a second way. Knowledge is this time considered in relation to the 'given.'

> 'We start from the very nature of truth. It is given us. We do not make it, we have to yield to it. The laws of our thought, the conditions of our knowledge are not framed by us. . . . Our mental constitution we find to our hand with a living *nisus* at every stage. There is no hope of anything if we do not obey it. . . . And unconscious

220

passivity precedes all our conciousness, and consciousness is but a growing appropriation of what was given us before consciousness arose. . . . All our knowledge arises upon us concretely out of certain actual relations in which reality approaches us. . . .

'The point is that the foundation of the intellectual life is itself given, revealed, and authoritative, though the full significance of the revelation appears in another quarter of our being. But the principle is not fatally different in each sphere. It is not as if the intellect (in its nature as distinct from its use) were incurably sceptical or self-sufficient, while the will witnessed to a will over us. In both regions we are dependent on what descends on us with a claim, on the authoritative.'[125]

Authority is no stranger to man's intellect, for the intellect must bow to the given and must be obedient to its own rules of thought. While man's basic dependency upon God is most clearly revealed in the conscience, even the intellect reflects this creatureliness. Man is a unity in his dependence upon authority.

Forsyth points out, in connexion with the intellect's obedience to the given and laws of thinking, that even the search for truth must be described in moral terms. He describes the pursuit of truth '. . . as a great and long moral act, resting on a dogmatic gift and a disciplined personality.'[126] In looking at the act of thinking, we also find the moral as a basic presupposition. Serious thinking is an act of the will and depends on a moral commitment to the truth. Here again we see the dependency of the intellect upon the interests and the commitment of the whole personality. The will is central and the intellect serves it.

In summary, the following seems of importance to Forsyth: the conscience, its commitment to moral norms and goals is the basic reality about man; the intellect finds its moral ground, its impulse, and also its task in serving man in his commitments in life.

The same basic conclusion is reached if we examine the manner in which man is certain of his knowledge:

'Certainty, therefore, is at bottom no matter of intellect alone, nor of thought; it cannot be there without an act of will, an act of appropriation by the personality. A process of thought apart from an act of will would bring us to no conclusion, to nothing that could be called certainty. . . . What is exhibited before us by thought must go through another process and must become our property; and we cannot affirm it till it do.'[127]

Forsyth first points out that the self must respond, must will to appropriate the data that it experiences. There is an act of commitment that is integral to certainty. Decision is involved for certainty to be actual; there is no certainty in a mere stream of consciousness, if such a thing were possible. To be *our* experience, there is an involvement of the self, an encounter and commitment. There must be interest and evaluation in certainty.

In stressing the active role of man in certainty or the wilful appropriation of certainty, Forsyth is not repeating the pragmatic idea of faith simply as the will to believe. This would lead us back into the subjectivity which Forsyth is so concerned to avoid. Faith, for him, is the organ of objective, personal knowledge. It is not true that man could morally will certainty, irrespective of reality, but rather the will appropriates the given. The following statement makes this clear:

'The thing willed is no product of ours. It is a given: what is ours is our appropriation of it, our self-committal to it, our identification with it, our self-expenditure on it. . . . The will is not the cause of truth but its recognition, its service. Even in God himself, his will is a perfect and eternal appropriation of his nature. It is eternal, for there never was a time when a divine nature began to impose itself on the divine will; it is perfect, because there is no part of that will that does not move by that nature. The causative process in our will is not so monopolist as to extend to the invention of truth (for which we have a short name) but only in its treatment.'[128]

The willed response of the self, necessary for certainty, is not independent of the data to which it is responding. Both personal commitment and moral obedience lie at the heart of certainty. Therefore, in certainty also, we see that the centre of man's person is the will which is served by the intellect as man appropriates the reality which presses upon him.

We can summarize this excursus as follows: only a view of man as intelligent will does justice to man's participation in revelation as the interpersonal communion between the holy God and sinful man in Jesus Christ. Intellectualism leads to man's participation in terms of right doctrine or right ideas. An aesthetic view of man which centres in the feeling leads to mystic union.[129] Only a rational voluntarism is adequate to what faith actually knows to be the case. In using the philosophic term 'voluntarism,' we must not forget that it receives its primary content, according to Forsyth, from the light of the Cross, from man's encounter with the *kerygmatic* Christ. Forsyth does not proceed from general philosophical principles but from revelation.

* * *

Let us now turn to the specific consideration of the role of the intellect in faith's knowledge of God, that is, in the act of man's knowledge in which God in Christ is the Object.[130]

6. The Role of the Intellect in Faith

Man participates in the 'eternal deed of the Cross' through the hearing and believing of the preached Word. The beginning of man's knowledge of God and of himself in faith is the heard Word of forgiveness in Jesus Christ. The evangelical experience of Christ as

223

the Redeemer and Lord of the conscience is both the beginning and foundation of man's knowledge in revelation.

> 'The first condition of forgiveness is not an adequate comprehension of the Atonement, and a due sense of the cost. That is not saving faith. Any adequate idea on that head comes only to the saved. The Cross becomes a theology only by beginning as a religion. The condition of forgiveness is answering the grace and freedom of it with a like free, humble, and joyful heart. It is taking the freedom of it home, and not the cost. It is committing ourselves to God's self-committal to us. It is taking God at his word—at his living Word, Christ—his urgent, reticent, gracious, masterful word, Christ.'[131]

It is obvious that we cannot, according to Forsyth, understand the basic role of the intellect in faith to be that of grasping and interpreting doctrine. The basic role of the intellect in faith is to inform the conscience of the personal grace and claims of Jesus Christ and to serve the commitment of faith to Christ in daily life. This function of the intellect has been central throughout our discussion of Christ in the conscience. There are, however, less fundamental but still essential functions of the intellect within faith, which we might consider as taking place within sanctification or growth in the knowledge of Christ.

We move from the initial experience of Christ to the broader plane of sustained life with him. We might say, keeping in mind Forsyth's earlier distinctions, that we move from the strictly dogmatic encounter into the realm of doctrine and theology. It is, however, under the impulse of grace that this transition takes place. The new man wishes to know more of his Lord and to serve him more truly. The moral unity of man's personality also makes the demand upon him to unify all of his knowledge in the light of Christ. The believer states, according to Forsyth: '. . . *credo ut intelligam*. I trust myself to his Person that I may understand his truth.'[132] There is an evangelical order of the knowledge of Christ, a certain necessary movement from encounter with Christ into knowledge about God, self, and the world in him. Forsyth describes this movement of belief as follows:

> 'So that in the order of importance we should go to the world first of all with the atoning Cross which is the Alpha and Omega of grace; second, with the resurrection of Christ which is the emergence into experience of the new life won for us on the Cross; third, with the life, character, teaching, and miracles of Christ; fourth, with the pre-existence of Christ, which is a corollary of his eternal life, and only after such things with the virgin birth, which may or may not be demanded by the rest. It is not a case of denying any of these points or even challenging them. They may all be accepted, but let it be in their true perspective, the perspective of faith. And they are offered to the public, and belief is claimed, in the degree of their relevancy to a vital Christian experience of the one Christian doctrine of grace. For when we carry reduction to its length we condense upon that one principle and power of grace which has in it the promise of the potency of all the soul's life and all Christian truth.'[133]

It is only fair to Forsyth's continual effort to overcome all individualism, to repeat what we noted in Chapter II; that the Church is the place in which this unfolding of grace takes place. Reflection and prayerful study take place both with regard to the long history of the Church's dogmatic knowledge of its Lord, and with the contemporary needs of the Church's common life and its relation to the world in view. Even though it is the individual who theologizes, it is not individualistic. As Forsyth states it:

> 'Theology in this large and expository sense does not belong to the individual but to something more universal,

225

to the Church. It is not the product or the property of any single person, nor even of any single sect or communion. It belongs to the Church as a whole, and for that Church it is a necessity.'[134]

We might therefore summarize the function of the intellect within faith with reference to its knowledge of God in the following manner: it is to serve the will, first in the primary, foundational encounter with the living Lord and Redeemer of the race. Then, within this response of man evoked by grace, that is, within this life-commitment, the intellect is to trace out the divine riches, the presuppositions and interrelations in the revelation of the Cross. It must be immediately added, in order to avoid misunderstanding, that this growth in faith, this pursuing of dogmatics, does not simply presuppose faith but takes place within faith. Faith remains the foundational response of the whole man to Christ; it is the living context of all of man's knowing in revelation.

We have moved from the role of the intellect in the encounter with Christ to the broader area of dogmatic knowledge in Christ. There is, however, an even broader use of the intellect within faith which Forsyth sees to be both possible and necessary. He can speak quite specifically of a Christian philosophy. Forsyth states his view as follows:

'A metaphysic of some kind is bound up with a Christ of this kind. Without some metaphysic you have not a base for that mystic adoration of Christ which is so much more than divine ethic, and which a whole class of churches has lost. ... Only it must not be a metaphysic of mere thought, brought up to faith and imposed on it. ... It must be a metaphysic of faith itself. ... A faith in metaphysic is one thing and the metaphysic of faith is another.'[135]

We have already seen at two places in this study the lines which Forsyth indicates that a metaphysic of faith in Christ must take. Both ontologically and epistomologically Forsyth offers some suggestions for a type of Christian voluntarism. He would, of course, claim no finality for his efforts, but he sees the possibility, even the necessity for faith to believe that its knowledge and hermeneutic method are rooted in God himself and thus in reality. Forsyth knows of no separation, no two-source view of knowing. Man knows rightly and really in faith. One could also, on the basis of Forsyth's understanding of man's cognitive participation in revelation, go on to speak of a Christian sociology, science, or any other discipline for these would be constituted by the interest and work of a Christian person in these fields. In other words, all the corners of creation and man's efforts to know them find their fundamental illumination in the light of the Cross. For Christ is the Redeemer-Creator. The ground plan of the creation is redemption.

In this study, however, we have limited ourselves to theology and primarily to the one doctrine in dogmatics of man's knowledge of God and of himself—revelation. Therefore, we must be content simply to note these other, quite legitimate and necessary interests to which Christian men and women might give themselves as part of their Christian work.

With this consideration of the role of the intelligent will in faith, we have completed our presentation of Forsyth's understanding of the experiential character of man's participation in the Cross. It has become clear that Forsyth's use of the term 'experience' is of such a special nature that we could only refer to it as an experience *sui generis* or, to use his own phrase, as the 'evangelical experience.' In our consideration of this it became clear that, above all, it was Christ who actually came to man and, in his coming, both granted, transcended and set the limits to faith's experience. It can be most succinctly stated: the evangelical experience is the response of faith to Christ the Redeemer, the Forgiver, and the Lord. And this response of faith is fundamentally a life lived under this Lord, committed to him, and in his grace. Faith is an act of the intelligent will, a cognitive act of obedience and thanksgiving.[136]

Now we turn to a theme that runs throughout all of Forsyth's writings and which reflects, as did his exposition of faith as man's experiential participation in the Cross, a clear witness to the living, historic Word of God in the face of the dangers presented by intellectualism and romantic pantheism. We refer to Forsyth's treatment of faith's knowledge of God and man in Christ as miraculous knowledge.

d—MAN'S KNOWLEDGE OF THE CROSS AS A MIRACLE OF GRACE

Forsyth's designation of man's knowledge of faith as miraculous was designed to proclaim that there is no epistomological bridge built by man to God. *Sola gratia, sola fide* is his one confession. Our task is to see how Forsyth exposits the sheer grace of our knowledge of God and of ourselves in Jesus Christ.

The word which Forsyth uses most often to characterize this aspect of man's participation in the Cross is the word 'miraculous.' Since this term is understood in various ways, it is necessary to see the sense in which Forsyth uses it.

'The true supernatural is not the miraculous, but the miracle for whose sake miracles exist. It is not prodigy in nature but the grace of God in history. It has no direct relation to natural law. Miracle is not a scientific idea but a religious. An event is a miracle not by its relation to law but to grace. The Incarnation would be equally a miracle, however Jesus entered the world. It is not nature that is the true region of the supernatural, but history; and history not as a chain of events, but as the spiritual career of the soul or of the race. That is the true region of the supernatural. It lies in the action of God's will upon men's wills, not upon natural law. It is the work of God's grace upon men's sin.'[137]

The miracle is grace itself, that is, miracle must be understood in the context of God's relation to guilty man and not in the context of the observed regularities of the cosmos. Is it not the Redeemer who in the Gospels commands nature to do his will? Is it not the forgiveness of sin in the name of Jesus by which the Apostles drive out demons and cure the physically sick? Is it not a contemporary miracle when, through the preaching of Christ, a sinner is called into communion with the God of holy love? It is not as if Forsyth were apologetically avoiding the eruptions of grace on the physical level, for we have seen earlier that he knows of no neutral nature; the ground plan of the creation is redemption and the redemptive is the real. No, Forsyth is pointing out that the miraculous is the presence of and the will of God in relation to his fallen creation; it is grace. Any other view of the miraculous simply remains on the level of historical positivism which seeks to establish inexplicable breaks in what man chooses to call the 'laws of nature.' To take one's starting point from the realm of physical nature and not from God's dealing with his creature man, is to seek to find a neutral point which does not exist. Even nature is a part of history.

Having seen that according to Forsyth the true miracle is grace itself, we can turn now to examine the ways in which he underlines the miraculous nature of our participation in the Cross. Forsyth first points out that only God is in a position to speak about God. He also asserts that there is no continuity between God and man by virtue of which man can judge or test

God in his revelation. Finally, Forsyth re-defines the term 'religious *a priori*,' a term used extensively at the time when he was writing, to indicate its dependence upon grace. We turn first to God as the sole author of the knowledge of himself.

> ' "Who shall tell me surely what to believe about Christ?" None can. No Church can. No book can; no saint, no theologian. None can but Christ himself in actual presence . . . by overwhelming my soul with its greatness and its evil, its judgement and its salvation, in his invincible word of death, resurrection, and glory.'[138]

> 'God swears by himself because there is none greater. Our final authority must be God himself in direct contact with humanity, i.e. with history. He cannot be proved, because there is nothing more real and certain to which we can bring him for sanction.'[139]

God being God, he is simply qualitatively beyond his creation, and as such he must be the author of his presence and his own guarantor. This means that his presence is self-authenticating, that the '. . . source of our certainty must be the object of it. To put it somewhat technically—the content of our faith must be constitutive for it.'[140] When God speaks, the formal and the material are one. We know who is speaking by what he says, for what he says points to himself as God with us. Only God can be the presence of God; only God can uphold a God-man communion; only God can speak the Word of God. The miracle is that God does speak his Word to man in Jesus Christ.

Having pointed out that God in his holy majesty is the only one capable of speaking for God, Forsyth turns his attention upon man in order to illustrate that man has no natural knowledge of God or any canon of general experience whereby he can test God's speaking.

'Experience in this region does not mean a prior standard in us by which we accept or reject the Gospel's claims. It does not mean that the Gospel submits to be tried by the code we have put together from our previous experience of natural things, even in the religious sphere. . . . Our very response to it is created in us before it is confessed by us. It creates assent rather than accepts it. . . . it is something miraculously created in us.'[141]

God's speaking is a free act of grace and not an immanent principle in man. Not only does God's personal majesty place him above his creation, but even more does man's sin make it clear that man is in no position to judge, from within himself, whether or not the voice be that of God.

Forsyth can ask: 'How is the natural man to verify a gospel which takes the confidence out of human nature and its instincts, and destroys the egoism which is its first certainty?'[142] At another place in his writings, Forsyth answers his own question: 'We may, moreover, take it that the authority of a holy Gospel cannot be proved to the natural man. The offence of the Cross has not ceased. It must first capture him and make him a super-natural man.'[143] If, however, we insist upon speaking of a criterion for judging revelation, Forsyth will agree only on the following terms:

'In the true sense of the word revelation must be final. If we possess a criterion of revelation it is the criterion that becomes the revelation. Revelation can only be judged by revelation.'[144]

To be sure, the believer is to 'test the spirits' but he is to test them by God-with-us, by Jesus Christ.

It is his understanding of revelation as grace that causes Forsyth to reject all natural revelation and all natural theology. The following quotation, written in opposition to the forms which natural theology was taking in Protestant thought contemporaneous with Forsyth, makes this clear.

231

'To make Nature the site of revelation, to seek it in the Kosmos rather than in the Ethos, is the very genius of Paganism, and it is the source of the humanist and scientific Paganism of our own day. And this is true, however refined our Kosmos may be. . . . If we will use the words carefully, there is no revelation in Nature. There can be none, because there is no forgiveness. . . . She is only aesthetic. Her ideal is harmony, not reconciliation. . . . For conscience, stricken or strong, she has no word. Therefore she has no revelation. . . . Christ is the only luminous smile upon the dark face of the world. . . .

'Nor can we find revelation . . . in the movements of our own pure, pious and genial hearts, in a natural piety, or even a Christian humanism. . . . It is not the men who have known the heart least that have been most distrustful of its verdict on things divine. It is too unstable. . . . But, still more, the heart's voice is the voice of a sinful heart. Sin is no accident, like blindness, which leaves the faculties and the conscience clear; and it is in the hour of our most thorough and guilty confusion that we chiefly turn to seek the certainty which a revelation exists to give. . . .

'Nor can a source for revelation be found in philosophic idealism or the principle of divine sonship severed from the person of Christ, any more than in the aesthetic Christ. The active contents of revelation, it must be reiterated, are not truths, ideas, or even principles. . . . The sole content of revelation, the power and gift in it, is the love, will, presence and purpose of God for our redemption.'[145]

These words of Forsyth allow no exception: only in the Christ of the Cross is there forgiveness. To man blind in his sin, only the light of the Cross is revelation. And only in revelation is there knowledge of God and of man in relation to him.

Seeing the care with which Forsyth points out the free grace of God's speaking and the miracle of man's hearing, it is with some surprise that we find him continuing to use the term 'religious *a priori*.' Its use by Troeltsch and others stood in direct contradiction

232

to Forsyth's position. Therefore we are faced by a double task. We must seek to understand what value Forsyth believes the term to possess and then we will note that, in his re-definition of the term he also demonstrates the grace of revelation.

First we turn to Forsyth's understanding of the positive value or nature of the religious *a priori*.

'First, we must own the justice of that demand for some *a priori* in the soul to which the revelation comes, and on which it strikes its proper note.'[146]

'There is such a thing, then, as a religious *a priori* in us, though it is not an authority but the power to own authority. It is not a passivity but a receptivity, a loyalty, an obedience. Revelation does not come to us as if we were blank paper, dead matter, or blind forces. It finds something to appeal to, to stir, to evoke. But this *prius* resides in the will and its power, not in the reason and its truth. It is a voluntarist *prius*, and not a noetic. . . . And that nexus is found in the norms which guide the will and make it more than a blind elemental force. They are *a priori*, because they are not produced by experience, but, on the contrary, are there to receive experience and make it possible. . . . Their authority, as I have said, is that of an ought and not of a must. . . . Revelation has its influence on the heart and will and not on the perceptions. It makes a man choose, else it does not reach the centre of his being but leaves him cold. But it is a receptive choice on our part, it is not a creative.'[147]

Here we understand Forsyth to mean that man, even in his fallen, sinful condition, remains man, an intelligent *will*. As a sinner he remains a living will owning a master, obedient to some satanic substitute of his own choosing. Sin is not to be explained as deprivation or as a neutral separation from God, but rather as a real rebellion against God himself. It is to this man, this creature who continually lives in terms of commitment and decision, that revelation comes in

233

Jesus Christ. The religious *a priori* is man himself and the value of using the term lies in its pointing to just this fact: man, within or apart from faith in Jesus Christ, remains an intelligent will. The creation may have fallen, the *imago dei* may be totally corrupted, but this does not allow us to speak in the passive terms of non-being or deficiency. Rather we must speak in the dynamic terms of perverse rebellion. One might say that the doctrine of sin and creation are protected by Forsyth's use of the religious *a priori*.

In his use of this term, Forsyth is careful to point out that it is grace which grounds and sustains our knowledge of God. Each time that he mentions the validity, even the necessity of the term 'religious *a priori*,' he goes on immediately to state that such a term does not in the least imply the idea that man can test the validity of God's speaking apart from faith.

> 'But, second, we must perceive that this *a priori* is not in the region of the reason but of the will. Its function is not criticism but obedience, not rational legitimation but moral response, not a voucher that the papers are in order, but an act of personal homage. It is not a case of new truth being fitly framed and built together into the truth we already possess, or a new process shown to continue the spiritual movement native to the soul.'[148]

> 'God has points of affinity and attachment in us which are not criteria. He does not appear before the bar of man; but the Father does say and we hear him say, "My son, give me thy heart." ...
> 'Yet it is quite true that our response to Christ is not a blind one; it is not impressionist, and not merely automatic. It does imply a judgement, or at least a preference. The point is that it does but imply it, it does not wait on it. The verdict is *in* the response, not *before* it. It is the verdict of the will in faith, not of intelligence. The verdict *is* faith, it is not a prior condition of faith. The judgement is latent in the act of faith, it does not precede it.'[149]

234

This careful re-definition and circumscription of the term 'religious *a priori*' by Forsyth is but another testimony to the *sola gratia* of revelation, of God's word of grace, spoken to fallen man. Man, while remaining man even in the depths of sinful distortion, can respond to God only by grace.

Forsyth sums up the whole miraculous nature of our knowing in revelation thus: 'The Gospel must *create* the power to believe it. Revelation here is so radical that in the same act it must be regeneration.'[150]

e—THE CHURCH'S KNOWLEDGE OF THE CROSS
   AND ITS TASK IN THE WORLD

Here just as in Chapter II, it is not our task to present an outline of Forsyth's doctrine of the Church. However, we must speak of the Church for, as we have continually seen in our study, the doctrine of the Church is implied by and, in large measure, determined by the doctrine of revelation. Up to this point we have observed that the Church and not individuals is the *vis-à-vis* of Christ in his Deed and Word. 'True, revelation can only speak the individual's *language*, but it utters much more than an individual *word*. The great truth is given and promised to a Church.'[151] We noted as well that faith or man's participation in revelation is personal *and* social. 'To join a Church is simply to give outward expression and obedience to a fact existing as soon as we became Christ's by faith.'[152] We also noted that it was the deed of revelation and its preaching which called the Church into being. Revelation is constitutive for the Church:

'A nation may survive regicide, but a Church cannot. In the State a revolution which thus renounced the past would not necessarily be treason. It might be but acute evolution. But in the Church that would be treason, and

235

it would embarrass accordingly. A historic, positive, objective and final salvation in Christ is absolutely constitutive for the Church. It is not merely regulative, or valuable for a passing stage or purpose. . . . His salvation is not a piece of the Church's primitive mythology, as some would Germanize it. It is of the Church's *esse*, and not simply of its *bene esse*.'[153]

But with these remarks, not all has been said that needs to be said about the relationship between the doctrine of revelation and the doctrine of the Church. One mark, one more note of the Church must be mentioned in relation to the Church's knowledge of God, its participation in revelation. This note is its apostolicity, its 'being sent' to the world. 'The apostle to society is a society.'[154]

With reference to this 'being sent,' Forsyth makes three points which we present briefly. He points out that the Church must be careful to retain its identity, to remain in faith, if it would serve anyone. It does not serve man in its own strength or insight but rather its service to man is utterly dependent upon grace.

'What makes Christianity Christian is that grace of God which marks it off from other creeds, makes it descend on the instincts of man instead of rising from them, and seeks from them absolute obedience as truly as sympathetic recognition.'[155]

From this first point comes the second: The Church's major task in society is not to build hospitals or to do other social services but to be an apostle of Jesus Christ, to execute the apostolic ministry of the Word. That is, the Church is to preach the Gospel of the Cross. The works of mercy will accompany a Church which is first of all concerned to preach the 'good news.' He who called the Church into being, marks it out as special and defines its primary service to society.

236

'The gospel of forgiveness is now the Church's central word, and it is the mainspring of its aggressive work. The Church can only be missionary as it is remissionary.'[156]

So it is that the Church must first be the Church by hearing the Word. And in so hearing the Gospel, through the power of the Holy Spirit it is led to confess Christ with its lips and reflect him in its common life and its love to the world. This is the great act of solidarity, the great act of love which the Church offers to society. 'The true priestliness of the Church is an abstraction if it do not work through living, convinced, and priestly persons.'[157]

Thirdly, this Church must also disperse and be a part of the society. There is a going to work, a living in neighbourhoods, and a sharing in the responsibilities of political citizenship. Here too the Church as individuals is to preach the Gospel and confess his name. The Church must go out into the world for a 'Principle which is to affect society works by permeation and not by insulation, by inspiration and not injunction.'[158]

These three points Forsyth understands to be implied in the Church's participation in the Cross. The Church is commissioned by the Gospel as a missionary to the society.

With these remarks concerning the missionary aspect of revelation, we have come to the end of the third chapter of our study—Personal Participation in the Fact of the Cross. We have first discussed our theme as the work of the Holy Spirit of the Cross, noting his twofold work of presenting the living Christ to man and of opening man's heart to Christ. In connexion with the Holy Spirit's regenerating work, we paused to consider the relation between the old and new creations. Then we turned our attention more directly to man in the Spirit, discussing first the fact

237

that faith's primary certainty is that it is known by God. Considering authority and certainty in faith's participation in the Cross, we found that this required us to speak of man's experience of the Cross which in turn led to a more detailed examination of the evangelical experience or man's encounter with Christ in the conscience. In order to complete our understanding of this encounter, we discussed the relationship of the intellect to the will. This brought us to a consideration of Forsyth's view of the primacy of the will in man. Then, after applying our findings to the role of the intellect in faith's knowledge of God and the world, we concluded with Forsyth's presentation of the miracle of man's knowledge of God and the missionary task of the Church in the world. Such is the path which we have trod in following Forsyth's thoughts on man's personal relationship to Christ in the Spirit.

This chapter concludes our presentation of Forsyth's thought on revelation and of the prolegomena questions which are usually treated in connexion with a doctrine of revelation. While this has been presented with a systematization foreign to Forsyth's style, and with a brevity which could not help but deprive the reader of many exciting statements by Forsyth, we hope and trust that we have accurately represented Forsyth's concerns at each point. He has dealt with difficult themes and often in a very unusual and surprising manner. He has, however, provided us with an exciting and profound exposition of God's final act of revelation in Jesus Christ and man's faithful participation in it.

No one statement by Forsyth can do justice to the whole of his thought concerning the doctrine of revelation, nor give full expression to the humble, consecrated spirit in which he wrote. However, the following statement, which appropriately appears in one of Forsyth's sermons, seems to us to be a suitable expression of his witness to God's revelation in Jesus Christ and of the spirit with which he carried out his theological reflections.

'The height of omnipotence was the power to humble himself, to empty himself, to go out of himself and his own bliss, he leaves his native and eternal blessedness and settles in a foreign world. The eternal Father expatriates himself, and in his Son becomes a Pilgrim Father to found a new world. Some speak of the world as due to emanations of the Divine. I would speak rather, if I reverently might, of the emigration of the Divine, of his going forth in his person, and not of his sending forth his waves. Might I venture on the expression that it was by a Divine emigration and settlement in Christ and his Spirit that earth became a colony of him and the Church a missionary colony upon the face of the earth? The real idea in the heart of creation was not by almighty magic to make something out of nothing, but it was by moral miracle to make himself of no account, to become a child and an alien on the earth, to suffer and to die. The thousand, the million, the Infinite, becomes a little one; and that is the way in which the little one ever becomes a thousand.'[159]

CHAPTER IV

A Critical Appreciation

FORSYTH has given good reasons why theology must be both critical and appreciative. A theologian must listen anew to the Word of God addressed to the Church in order that he might assist the Church in making its proclamation more faithful to that Word and more relevant to the moral question of the hour. To be critical is to be both positive and negative; it is to purge out the foreign elements and to build upon the genuine. But this is not the work of a moment, nor of the contemporary generation alone. It is a service which the Church has from the beginning sought to render to God's Word. Therefore the theologian is called to sit humbly at the feet of those around him and those who have gone before him. Here too he is to listen critically but appreciatively, sympathetically. For these reasons and in this attitude we seek to evaluate the theology of Forsyth as we have come to understand it.

This chapter is divided into three sections. Part I seeks to identify the centre of Forsyth's theology and to compare it with other possibilities which are presently being suggested by some contemporary theologians. Part II discusses the implications of this centre for the wider range of theology, and seeks to indicate how Forsyth's theology stands in relation to the revival in contemporary Biblical and dogmatic theology. Lastly, Part III points out some dissatisfactions which we have with regard to Forsyth's theology.

241

Due to the scope of this study it has been necessary to limit the material in this chapter in several ways. We shall be more concerned with general tendencies and emphases than with a detailed presentation of any one contemporary theologian. Also no effort is made in this chapter to summarize all of the pertinent material which has been presented earlier in this study. Summary statements have been provided throughout the study usually at the end of each major section and at the end of the chapters. And finally, we have not sought to be exhaustive. A full comparison of Forsyth's theology with contemporary theology would require a study in itself. Rather we have sought to be representative, and to indicate the dominant themes in Forsyth and in the contemporary scene.

In an evaluation such as this it will not be amiss to inform the reader beforehand of the writer's own position. We find ourselves in full agreement with such theologians as Brunner and Mozley when they refer to Forsyth as the greatest dogmatic theologian Great Britain has given to the Church in modern times.[1] It is hoped that the material in this chapter will indicate the reasons which justify such high praise. We shall seek an answer to the question as to why Forsyth continues to speak in a fresh, stirring manner despite his lack of system and difficult style when so many theologians who were his contemporaries no longer speak to the Church. What is it that lifts Forsyth into that select company of theologians who remain contemporary despite the passing of the years? Were Forsyth alive he would no doubt answer that it is not the theologian who remains contemporary, but the Gospel. Only in so far as a theologian's writings are sacramental to that Gospel are they given power to span the years. It was for this reason that Forsyth consciously sought to be an evangelical theologian.

And it is our conviction that he was evangelical. He was not evangelical in the sense of adopting some system of theology which might go by that name, but rather in the sense of seeking before all else to hear and serve the evangel of Christ, the apostolic preachment. He sought to give it clear and fresh exposition for his generation. And it is because of the faithfulness and profundity with which he was granted to carry out that service that Forsyth has a word for today. It is therefore in a spirit of basic agreement that we offer these concluding observations.

The Centre of Forsyth's Theology

Theology, as well as all interpretative thought, proceeds from a centre. Some basic point of reference, perhaps some image underlies and colours all that a man does and thinks. It gives uniqueness and perspective to a man's writings. It sets him apart or in a communion. It is the primal vision through which all is seen, felt, and willed. Three phrases describe the centre of Forsyth's theology and indicate what makes him unique. They display what he himself considered to be his contribution to modern theology and to a deeper penetration into the mind and heart of St Paul. They are: Holy Father, evangelical experience, and the moralizing of dogma. The first two point to the event in which God gives himself to man and the last indicates the implication of this event for theological methodology.

The centre, stated objectively, is God the Holy Father giving himself as Holy Love in and through the atoning Cross of Jesus Christ. Stated subjectively, it is the 'evangelical experience' in which man, through the power of the Holy Spirit is enabled to hear God's Word in the Good News of the Cross and thus also to know himself as a forgiven sinner now living a new life under the Lordship of the Risen Christ. It is the redeemed conscience hearing, praising and serving its Holy Lord.

In the closest connexion with this event or centre, is the moralizing of dogma, which is Forsyth's conviction that all our knowledge of God, of ourselves and of the world arises from and is qualified by this moral encounter. Thus all dogma is morally known, and must be morally explicated. In the light of this centre God is known as Holy Love, man as intelligent, redeemed conscience, and the world as the background for personality. The world is teleological as is history. Or to put it inclusively and somewhat metaphysically, the real is the redemptive. Thus we can say that the moralizing of dogma is the understanding and interpreting of all theology in the light of the one theonomous centre—Christ in the conscience.

Such, briefly stated, is our understanding of the centre of Forsyth's faith and theology. Here is the source of the amazing single-mindedness and unity which pervades all that he has written. The following three questions will help us to place Forsyth's view of the Gospel in dialogue with the contemporary theological scene, thereby giving us a chance to evaluate its adequacy. First, is this centre absolute, or ought we to expect in the course of the Church's history other equally valid interpretations of the heart of the Gospel, interpretations more relevant to the historic hour? Second, does not this centre place the believing subject too much in the centre? Does it not lead to subjectivism and individualism? And lastly, is this centre able to provide by its correlate, the moralizing of dogma, a method adequate to the scope of man's knowledge of God, himself and the world? Is it an adequate theological methodology?

244

It is one of the central contentions of the theology of Paul Tillich that the material norm of theology is itself historically determined and varies in relation to the basic questions which man asks at a particular historic period and in a particular culture. In the period of the Greek Fathers the question concerned fate and death and the theological norm was Christ who brought man the medicine of incorruptibility and a place in God's providence. In the Middle Ages and at the Reformation the question was the problem of guilt and condemnation and the norm was Christ the sacrificial bearer of divine forgiveness. And today the question is one of existential emptiness and meaninglessness and the norm is Christ the bearer of the new creation who gives man participation in the New Being, a spiritual centre and the courage to be. Tillich does not suggest that these three elemental forms of anxiety are capable of separation. All three forms are interrelated and all are always involved in every period. But each historic period has its dominant threat to man's existence. And the Church finds in the Gospel the Christ who deals with all the forms of anxiety in terms of the one central question basic to the age. Thus we can say that the material norm or centre shifts, that it too shares in historic change as new questions elicit new answers.

This places in question Forsyth's interpretation of the *kerygmatic* Christ. For Forsyth the atoning Cross remains the absolute centre. There can be for Forsyth no basic shift. God is always the Holy Father and man the redeemed sinner. Grace overcoming guilt or justification by faith is always the dominant or ultimate concern of the Gospel.

Rudolph Bultmann too has shifted the centre of theology. For him it has moved from the atoning

Cross in the direction of man's fear of death, man's anxious flight into inauthentic existence which has trapped him in a false self-understanding. It is not forgiveness *per se* that is called for so much as a grace which will free man from his anxious efforts of self-preservation. It is a grace which will free man to face the future trusting in the power of God, that is, which will open man to the intangible realities. Here too the problems of man's self-confusion, man's self-contradiction, and man's need for a true self-understanding place in question Forsyth's centre, the atoning Cross of Christ. Modern theology asks Forsyth if he has not falsely absolutized the Atonement in his exposition of the Gospel. Tillich asks if the Cross is not to be seen today as the perfect symbol of the wholeness and meaningfulness resident in the ground of being emerging into existence and overcoming its emptiness, its loss of purpose and courage. Bultmann sees the preaching of the Cross as the eschatological call of God, calling man to a new self-understanding, bestowing upon him a new freedom and trust which allows him to live meaningfully and authentically in his being-unto-death. What are we to say? Has Forsyth absolutized an historically limited interpretation of the *Kerygma*?

We must take note that, according to Forsyth, this centre is the footing of theology, its foundation and not theology itself. The Gospel alone is the absolute point at which the Living Lord encounters man. There is no final theology. Theology can only be the Church's confession and exposition of this absolute point at different periods in history. Forsyth does, of course, state that each historic hour formulates the moral question differently, but he does not doubt that it is always the moral question that is primary. It is always the Gospel of an atoning Christ that evokes the faith which theologizes within that company of God's people, the

Church. No matter what man might conceive his existential problems to be in any age, when he is confronted with the Cross of Christ all of his problems are seen to be but forms of his guilty rebellion against the Holy Father who meets man in Christ as Holy Love. Christ does not answer our questions but he questions our questions and he answers first of all God's question—a question posed by Holy Love in the face of sin. Such would be Forsyth's answer.

What evidence can be brought to bear on this issue? First there is the central witness of the entire Scripture. Can there be any doubt that from Genesis to Revelation the Bible bears witness to a great redemptive drama in which God redeems a guilty, rebellious people? Is it not true that the Cross dominates the entire New Testament? This is true even when the particular theology of the individual writer is not able to grasp the centrality of the atonement. St Luke, for example, is forced to centre massively on the Cross even though he seems least conscious of its atoning significance. And thus he bears particular witness to its centrality despite his personal predilection. It is fair to state that the witness of the Scriptures taken as a whole finds its centre in grace overcoming guilt in the atonement and that it knows no other centre. Could it not be an extension of liberalism's weak doctrine of sin that seeks some other centre?

Also Forsyth points to the theonomous event of revelation in which man knows himself to be forgiven and claimed by God through the Cross of Christ. This is the certainty of faith and it rests on nothing beyond itself. God's Word of grace is received by the redeemed conscience. Thus man's fundamental knowledge of God and of himself is directly given and certified in the preaching of the mediator's Cross. At the same time the reception of this Good News restores man to his destiny, to himself.

247

On the basis of the concerted witness of the Scripture and on the basis of the self-knowledge given in the faith which arises as a response to the proclamation of the Gospel, Forsyth claims that grace overcoming guilt remains the abiding centre of all theology. It is the *prius* of all history even though the moral question must take its form from the historic hour. At every moment in history man's self is not a *datum* but a *mandatum*; at every moment of history the real is the Redemptive.

At this point it becomes clear that a theologian must make a choice as to the central symbols and analogies which he will use. It becomes necessary either to interpret the impersonal symbols in the light of the personal ones or vice versa. Forsyth opts for the primacy of the anthropomorphic analogies of Scripture. He speaks primarily in terms of will and of personhood and interprets the impersonal symbols in that context. Nature is discussed teleologically. It is in the moral, interpersonal realm that man encounters grace which is the reality of all that is. This choice of the primary symbols, analogies, and images is not based upon the caprice of the theologian. It is rooted in the nature of that encounter in which God reveals and gives himself to man and in which man finds his fulfilment. A faith in the God of the atoning Cross calls for the primacy of the moral analogies and provides the only context for their proper understanding.

With regard to this question of the absolute centre of theology we find ourselves in agreement with Forsyth. As we understand it, to shift the centre from grace overcoming guilt to some other centre does not merely bring a new facet of the Gospel to light but eventuates in an understanding of man and of God which departs radically from the general witness of Scripture and from the knowledge of God and man given in faith.

b—IS THIS CENTRE TOO SUBJECTIVE AND INDIVIDUALISTIC?

Karl Barth has made it clear that an introspective pietism is one of the most subtle and dangerous falsifications of faith. It places man and his affections in the place of God and his deeds. It reverses the entire perspective of Biblical faith. Further it tends toward an individualism which is foreign to the Biblical witness. In the light of Barth's impassioned plea for the rejection of such pietism it is important to ask if Forsyth's understanding of the centre of theology results in an over-concentration upon the individual's piety.

There are at least three primary indications that Forsyth is not driven to individualistic pietism. First his use of 'experience' is not tied to feelings interior to man but rather he speaks of the 'evangelical experience' which is a moral conviction, a belief. In the light of the Cross man is not driven to simply peer within but rather he finds himself confronted by another, convicted of sin, redeemed and claimed by Christ the Lord. The eyes of faith are directed toward Christ and only in the light of his deed is man given self-understanding. It is important to keep this unique use of the term 'experience' in mind. It is not an experience of the self but a relationship, a personally present Lord which the conscience knows and serves. To be sure, it includes a conviction about the self, but this conviction is mediated through the knowledge of Christ. Forsyth preaches Christ not faith.

As to the question of individualism, we need only think of Forsyth's view of a racial salvation, and of his understanding of the Church. To be saved is to be saved in a salvation which includes the new humanity, a world. And to be saved in Christ is at the same time to be placed into his Church. Indeed the whole of

249

history is guided to the fulfilment of God's purpose, which is to hallow his own name by claiming and renewing all men for himself. At this point, however, we note a paradox. We are all saved if we will be saved. Faith is the reception of salvation. Forsyth knows of no purely objective salvation, for salvation is communion with God and communion is interpersonal. Thus Forsyth offers us no rational solution. But by keeping the paradox he is able to affirm both *sola gratia* and *sola fide*. There is a tendency in modern theology to speak of salvation as accomplished in such a fashion that faith is simply becoming aware that with or without faith one is saved. This is too impersonal, too objectivistic for Forsyth. Faith is our entrance into the salvation already prepared for us in Christ. By faith one enters into salvation, receives forgiveness and renewal, and seeks to serve a new Lord. The centre of Forsyth's theology is the eventful self-giving of God to man. It is a personal relationship and thus it forces Forsyth to include faith within salvation as man's participation in this personally given and received communion. The Gospel is above all the power of God, but paradoxically, to them who believe.

It is our opinion that Forsyth is faithful to the Biblical view of faith by presenting it as the response whereby man enters and participates in salvation, and also by making the primary focus of faith Jesus Christ and not the inner affections of the believer. He has thereby avoided a one-sided subjectivism without falling into objectivism. Further there is a full appreciation of the corporate as well as the individual in Forsyth's exposition. And it is our conviction that it is Forsyth's understanding of the centre of theology which has made this possible.

Here we are concerned with Forsyth's programme for the moralizing of dogma. Is it possible to base all our knowledge of God, ourselves and the world on the moral centre of grace overcoming guilt? Can we find clarity as we seek to let this centre determine our theological exposition? In order to explore these questions we shall discuss the question of demythologizing as raised by Bultmann, the idea of natural theology as affirmed by Neo-thomists such as Przywara and Liberals such as L. H. DeWolf, and the possibility of a Christian philosophy as suggested by Forsyth.

Both Bultmann and Forsyth are *kerygmatic* theologians. But it is clear that on the question of demythologizing they do not agree. Forsyth centres all on an objective atonement taken home by the conscience whereas Bultmann describes the atonement as a mythological manner of thinking no longer acceptable to modern man and does not hesitate to excise it from his understanding of the *kerygma*. This he dismisses along with the Incarnation, the pre-existence of Christ and the personal Resurrection of Christ, all of which are affirmed by Forsyth. However it is also clear that Forsyth was no Biblical literalist. He praised Biblical criticism and was not at all concerned to defend the scientific accuracy of the Biblical world-view, or its historical accuracy at every point. The question arises as to why these two men who both seek to exposit the Biblical *kerygma* for their generation differ so profoundly as to what is and what is not susceptible of demythologizing. The answer lies in the character of their centres, of their respective understandings of the *kerygma*. For Forsyth it is moral, historic, and interpersonal, whereas for Bultmann it is closely identified with self-understanding as a decision in response to God's call in the fleeting point of the eschatological 'now.' The connexion between the centre and the scope of demythologizing is clearly illustrated with regard to the atonement. For Forsyth, God's call is in actuality a gift of himself to sinful man, the re-establishment of communion through the event of the Cross. It involves God's action in history in such a fashion that God himself must enter it to atone himself, to set man free for his Lordship and thus, in principle, to overcome the demonic forces which seek to hinder God's purposes for all history. There can be no demythologizing of history which conceives of all talk of God's entering into history as but the mythological description of man's action in history. God has actually been encountered in history in and through man's action in history—ultimately in and through Jesus Christ but secondarily in and through human witnesses to him. Bultmann, who somewhat arbitrarily links God's call with the preaching of the Cross, is willing, however, to see in this preaching simply the call to man to trust in God, to decide to place his security in God's hands. The fact that the dimension of the atonement is missing here allows Bultmann to conceive of history in terms comparable with the autonomous view of modern man. There is no entrance by God into history in Jesus Christ; there is only the momentary juxtaposition of God's call in and through the proclamation of the Cross. Bultmann's centre does not force him to moralize history. And above all he is not compelled to proclaim the offence of the uniqueness of God's entrance into history in Jesus Christ to deal with his wrath and with sin.

In the closest connexion with this is Forsyth's view of man's self-understanding as contrasted with that of Bultmann. Here again Bultmann is free to allow wide range to modern man's self-understanding as an autonomous being, one who must bear the penalty of his own failures, and whose spirit is in no sense penetrated by God's Spirit. On the other hand, Forsyth is forced to go beyond the somewhat idealistic idea of self-understanding to speak of an encounter in history in which God's Spirit opens man's spirit to God's self-giving in the Cross. Man's self-understanding is the reflex of this action by God in history through the Spirit of the Cross. It is, therefore, a self-understanding which is in radical opposition to the autonomous view of modern man. It is a self-understanding as a redeemed conscience, as a self living in historic communion with the Lord of History and Nature.

In summary we can say that Bultmann's norm for demythologizing envisions autonomous man who is called to respond to the call of God in the face of death. However, Forsyth's norm, based as it is on God's moral action of the Cross and in the conscience, forces him to an understanding of God in history and to an understanding of man's self which challenges the autonomy of modern man. Once again, in our opinion, it is a weak doctrine of grace and sin perhaps retained from Bultmann's teacher Wilhelm Herrmann, a remainder of Liberalism, which separates Forsyth's moralizing of dogma from Bultmann's programme of demythologizing. Actually it is precisely fallen man's autonomous self-understanding, whether it be that of idealism, or of naturalism, or of existentialistic moralism, which is challenged by the Gospel. In Forsyth we find a centre which provides him with a theological method that makes this challenge clear.

We have noted in our study that Forsyth has rejected all natural theology. The present resurgence of Neo-thomism and the use of the principle of rational coherence by some liberal theologians also questions Forsyth's programme of moralizing of dogma. For Forsyth our knowledge of God is personal knowledge and not intellectual knowledge. It arises from the restoration of personal communion between a Holy God and sinful man. Apart from this restoration there is no true knowledge of God or of self. And this restoration is a miracle of grace. Any use of the intellect which seeks to deduce or induce God, or which seeks to prove his existence on rational grounds, is first of all a misunderstanding of the role of the intellect within the personality and secondly a misunderstanding of the reality of sin. While it is true that Forsyth is strangely silent with regard to those Pauline texts usually quoted in support of natural theology, it cannot be denied that he has the central witness of Scripture in his favour. Even those texts so often quoted militate not for but against the possibility of natural theology. At most they can be interpreted in favour of a general witness to God in nature and in the conscience, but it is a witness which is not heard by sinful man, as these very texts point out. Here again the miracle of grace which is Forsyth's centre provides him direction as he grounds all of man's knowledge of God in the revealing event of the Cross.

Lastly, to illustrate the scope which Forsyth's centre gives his theology, we note his call for a metaphysic of the conscience. He envisions the possibility of a Christian philosophy. To be sure this does not mean a final philosophy or even a *philosophia perennis*, but rather a philosophical style or stance in which the Christian working in philosophy proceeds from his conviction that the Real is the Redemptive. Here we see the totality of man's knowledge embraced in the scope of the moralizing process. To work this out in concrete philosophical problems is the task of a Christian in philosophy. Forsyth stands, therefore, in the honoured tradition of St Augustine.

Forsyth and the Contemporary Biblical and Dogmatic Revival in Theology

Another way of evaluating the theology of Forsyth is to observe how his exposition of the Gospel compares with the findings of the present theological revival. Does his *kerygmatic* centre allow him to give full expression to what the Church is hearing in the Gospel today? In order to make this comparison we shall briefly comment on six of the dominant themes of contemporary theology.

a—THE SOVEREIGNTY OF GOD

If modern theology has repudiated the three-level cosmology of the Biblical world-view it has restored a three dimensional view of history. Once again we hear of God as the Lord of creation and history and of the reality of the demonic. The Gospel is now a Word from God and not a religious insight of man. God is transcendent and Holy and not simply immanent in natural process. And all of this is central to Forsyth, for the sovereignty of God, his Will, his Kingdom, his Word and Deed—these were of primary importance to him. It is true that later in his life he was drawn anew to Calvin and the Puritans, especially to Goodwin,[2] but they did not introduce him to the sovereignty of God. This is rooted in God's very act of revelation, in the Cross. Forsyth's view of revelation, from his early writings to his last, exposits a Word of God which descends upon man before it rises up from him. It is a Word which is initiated in God's gracious Will and is miraculously heard in the Spirit. It is an act which not only meets man's profoundest need but hallows God's Name. It is a sovereign act whereby all history is ordered by its Lord. It is an act which effects

255

God's authority upon earth, an authority which is mediated through men but never placed in their possession. At a time when theologians were centring upon man, Forsyth sought first the Kingdom of God. His is a theocentric theology.

b—CHRISTOCENTRISM AND THE DOCTRINE OF THE TRINITY

If Liberalism recovered the lineaments of the human figure of Jesus, they tended to lose the divine Word addressed to man in him. Contemporary theology has recovered Christ, the Word of God. The acts of Christ are the acts of God. And, in this recovery, the doctrine of the Trinity has found new relevance. Since faith in Christ is faith in God, all theology must be trinitarian throughout. No longer are we called to believe like Jesus but to believe in Jesus Christ. And such belief is possible only by the power of God in us, in the Spirit.

In Forsyth we find this trinitarian connexion between God, his Word and the Spirit. We have heard him state that theology is only possible upon a trinitarian basis. We note that revelation is triune. 'The Father who *spoke* by his prophets must *come* to save in the Son and must *occupy* in the Spirit.'[3] The act of the atonement involves the whole Godhead. Also there can be no talk of the Spirit apart from Christ the Word. He is the Spirit of the Cross. But neither can there be any understanding of Jesus apart from the Word, the Lord the Spirit. In contemporary theology there is some discussion by men such as G. E. Wright of a 'God who acts theology' which so stresses God's action as revelation as to de-emphasize the interpreting Word and Spirit. This is to fail to do justice to the central significance of Biblical prophecy and of the interpretive role of the Spirit. In Christ we meet the

God who acts and speaks the Word which is spoken. And it is the Spirit who calls forth a community of response to God's active Word.

Forsyth not only speaks of Christ as the Word of God but he is Christocentric. The Cross, which is Christ in the culmination of his ministry, is the centre of all Forsyth's thought. It is in Christ alone that we encounter the grace which overcomes our guilt and claims us anew. Scripture, preaching, the witness of the life of the congregation, creed and theology are all significant only to the extent that they are sacramental to the grace of Christ's Cross. It is due to this fact that Forsyth concentrated his ministry on the dogmatic task rather than on the apologetic, for he felt that the most powerful way to men's hearts and minds lies through the Cross. It is a further illustration of Forsyth's Christocentrism that he never sought to define 'religion' and to use it as a regulating concept as was common in his day.[4] Faith as man's response to God's grace communicated in the Cross of Christ must find its norm there and not in some general abstraction called 'the essence of religion.'

In this concentration upon the *kerygmatic* Christ, Forsyth has done what the writers of Scripture have done, either by anticipation or recollection.[5] And in this respect too, he finds himself in agreement with a major tendency in contemporary Biblical and dogmatic theology.

c—GRACE

If modern theology has recovered the Biblical notes of God's sovereignty and its full exercise in Christ, it has thereby come to a new awareness of what he sovereignly proclaims in Christ his Word. His is a Word of grace. The covenant mercy of God is the ground of his creation, his Cross, and his promised new heaven and new earth. God personally bending down to rebellious man in sovereign mercy is both the good news of the Gospel and the voice that proclaims that Gospel. Grace is God's personal presence given in sheer mercy to undeserving man, bestowing and creating value where he finds none.

Along with this recovery of the centrality of grace comes concomitantly a deeper awareness of man's sin. The tragedy and misery of man are exposed by the grace of God. Terms long neglected such as 'the fall' and 'original sin' have become common coin again. They are, however, interpreted less biologically than the Augustinian tradition interpreted them.

Also in this connexion the significance of Christian ethics has been placed in a new light. For grace not only forgives but claims man's whole life and renews him for a life of obedience and service. Grace calls man into a communion of love, love for God and for neighbour.

We have already heard that it was Forsyth who sought to recover the term 'grace' for his generation. At a time when others spoke of the love of God, Forsyth spoke of the grace of God, of the Holy Love of God, victorious over man's sin and Satan. It is grace that regenerates man into the communion with God which is his Kingdom. Jesus Christ is the Word of God precisely in that he came to seek the sinner and to restore him to God through his Cross.

It has long been a tendency in the Church to distort the concept of grace in two ways: as an impersonal power or virtue and as sentimental love. Forsyth fought both of these tendencies. The latter was represented by much of the Liberalism of his day and the former was and continues to be held by the Church of Rome. But to see grace in the light of Christ's Cross is to see it as God's personal action. Further, to see it in an atoning Cross, is to see it as Holy Love in powerful action, dealing sovereignly with the sin of man and the powers that bind him. It is no powerless wringing of the hands, no willing but weak display of affection.

Nor could he who was turned from a lover of love to the recipient of grace be unaware of the depth of sin and its universality. It was not for naught that Forsyth referred to the doctrine of sin as the watershed between Liberalism and the Gospel. To speak of grace is to speak of the Holiness of God and of the sin of man, for grace is the Holy Love of God meeting sinful man.

Neither should we fail to mention that Forsyth saw here the closest connexion between grace and ethics.[6] In this he anticipated the work of modern Biblical theologians and dogmaticians such as Karl Barth. It was Ritschl's ellipse which separated the two that called forth Forsyth's most profound criticism of his theology. As we have noted, Forsyth tells us that 'the source of Christian Ethics is theological.'[7] It is grace which bestows all upon man freely, but it is grace which claims all of man completely. God's grace calls man into communion, not into an easy chair. To separate the command of God from his grace is to speak of another god than he who sovereignly gives himself to man in Jesus Christ as Lord and Saviour.

d—HISTORY AND THE KINGDOM OF GOD

The fact that history stands under the judgement of God, that all of our social structures and all of our efforts will not bring in the Kingdom of God is a dominant theme of modern theology. The false Utopianism of an earlier generation has been dented if not shattered. Biblical scholars have made it clear that there is no social pattern or programme in the Bible. The complexity and seriousness of social problems, compounded as they are by man's abiding

259

sin, allow, at most, only proximate solutions. The Church's task is to seek to contribute to a more 'just' society and not to incarnate the Sermon on the Mount in social institutions. And it is to do this in repentance while waiting for God's gift of his Kingdom proleptically now and ultimately at the end of history, an end to which he, as its Lord, is sovereignly guiding all history.

In his doctrine of the Cross as the Final Judgement, as the gift of the Kingdom now working itself out teleologically within history through judgement and crisis and in his distinction between grace as mercy to persons and as public righteousness, Forsyth stands in agreement with present-day theology. We make no attempt to be complete here; however we would like to point to a certain naïvety in Forsyth's treatment of grace as public justice on the social and international level. He seems to have been little aware of the shades of grey which exist in any international conflict. Can we really say that in any war one side exhausts all of the evil involved? Also he never deals specifically with the question of justice. What is justice? How does *agape* transpose itself into justice on the social level? Would Forsyth stand closer to Barth's Christocentric approach or to Brunner's approach based on the Orders of Creation?

e—BIBLICAL INTERPRETATION

The fact that the Biblical authors write portraits of faith, that they do not provide us with modern biography, the fact that all interpretation is done by a living subject and thus includes, of necessity, the subjectivity of the interpreter, the value of Biblical criticism, and the unity of the Bible in Christ—all of these themes of modern Biblical interpretation and more find their place in Forsyth.

It was he who in the very face of the search for the historical Jesus, said that we cannot get behind the apostolic writings, a verdict confirmed afresh by subsequent form criticism. He had already seen the unity of the Old and New Testaments to lie in the faithfulness of God who consistently acts redemptively and whose redemption culminates in Jesus Christ, the centre of Scripture. This consistency of God's purpose and action in the broader framework of promise and fulfilment as viewed from the Cross makes clear the unity of all the Biblical writings. They all testify of him, the God of Holy Love. Such contemporary writers as J. D. Smart, Werner G. Kümmel, Oscar Cullmann, Karl Barth, Emil Brunner and others hold similar views. In our excurses on Biblical interpretation we indicated how profoundly Forsyth involves the subjectivity of the interpreter in the act of interpretation. All human knowing is subjective, and this subjectivity reaches its peak in the knowing of One who claims the conscience and awakens a true self-knowledge in man. Here, too, Forsyth stands in a line with Barth, Brunner and Smart, though not with the way in which Bultmann includes man's subjectivity. True self-knowledge is a reflex of the Gospel, an awareness of faith, and it cannot be gained nor approximated apart from faith. Nor would he accept the objective approach to exegesis represented by Cullmann. Also we note Forsyth's appreciation of Biblical ethics, his concern to find a *kerygmatic* centre in Scripture when the critics seem dedicated to its dissection, but also his appreciation of the truly critical role of Biblical criticism when it did not pretend to an objectivity which is neither possible nor desirable. In addition Forsyth's feeling for Biblical eschatology (though he dealt with it in terms of teleology), his awareness of the Biblical attitude toward religion, his perception that Christ in speaking

261

of the Kingdom spoke of himself, his treatment of the parables, and supremely his understanding of the authority of God mediated through Scripture and preaching, are all of fundamental importance to him and stand in harmony with the views of much of modern Biblical and dogmatic theology.

f—REVELATION

Since this study has dealt primarily with Forsyth's doctrine of revelation we need only point out here how he anticipated the recovery of the personal and historic character of revelation as it is presently being interpreted by theologians. His understanding of Scripture, preaching, and Church reflect this doctrine of revelation. We might say that he stands close to Barth and Brunner, though perhaps closer to Brunner. Here, too, Forsyth finds himself in eminent contemporary company.

A great deal of significant material has gone unmentioned. We think, for example, of Forsyth's vital concern for ecumenicity long before the movement got under way. Surely, however, this quick sketch has convinced us that Forsyth's centre has allowed him to anticipate in the most remarkable and impressive manner so much of what the Church has only lately come to hear in the Gospel. It has strengthened us in our conviction that grace overcoming guilt or the atoning Cross of Christ is the true centre of the Gospel.

PART III

Some Dissatisfactions with Forsyth's Theology

In our concern to indicate a fundamental agreement with the centre of Forsyth's theology we would not want to give the impression that Forsyth is above reproach. There are a number of questions and reservations that arise when one is reading Forsyth. One cannot but wonder why it is that Forsyth, a man who centred his whole theology on the Biblical Christ, presents so little exegesis in his writing. Had he done so some of the Biblical themes which receive inadequate treatment would have intruded themselves upon him. We have in mind such themes as the covenant, creation, etc. Also he would not have ignored texts relevant to the themes which he did handle in detail. Texts such as Romans I and II never receive treatment, as far as we know, and yet they are considered as classical *loci* for the doctrine of revelation. Further, he would have avoided giving the impression that he was arguing from philosophic principles, an impression which he gives from time to time.

Another question arises as to why Forsyth allowed himself to be so inconsistent in his terminology. It is not that we do not appreciate his suggestive, expressive literary style. Surely, however, that does not require inconsistency. Basic terms such as revelation, gospel, religion, moral, etc., are all used with two or three meanings. While this is not an insurmountable obstacle it unfortunately makes the reading of Forsyth unnecessarily difficult.

Forsyth's use of the term 'Cross' also gives occasion for misunderstanding. There was, to be sure, an excellent reason why he felt it necessary to replace the title 'Christ' by the word 'Cross.' He did this to point to the Christ of the Gospel in opposition to liberal, non-*kerygmatic* interpretations of Christ. But by so doing he can be understood to reduce the Cross to an impersonal principle and also to separate the Cross from the whole ministry of Christ as well as from his Resurrection. Such a reading would be false and can be corrected by a careful and full reading of his writings. However it does cause initial difficulties.

Also one wonders whether Forsyth really does justice to the significance of the physical realm, to creation. He treats it teleologically, under the rubric of history but does he really reflect the Biblical appreciation and joy in the earthly blessings of the Lord? Perhaps he has remained too much under the influence of Ritschl at this point. It is good to be a redeemed person, but redeemed in the body.

We have already mentioned the naïvety with which we feel Forsyth approaches the whole area of public justice. Also it is important to realize that much which Forsyth treats is only suggested or outlined. It is never dealt with in detail. But we dare not ask too much of one who worked so industriously and who has given us so much.

A Concluding Remark

We do not wish to end upon a negative note. The dissatisfactions we have are but minor compared with what we have received from this theologian of the Cross of Christ. His re-affirmation of the insights of the Reformers, especially of Luther, though modified by Calvin, is based upon a personal encounter with the *kerygmatic* Christ, is thought out in dialogue with the mind of his day and is based upon a serious appreciation for the Church's theological tradition. He thus provides us with a stirring example, with a challenge to go and do likewise, and with profound insights into the Gospel. To read Forsyth is not simply to learn much but to be directed to him who made Forsyth an apostle of grace.

APPENDIX

P. T. Forsyth, his Relation and Attitude to Philosophy

THIS appendix grew out of a need which the writer felt in his study of Forsyth's writings. Often Forsyth expresses his thoughts in a manner conditioned by his philosophical inclinations. He does this, however, without ever giving a specific description of the philosophical tendencies which have influenced him. Only in the most general way[1] does he indicate what it was in modern thought that he found helpful in his exposition of the Gospel. For this reason, in the first reading of Forsyth's works, many of his statements remained difficult, if not incomprehensible to the writer. It was necessary to do two things: first to examine the philosophical thought contemporary with Forsyth and then to compare those passages in Forsyth with one another and with the thought of the time, in order to see more clearly Forsyth's own position in relation to it. This proved to be most helpful in clearing up the initial difficulties encountered in reading Forsyth.

As an aid to the reader we briefly present here the fruit of our study. Our remarks are in two sections. The first will deal with Forsyth's place in the philosophical thought of his time, showing the general themes which seemed to have influenced him. The second section will deal with Forsyth's own metaphysical insights and his attitude to the use of philosophy in theology. We are not concerned at this point to be critical so much as to be descriptive.

265

We do not propose to discuss in detail the thought of individual philosophers but rather to point out those schools and men who might have influenced Forsyth. In order to do this we have adopted two procedural rules. We shall mention only those philosophers who are *actually cited* in Forsyth's writings and who cast a light on his own position. Secondly, we shall mention only those aspects of their thought which influenced Forsyth, either by his acceptance or his rejection of them.

Forsyth, living in England and acquainted with German thought, was in a position to be influenced by the philosophical thought of America, England and Europe at the turn of the nineteenth century. This was a time of transition in philosophical thought and there were, therefore, both new streams of thought and older eighteenth century forms of thought competing for man's allegiance. This sense of transition and flux is itself a factor which must be kept in mind.

It immediately strikes the reader that Forsyth does not share the well-known British empiricism, in fact, that he does not even find it a worthy opponent with which to do battle. The second factor that stands out is Forsyth's voluntaristic type of thought. The primary impulse to Forsyth's personalistic-voluntarism derives from his faith relationship with Christ, but there were also factors in the thought of his time which helped him give expression to this relationship in terms of the will. It is therefore important to discuss the influences on Forsyth which kept him from scientific empiricism and those which supported him in a form of voluntarism.

British empiricism, founded in the seventeenth century, developed in the eighteenth century, and

266

influencial today in positivistic types of linguistic analysis, has always been accompanied by a British Platonism. At the end of the nineteenth century and during the first quarter of the twentieth however, British Idealism was the most influencial philosophical school in England.[2] Therefore empiricism did not hold the position which it held earlier nor which it holds today.

Leaving out of consideration the social problems in England at the turn of the century which drew attention to man and his needs, that is, which served to give thought a more personalistic and less mechanistic-empiricistic direction, we must also in this connexion take note of the new findings in physics, mathematics and of the critique of scientific methodology.[3] Since rationalism throughout the eighteenth and the nineteenth centuries was closely associated with the model of mathematics and the natural sciences, this also produced a crisis for rationalistic empiricism.

In the field of physics, the mechanistic view of Newtonian physics was placed in doubt. The determinism, unquestioned by Kant and the whole of British empiricism, was no longer tenable. Accompanying this confusion caused by the change in physics, was the critique of the scientific method by the empirocritics in Germany and France. The role which the subjectivity of the observer must of necessity play in observation was pointed out. Science as a method was described as an instrument for explaining experience, but not of absolute value. It was not able to deal with the questions of truth and value. A certain relativism was thereby introduced. When we add to this the fact that even mathematical theory began to show uncertainty, for paradoxes and discrepancies had appeared even in that citadel, then we can understand that scientific empiricism was not in a favourable position to strongly influence Forsyth's thought.

What were, then, the philosophical tendencies which did influence Forsyth's thought in some measure, either positively or negatively? The following factors are important: Kant and the neo-Kantians, a group which Forsyth refers to as the pessimists, the two voluntarists Paulsen and Wundt, the life-philosophers, the general romantic mood of the time, Hegelianism, Sören Kierkegaard, and naturalistic evolutionism. Of these, the most important which positively influenced Forsyth are without a doubt the Kantian-neo-Kantian influence and the writings of the life-philosophers. The most important negative influences on Forsyth were Hegelian Idealism and non-teleological evolutionism. We shall indicate quite briefly what influence we understand each of these factors to have exercised on Forsyth.

Beginning with the negative, we note Forsyth's frequent reference to Hegel's thought and to German Idealism in general. Schelling, for example, is mentioned specifically. In almost every case it is in connexion with Forsyth's repudiation of rationalistic metaphysics.[4] This fight against Idealistic metaphysics (and we must not forget that such metaphysics had gained the upper hand in England during Forsyth's lifetime), against its intellectualism and impersonalism, served to sharpen the issue for Forsyth. It led him to look for a counter-position in the voluntaristic and life-philosophical writings. In this connexion it should be mentioned that Forsyth was acquainted with another, now more famous opponent of Hegel, Sören Kierkegaard. Also we must not limit Forsyth's reaction against rationalism only to the rationalism of Hegelian metaphysics. Forsyth was acquainted with and wrote directly against the views of Lessing, for example.

Secondly, Darwinian evolutionism had continued to find expression in England and on the continent, to some extent even in Nietzsche. This tendency to find a sufficient explanation for the higher forms in the lower, was rejected by Forsyth. His references to evolution are generally written to point out that it is inadequate because it is non-teleological. When taken seriously, it leads to a self-contradictory relativism, since there are no real constants by which one can measure evolution. Forsyth also points out that evolutionism is constituted by using mechanistic conceptions in areas where they do not fit. He was more than willing to speak of evolution, of movement, but it took place within an order.

What were the positive influences? These were primarily Kantianism and Life-philosophy. We should, however, mention the general romantic mood of the time. Earlier in the nineteenth century, in reaction to a strict mechanistic and rationalistic view of reality, romanticism had expressed the conviction that emotion, life and religion were important ways through which man comes into contact with reality. This reaction remained alive and received support from the crises in the scientific realm. Having blended itself with Idealism, it was now a strong constituent in the general mood of the time. Actually, in this romanticism as in all of the positive influences we have mentioned and shall mention, there are elements which Forsyth fought against strongly. But what is important in our present context is that romanticism was a positive influence in that it provided a milieu in which the intellect was not conceived of as playing the leading role.

The Kantian-neo-Kantian movement, especially the writings of Kant himself and of the Baden School, e.g. Windelband, is one of the most decisive of the philosophical influences upon Forsyth. From this line of thought, which considered the will as man's contact with reality, Forsyth received constant support for his own view. The Baden or axiological school stressed values, i.e. moral, aesthetic, and religious, as actualizing themselves in man's judgement by making themselves felt in man's life as a claim on him. In such a view man would know God, not syllogistically, but by God's claim on man through the religious values. Coupled with this accent on the will, there is in neo-Kantianism a conceptualist view of the intellect. Knowing is a creative act in which the intellect is active as synthesizing, but not as intuiting essences. Forsyth shared in this rejection of rational intuition.

Also influencing Forsyth in the direction of voluntarism, were the two psychologist-philosophers, Wundt, and Paulsen. Both of these men were voluntarists themselves and wrote in the field of metaphysics. We note, for example, that Forsyth was acquainted with Paulsen's *Ethik*. Forsyth also quotes with approval Wundt's stress on the distinction between an unconscious or instinctive motive and a conscious or imperative motive.[5] The conscience, he agreed, was not to be neutralized by unconscious drives which were mechanically interacting with one another in a power struggle, as depth psychiatry at its inception was prone to explain human decision.

Having discussed the strongest influences with regard to the primacy of the will in Forsyth's thought, we must turn to those influences which related this will to the whole man in life: to the Life-philosophers and the pessimists. We find Bergson, Eucken, James, Nietzsche, Schopenhauer and von Hartmann mentioned in Forsyth's writings. Considering first Bergson, Eucken and James, the Life-philosophers, we find that they have the following general emphases in common. They are actualistic; the accent is on action, movement, becoming and life. Also they share an organic view of reality; life does not move mechanically but it pulsates as an organism. It is historical, as Eucken and Bergson, each in his own way stresses. Thirdly, they are all, in the strict philosophical sense of the word, irrationalists; this does not mean that they have no interest in reason or that they can see no function for reason, but rather that the tests for reality are not rational. Their criteria are the tests of practicality, of personal intuition or of a vital understanding of history. Their conception of the intellect is instrumentalist; it serves life's interests. The intellect is an instrument of the personality. Lastly, they all tend to an objective, pluralistic, and personalistic view of reality.

The other three men we named are those whom Forsyth appreciated because of their grasp of the tragic sense of life. We refer to Nietzsche, Schopenhauer, and von Hartmann. Forsyth in no sense accepted Nietzsche's relapse into naturalistic evolutionism nor von Hartmann's discussion of redemption as an impersonal process. But he valued them in that they gave expression to the fact that life called for redemption, for a moral and not for an intellectual answer. He also speaks of Ibsen in this connexion.

These two groups provide the background for such words in Forsyth's writings as 'life interest,' for his distinction between *Geschichte* and *Historie*,[6] for his understanding of the life-relatedness of the intellect, for his dismissal of 'faculty' psychology and for his actualism.

One word of caution is in order before we close this first section. In his writings we find no full discussion of the schools of philosophy or of the men with whose thought he was acquainted. Those names which we have mentioned in this section appear only as footnote material in Forsyth's writings. He was not interested in philosophy *per se*, or if he was, he does not indicate this in his writing. Therefore the background material which we have just presented in a most general fashion is only a conjecture. It serves the practical purpose of helping us to understand the cultural background of Forsyth's terminology, but it is in no sense to be considered as a genetic study.

b—AN OUTLINE OF FORSYTH'S USE OF PHILOSOPHY AND ITS RELATION TO THEOLOGY

The title given to this section is somewhat presumptuous or, if it is not, it is only because the primary accent must be on the word 'outline.' Only a sketch or an outline is offered at this point because the material which we have at our disposal only permits of such treatment. Forsyth did not provide us with more. For this reason this outline is cast in the form of a discussion of Forsyth's use of certain philosophical terms. This will avoid the impression that we are dealing with a system. Actually, we are dealing with some philosophical insights and with a consistent tendency.

We are concerned to examine the interrelatedness existing between Forsyth's use of the terms 'real,' 'final,' and 'moral act.' We offer first a definition of each term and then we shall discuss their meanings and their relatedness. The definitions are our formulations based on a comparison of the way in which Forsyth uses these terms in different passages.

The *Real*, described objectively, is the Holy, or, described in relatedness, the Redemptive. The *Final* is the central act of the Holy which has completely determined the destiny of man or has set the course of history. *Moral-act* is the decisive response of the whole self to that Lord who claims the total person or the conscience.

It is important first of all to note that Forsyth received his axiomatic starting point with reference to

272

philosophy from theology. He starts from the givenness of the redeemed conscience. He then turns to construe the universe in terms of its highest product—the soul redeemed by the creative morality which is grace. This leads us to an exposition of the philosophical implications of 'the Holy.' That which ordered and continues to shape and order reality is the Redemptive. A redeemed conscience accepts axiomatically that the Holy, as the Creator and Norm of the redeemed conscience, must be identified with the ultimate reality of the world. Thus we are in the realm of metaphysics. 'The true metaphysic is the metaphysic of the soul, of the religious soul in a moral universe, of redemption.'[7]

Forsyth points out that such a starting point contains within itself a paradox. The conscience knows itself to be redeemed by ultimate reality from sin, but sin is itself a part of reality. Sin must be both in the Holy and anti-thetical to the Holy. This is not thinkable. However, it is not only knowable, but basic to faith's consciousness of itself and of the Holy. Thought demands monism and faith demands a dualism of reconciled wills. That is, we have a metaphysic which is pluralistic, interpersonal or voluntaristic, and paradoxical to thought.

In connexion with this it is helpful to see where Forsyth agrees and disagrees with the Kantian-neo-Kantian influence.[8] In his stress on the practical side of the soul in its relation to reality, Forsyth stands in the Kantian line. This also holds true in his conclusion that reality cannot be thought without ending up in paradox. Forsyth differs from the Kantians in that the nature of things is not moral law, but the Holy as the Redemptive, which is interpersonal and not simply axiological.

In order to relate the above to the other two terms, the Final and Moral-action, we shall start with the latter. A view of ontology as the Holy implies, according to Forsyth, actualism. He maintains that reality is action and not essence. He places action over thought, feeling, and personality. By moral-action Forsyth refers to that action which springs from the self's *prius* in the redeemed conscience. Such action, then, is deeper than, but involves the feelings and the intellect and it is through such action that the self gives shape and form to the character or personality.[9] This moral-action is a response to the action of reality or of the Holy as redemptive upon the self. Redemption is an act and not a process, as von Hartmann would have it. We find this stress on divine and human action throughout Forsyth's writings. The following statement with regard to revelation is typical:

> 'If only we could grasp the idea of revelation as something done instead of something shown, as creation instead of exhibition, as renovation instead of innovation, as resurrection instead of communication.'[10]

Here we note the background of the actualism of life-philosophy, its instrumentalist view of the intellect and its personalism. Thus Life-philosophy, combined with Kantianism provided support for Forsyth's emphasis on the centrality of moral action.

The Final is related to the other two terms as the determinative act of the Holy. The Holy or Reality has so acted within history as to determine the destiny of creation. Thus Forsyth can refer to Butler's statement, 'Morality is the nature of things'[11] in a far different sense from platonic-idealism. He is referring to the Holy as redemptive, final action. The redeemed conscience is conscious of itself as standing in relationship to the Holy which is based on the final act of the Holy, and as continuing in a history of action which participates in this final redemptive act.

When he discusses the Final with reference to history

and to the redeemed conscience, we find Forsyth speaking similarly to the thought of the Life-philosophers. History as the scene of spiritual actualism was of great importance to them.

In conclusion a word indicating Forsyth's attitude to the role of philosophy or reflective thought in theology is in order. He poses the problem as follows:

> 'I am asking whether he (the preacher) should do much or little in construing his own conception of his message in the mental vernacular of his time. . . . Shall he become here all things to all men? . . . Or shall he, at the other extreme, deliver a message manifestly, and almost aggressively, independent of the fashions of thought, with small concern whether men hear or forbear?'[12]

Later he answers his question thus:

> '. . . if history teach us rightly, does it not teach us that the main policy of the Church must be . . . autonomous, independent. I say the main policy, for the accommodations to modern knowledge and modern criticism must be many. But amid all these adjustments to the world of natural and rational culture, the Church must in principle be detached. She must descend on the world out of heaven from God.[13]'

Forsyth does not refuse to listen and adjust to the natural and rational culture. He is convinced that in these secondary realms there is a possibility for knowledge and a growth in knowledge. He would repudiate any claim coming from these quarters to know the final truth, but he is concerned to read and embrace the valid insights of modern thought, and to use them in so far as they are compatible in giving expression to the Gospel.[14] One might almost say that Forsyth posits a work of the Holy Spirit in the cultural realm, for he states that the believer or theologian can learn to see more deeply into his own Gospel in and through the new developments in the principles of the

275

culture. Freed from the idolatrous claims of philosophical thought, the believer is free to learn about the things of God from it. As Forsyth states:

'In the face of modern *theories* or dogmas the Word of revelation is autonomous. . . . But in the face of modern *principles*, it discerns in them, and often through their means, the hidden treasures of its own wealth.'[15]

NOTES

Footnotes to Introduction

Page 1

[1] James Orr, *The Progress of Dogma* (Grand Rapids, Michigan: W. B. Eerdmans Publishing Company, 1952), p. 138.

[2] The most complete treatment of Forsyth's life will be found in William Lee Bradley's *P. T. Forsyth, The Man and his Work* (London: Independent Press Ltd., 1952); cf. the delightful memoir written by Forsyth's daughter in P. T. Forsyth's *The Work of Christ* (London: Independent Press Ltd., second edition, 1958); biographical sketches in Robert McAfee Brown, *P. T. Forsyth: Prophet for Today* (Philadelphia: Westminster Press, 1952), Harry Escott (ed.), *Peter Taylor Forsyth 1848–1921 Director of Souls* (London: Epworth Press, 1948) and the article 'Die Bedeutung des Kreuzesgeschehens für Lehre und Bekenntnis nach Peter Taylor Forsyth' by Klaus Rosenthal in *Kerygma und Dogma* 7 Jahrgang, Heft 3, Juli, 1961.

Page 2

[3] cf. Bradley, op. cit., p. 21.

Page 3

[4] The writer feels that he must differ from Bradley's assertion that both Forsyth and Maurice have a concept of 'universal man.' Bradley, op. cit., p. 96. It is true that Forsyth does think in terms of the human race as a unity but he arrives at this conclusion on different grounds than the platonic one which is Maurice's! We will consider this concept of Forsyth's in Chapter I. In all fairness to Bradley, the writer notes that he is hesitant at this point and stresses Forsyth's uniqueness.

Page 4

[5] One of the most serious shortcomings of the existing studies on Forsyth's thought is the lack of a sustained discussion of Forsyth's relation to Kantian, neo-Kantian, and Ritschlian thought. Such material is of the greatest help in understanding Forsyth. cf. the remarks of R. C. Johnson in his book *Authority in Protestant Theology* (Philadelphia: Westminster Press, 1959), p. 104.

[6] Forsyth, *Work of Christ*, p. x.

[7] Forsyth's book *The Christian Ethic of War* (London: Longmans, Green & Co., 1916), was written with Germany, German theology and naïve pacifism in mind. cf. Karl Barth, *Evangelische Theologie im 19.*

Jahrhundert (Heft 49 of *Theologische Studien*, ed., Karl Barth & Max Geiger, Zollikon-Zürich: Evangelischer Verlag AG., 1957), p. 6, which includes similar remarks regarding Barth's German theological teachers.

Page 5
  [8] Bradley, op. cit., p. 27.

Page 6
  [9] Forsyth, *Positive Preaching and the Modern Mind* (London: Independent Press Ltd., first ed., fifth impression, 1957), pp. 192–3. Hereafter referred to as *Positive Preaching*. One cannot but be reminded of Luther when reading this confession by Forsyth.

Page 7
  [10] cf. The discussion of Forsyth's view of higher criticism in the excursus on Biblical Interpretation in Chapter II.
  [11] Forsyth, *Work of Christ*, p. xv.

Page 8
  [12] Proceedings of the Second International Council, 1899, pp. 57–63. Cited from Bradley, op. cit., p. 49.

Page 9
  [13] For a list of all of Forsyth's books the reader is directed to the bibliography; for a list which includes a selection of his periodical articles, see Brown, op. cit., pp. 171–4. There is also a bibliography at the conclusion of the memoir written by Forsyth's daughter in *Work of Christ*, p. xxix.
  [14] We shall make no effort here to describe the contents of each of Forsyth's writings (this is done in Bradley, op. cit., pp. 64–90) but rather are concerned to comment on their scope and nature and on Forsyth's controversial style.
  [15] He was very concerned to be a pastor to the students in the college. See Escott, op. cit., pp. 119–131.
  [16] Campbell was deeply influenced by the great English Modernist George Tyrell (1861–1909).
  [17] cf. Forsyth's essay in *The Old Faith and The New Theology*, Charles H. Vine, (ed.), (London: Sampson Low, Marston & Company, 1907), pp. 47–61. It is interesting to note that in 1911 Campbell withdrew his book from publication and in 1916 he entered the ministry of the Church of England.

Page 12
  [18] Forsyth, *The Cruciality of the Cross* (London: Independent Press Ltd., third impression of second ed., 1955), p. 36, hereafter referred to as *The Cruciality of the Cross*.

Page 13
[19] Forsyth, *Positive Preaching*, p. 12. cf. J. K. Mozley, *The Heart of the Gospel* (London: Society for Promoting Christian Knowledge, 1925), p. 71.
[20] Forsyth, *Work of Christ*, p. xxvi.

Page 14
[21] Forsyth, *Positive Preaching*, p. 197. cf. ibid., pp. 76–7, 83. Forsyth's understanding of dogma as *kerygma* will be discussed in Chapter II.

Page 17
[22] Forsyth, *The Old Faith and the New Theology*, p. 57; and Forsyth, *Positive Preaching*, pp. 80–1.

Page 18
[23] Forsyth, *The Justification of God. Lectures for War-time on a Christian Theology* (London: Independent Press Ltd., second impression, 1957) p. 11. cf. ibid., pp. 106, 176. Hereafter referred to as *Justification of God*.
[24] Forsyth, *Faith, Freedom and the Future* (London: Independent Press Ltd., second impression, 1955), p. 286. cf. his discussion of Pharisaism as anthropocentrism in *Justification of God*, pp. 114–16.
[25] Forsyth, *The Cruciality of the Cross*, p. 35.

Page 19
[26] ibid., p. 30.
[27] Forsyth, *Positive Preaching*, p. 81.

Page 20
[28] Forsyth, *The Cruciality of the Cross*, p. 32.
[29] Forsyth, *Justification of God*, pp. 85–6.
[30] Forsyth, *Faith, Freedom and the Future*, pp. 273–4.

Page 21
[31] Forsyth, *Work of Christ*, pp. 141–2. cf. Forsyth, *Positive Preaching*, p. 242.
[32] Forsyth, *Positive Preaching*, p. 163.
[33] Forsyth, *Work of Christ*, p. 24.

Page 22
[34] ibid., xxxii. cf. *The Christian Ethic of War*, p. 4; Forsyth, *The Church and the Sacraments* (London: Independent Press Ltd., fifth impression, 1955), pp. 16–21, 31, 99 and Forsyth, *The Principle of Authority in Relation to Certainty, Sanctity and Society. An Essay in the Philosophy of Experimental Religion* (London: Independent Press, second ed., 1952) p. 71. Hereafter referred to as *Principle of Authority*.
[35] cf. Forsyth, *Positive Preaching*, p. 82.
[36] cf. Chapter I—Kingdom of God, and Appendix.

19—TTOPTF

Page 23

37 Forsyth, *The Cruciality of the Cross*, p. 23.

38 Forsyth, *Positive Preaching*, 118–19. cf. Forsyth, *Missions in State and Church* (London: Hodder & Stoughton, 1908), pp. 102–3 and Forsyth, *The Church and the Sacraments*, p. 23.

39 Forsyth, *Justification of God*, p. 198.

40 Forsyth, *Christian Aspects of Evolution* (London: Epworth Press, 1950), *passim*.

41 cf. Section on history in Chapter I.

42 Forsyth, *The Christian Ethic of War*, p. 97. cf. Forsyth, *Justification of God*, p. 110.

43 cf. Forsyth, *Faith, Freedom and the Future*, pp. 263–4. cf. ibid., pp. 205–6, 339; Forsyth, *Positive Preaching*, p. 97, and Forsyth, *The Church and the Sacraments*, p. 28.

44 Forsyth, *Christ on Parnassus. Lectures on Art, Ethic and Theology* (London: Independent Press Ltd., second impression, 1959), p. 48. (Hereafter referred to as *Christ on Parnassus.*) cf. Forsyth, *Faith, Freedom and the Future*, pp. 205–6; Forsyth, *et. al.*, *The Atonement in Modern Religious Thought* (London: James Clarke & Co., 1902), p. 62 (hereafter referred to as *The Atonement*) and Forsyth, *The Church and the Sacraments*, pp. 35–7.

45 Forsyth, *The Cruciality of the Cross*, p. 34 and Forsyth, *The Church and the Sacraments*, p. 38.

46 cf. Chapter III, Part II *passim* and Forsyth, *Faith, Freedom and the Future*, pp. 88–9, 98–9.

47 For the purposes of this study we follow what has become a common designation which includes the first quarter of the twentieth century as part of the nineteenth century theology. Perhaps the best way to limit the period is to designate Troeltsch as the *terminus ad quem*. cf. Barth, op. cit., p. 6.

48 Mozley, op. cit., p. 69.

Footnotes to Chapter 1

Page 25

1 The basic division of our exposition is a reflection of the trinitarian foundation of Forsyth's thought. cf. Forsyth, *Person and Place*, p. 327.

Page 26

2 Forsyth, 'Revelation and the Person of Christ' in *Faith and Criticism Essays by Congregationalists* (London: Sampson Low Marston & Company Ld., 1893), pp. 116–17. Hereafter referred to as *Faith and Criticism*.

Page 27

3 cf. Forsyth, *Faith and Criticism*, pp. 104–5. cf. ibid., pp. 121–2. It should be added here that Forsyth is not always consistent in his terminology. At times he places revelation and faith or religion in polarity; in such cases 'revelation' refers to God's self-manifestation and 'faith' or 'religion' to man's response. In this less exact form, Forsyth can refer to non-Christian religions as based on revelation, though the

280

response in such religions he refers to as 'religion,' seldom as faith. Faith is primarily the response of man to God in Jesus Christ and, as such, is not capable of inclusion under the general term 'religion.' The reader will be able to discern from the context whether Forsyth is using revelation in its deepest sense, as that act in which God successfully calls man into communion with himself in Jesus Christ, or whether he is using it only to designate the Godly side of the polar relationship. cf. Forsyth, *Rome, Reform and Reaction* (London: Hodder & Stoughton, 1899), p. 125.

[4] cf. Forsyth, *Positive Preaching*, p. 239.

Page 28

[5] Forsyth, *Person and Place*, p. 354. cf. P. T. Forsyth, *The Soul of Prayer* (London: Independent Press Ltd., 4th impression, 1960), p. 37; *Positive Preaching*, pp. 10–11 and *Faith and Criticism*, pp. 119–20, *et passim*.

[6] The reader is referred to Forsyth's rejection of the views of Harnack and Troeltsch in his essay 'Christ and the Christian Principle' in *London Theological Studies*. (London: University of London Press, 1911), pp. 133–66 (hereafter referred to as *London Theological Studies*) in which he criticizes all efforts to separate a Christian principle, i.e. redemption as a teaching that God is a loving Father and man is capable of sonship, from the person of Christ. Jesus Christ *is* the revelation in person and in deed. Christ is not the *primus inter pares* of nineteenth-century liberal theology.

[7] cf. Forsyth, *Church and Sacraments*, p. 101.

Page 29

[8] cf. Forsyth, *The Atonement*, p. 80.

[9] Forsyth, 'The Evangelical Churches and the Higher Criticism' in *Contemporary Review*, LXXXVIII (July–Dec., 1905), p. 578. (Hereafter referred to as 'Higher Criticism'.) Forsyth refers to such a view of revelation as typically Lutheran in *Faith, Freedom and the Future*, p. 40.

[10] Forsyth, *Faith and Criticism*, pp. 116–17.

Page 30

[11] We have in mind the minimizing of the Holiness and Wrath of God and the corresponding semi-Pelagian view of sin which we find in the Ritschlian School. This is true despite their emphasis upon the moral consciousness and on the social nature of sin, i.e. kingdom of sin. Even Herrmann, who was aware of the interpersonal nature of revelation, never transcended a moral-aestheticism. cf. Albrecht Ritschl, *The Christian Doctrine of Justification and Reconciliation* (trans. Mackintosh & Macaulay, Edinburgh: T. & T. Clark, 1900), pp. 273–4 (hereafter referred to as *Justification and Reconciliation*) and Herrmann, op. cit., pp. 59–93 *passim*.

Page 31

[12] Forsyth anticipated the modern objections to speaking of the

attributes of God. cf. Forsyth, *The Cruciality of the Cross*, p. 104; George A. F. Knight, *A Christian Theology of the Old Testament* (London: SCM Press Ltd., 1959), p. 89; Emil Brunner, *The Christian Doctrine of God Dogmatics*, V. I (trans. Wyon, London: Lutterworth Press, 2nd impression, 1955), *passim* and, for different reasons, Karl Barth, *Church Dogmatics* V. II, first half-volume (ed. Bromily & Torrance, Edinburgh: T. & T. Clark, 1957), pp. 322 ff.

[13] Isaiah 43:3. We do not mean to infer that it is only in the New Testament that God manifests himself as the holy love. In both covenants, God *saves* his people for his *name's sake*, for his glory. See especially Isaiah 6:3 ff. where holiness and forgiveness are seen in unity. cf. Knight, op. cit., p. 94.

[14] I John 4:8.

[15] Two things need to be noted about the fact that Forsyth does not use the term '*agape*.' This term has found its way into dogmatic usage primarily through the excellent monograph written by Nygren, *Agape and Eros* (English ed., 1930) which was published after Forsyth's death. Secondly, there is in Forsyth's usage of the term 'holy love' more emphasis placed on its moral foundation than is usually found in the modern usage of the term '*agape*.' Modern usage tends to stress its difference from '*eros*' and thereby emphasizes *agape* as a selfless love which moves toward an unlovable object, i.e. fallen man. Forsyth would add— 'for his name's sake.'

[16] Forsyth, *Cruciality of the Cross*, p. viii.

[17] Forsyth, *Faith and Criticism*, p. 142.

[18] Forsyth, *God the Holy Father* (London: Independent Press Ltd., 1897, re-issued 1957), p. 3.

[19] In the New Testament witness to the Holy Spirit, Forsyth finds evidence of the centrality of God's holiness in the New Testament. cf. Forsyth, *Positive Preaching*, p. 253.

Page 32

[20] P. T. Forsyth, *This Life and the Next. The Effect on this Life of Faith in Another* (London: Independent Press Ltd., 1918, 4th impression, 1953), p. 28. Hereafter referred to as *This Life and the Next*.

[21] Forsyth, *The Cruciality of the Cross*, p. 23.

[22] cf. Forsyth, *Christian Aspects of Evolution*, p. 24; Knight, op. cit., pp. 108–9; Emil Brunner, *Revelation and Reason* (trans. Wyon, London: Student Christian Movement Press Ltd., 1947), pp. 33–4, in footnote.

Page 33

[23] cf. Forsyth, *Principle of Authority*, pp. 180-1.

[24] cf. Forsyth, *Work of Christ*, p. 167; *Justification of God*, p. 117.

[25] cf. Forsyth, *Work of Christ*, pp. 204–6; *God the Holy Father*, pp. 4–5.

[26] Forsyth, *Positive Preaching*, p. 241.

[27] Forsyth, *The Cruciality of the Cross*, p. 78, in footnote.

Page 34
[28] Forsyth, *Positive Preaching*, p. 207.
[29] Forsyth, *The Atonement*, p. 79.
[30] cf. Forsyth, *Justification of God*, p. 40.

Page 35
[31] cf. Forsyth, *Congregationalism and Reunion*, (London: Independent Press Ltd., reprinted 1952), p. 38.
[32] Forsyth, *Justification of God*, p. 108.
[33] cf. Forsyth, *God the Holy Father*, p. 11; *Principle of Authority*, pp. 418–19; *Work of Christ*, p. 159.

Page 36
[34] Forsyth used the term 'aestheticism' broadly. He included in it neo-platonic Roman Catholic mysticism, romantic idealism and the vulgar idealism of his day. cf. Forsyth, *This Life and the Next*, p. 13.

Page 37
[35] Forsyth, *The Church and the Sacraments*, pp. 93–4. The following will serve to give the reader a good cross-section of his objections: *Justification of God*, 107–9, 123–4, 170–1; *The Christian Ethic of War*, 167, 169–70, 176, 178, 192–3; *Congregationalism and Reunion*, 41; and *This Life and the Next*, 22, 27, 28.
[36] Forsyth, op. cit., p. 28. cf. Barth's treatment of God's grace and love for a discussion which also allows no tension or separation between God's holiness and God's love. Barth, 'The Doctrine of God' in *Church Dogmatics*, V. II, first half-volume, pp. 351–68.
[37] Forsyth, *The Cruciality of the Cross*, p. 23.
[38] cf. Hendrik van Oyen, *Evangelische Ethik I, Grundlagen* and *II, Liebe und Ehe* (Basel: Verlag Friedrich Reinhardt AG.) no dates; *Theologische Erkenntnislehre* (Zürich: Zwingli-Verlag, 1955), *passim*.

Page 38
[39] Forsyth, *God the Holy Father*, p. 26.
[40] The term 'divine' is used here consciously, as representing a favourite word and attitude of nineteenth-century theology.
[41] Forsyth, *This Life and the Next*, p. 29.
[42] cf. Forsyth, *Positive Preaching*, p. 162; *Christian Aspects of Evolution*, p. 22.

Page 39
[43] Forsyth, *Positive Preaching*, p. 252.
[44] Forsyth, *Work of Christ*, p. 78.
[45] Forsyth, *The Christian Ethic of War*, p. 131.
[46] Forsyth, *Work of Christ*, p. 84.

Page 40
[47] Forsyth, *Missions in State and Church*, pp. 61, 56–7.

⁴⁸ Forsyth, *Rome Reform and Reaction*, p. 243. cf. *The Cruciality of the Cross*, pp. 19, 21 and *The Church and the Sacraments*, pp. 298-9.
⁴⁹ Forsyth *Justification of God*, p. 31.

Page 41
⁵⁰ P. T. Forsyth, *Religion in Recent Art being Expository Lectures on Rossetti, Burne Jones, Watts, Holman, Hunt, and Wagner* (London: Simpkin, Marshall & Co., 1889), p. 280. Hereafter referred to as *Religion in Recent Art*.
⁵¹ Forsyth, *Positive Preaching*, pp. 242-3.
⁵² Forsyth, *The Church and the Sacraments*, p. 195.

Page 42
⁵³ We see this clearly in the pronouncements of the Council of Trent. Ludwig Ott, *Fundamentals of Catholic Dogma* (trans. Lynch, Cork: The Mercier Press Limited, 1960), p. 260 as quoted from Henrici Denzinger, *Enchiridion Symbolorum*, Barcinone, Friburgi Brisg., Romae; Herder, 1960), p. 800.
⁵⁴ Forsyth, *Positive Preaching*, p. 173.

Page 43
⁵⁵ Forsyth, *Work of Christ*, p. 65.
⁵⁶ ibid., p. 186.

Page 44
⁵⁷ Forsyth, *Christ on Parnassus*, p. 100. cf. Forsyth, *Work of Christ*, pp. 77-8.
⁵⁸ Forsyth, *Work of Christ*, p. 82.
⁵⁹ Forsyth singles out Hegel and Ritschl as two men who attempted to develop a doctrine of reconciliation without retaining a doctrine of the atonement. cf. Forsyth, *Work of Christ*, pp. 66-7; Forsyth *Person and Place*, p. 131; Forsyth, *Positive Preaching*, p. 84; Forsyth, *Work of Christ*, p. 154.
⁶⁰ ibid., p. 103.

Page 45
⁶¹ ibid., p. 86.
⁶² ibid., p. 199.

Page 46
⁶³ Forsyth, *Justification of God*, p. 175.
⁶⁴ ibid., p. 116.
⁶⁵ For a full description of Forsyth's view of Christian perfection. cf. *God the Holy Father*, pp. 97-148.
⁶⁶ Forsyth, *The Church and the Sacraments*, p. 296.
⁶⁷ Forsyth, *The Christian Ethic of War*, pp. 142-3.
⁶⁸ cf. Forsyth, *The Cruciality of the Cross*, p. 104.
⁶⁹ By stressing the Cross Forsyth does not mean that there is a separation between Christ's life and his death. It is rather that the unity of the two, including even the pre-existent decision to become incarnate, is

seen in the Cross and through the resurrection. cf. Forsyth, *Work of Christ*, p. 153, and *Missions in State and Church*, p. 13.

Page 47
   [70] cf. Forsyth, *The Soul of Prayer*, p. 14.
   [71] Forsyth, *The Atonement*, p. 82.
   [72] Forsyth, *The Cruciality of the Cross*, p. 98. cf. Forsyth, *Work of Christ*, pp. 228–9.
   [73] ibid., p. 135. With 'punishment,' Forsyth refers to the physical and spiritual agony of Christ on the Cross.
   [74] cf. Forsyth, *Positive Preaching*, p. 249.

Page 48
   [75] cf. Forsyth, *The Cruciality of the Cross*, p. 29; *The Christian Ethic of War*, p. 30.
   [76] The term 'necessity' is used frequently by Forsyth to indicate that the judgement on the Cross is required by God's *holy* nature.

Page 49
   [77] Forsyth, *Missions in State and Church*, p. 52. cf. ibid., p. 77.
   [78] Forsyth, *The Cruciality of the Cross*, pp. 85–6. The reader is referred to Forsyth's full and significant treatment of this subject in the final chapter of this book. cf. His remarks concerning the painting 'Scapegoat' by Holman Hunt in Forsyth, *Religion in Recent Art*, pp. 207–31.
   [79] Such a view of sacrifice indicates its theocentric character in the Bible. cf. Forsyth, *The Christian Ethic of War*, p. 9.
   Forsyth, in his view of sacrifice as personal obedience to God, rejects the cult of self-sacrifice. cf. ibid., pp. 51, 139; *The Cruciality of the Cross*, p. 87.

Page 50
   [80] cf. *Work of Christ*, pp. 169–70.
   [81] ibid., pp. 189–90.
   [82] Forsyth, *The Atonement*, p. 82.

Page 51
   [83] cf. Forsyth, *Work of Christ*, pp. 189–90.
   [84] Forsyth, *The Old Faith and the New Theology*, p. 56. cf. Forsyth, *The Cruciality of the Cross*, p. 19.
   [85] ibid., p. 104.
   [86] Forsyth, *God the Holy Father*, p. 16 and *Work of Christ*, pp. 92–3.

Page 52
   [87] Forsyth, *The Church and the Sacraments*, p. 263. This statement is surely a rebuttal of Ritschl's analytic attitude to atonement. cf. Forsyth, *God the Holy Father*, p. 19.
   [88] Forsyth, *The Atonement*, p. 83. Forsyth speaks of Christ's sacrifice as penal but not as a punishment. God did not punish Christ in whom he was always well pleased but rather Christ took the penalty of sin upon himself. cf. ibid., pp. 84–5; Forsyth, *Work of Christ*, pp. 146–7, 162.

Page 53
[89] ibid., p. 188. cf. ibid., pp. 190–3.

Page 55
[90] ibid., p. 151. For this reason Forsyth feels that the views of the atonement which lay the emphasis upon Christ as confessing man's sin are false. (Moberly, Campbell), Christ's primary confession is of God's holiness. cf. ibid., pp. 148 ff.

Page 56
[91] Forsyth, *The Atonement*, p. 86. cf. Forsyth, *Missions in State and Church*, pp. 100–1.

Page 57
[92] Forsyth, *Work of Christ*, p. 201. Words in brackets are our additions.
[93] ibid., p. 202. cf. ibid., p. 222.

Page 58
[94] ibid., pp. 80–1. It will help us to appreciate the uniqueness and value of Forsyth's exposition of Christ's reconciling work on the Cross if, before leaving our consideration of the work of Christ, we note the similarities and differences between Forsyth's view and the well-known Anselmic-Reformation view of the Cross.

The first point to be observed is the inclusiveness of Forsyth's treatment of the Cross. He deals with it in terms of reconciliation and not only in terms of atonement. This means that he is able to incorporate the triumphant and regenerative aspects of Christ's work as well as the satisfactory aspect upon which the Anselmic-Reformation tradition concentrates. This threefold, interpolar treatment gives a fullness and unity to Forsyth's exposition which enables him to affirm more of the Biblical witness than is possible when atonement is considered in isolation. Because Forsyth was not willing to simply classify and list Biblical and theological theories of the atonement (i.e. subjective, objective; or Greek, classic and Latin; or Athanasian, Anselmic, and Abelardian; or redemptive, substitutionary, and regenerative) but sought to see these aspects in their unity in the light of the *kerygmatic* Christ, he has provided dogmatic thought with a new challenge in its reflection upon the work of Christ. It is the writer's opinion that any present-day treatment which is content to go back to simply cataloguing or listing unrelated theories of the atonement has fallen below the level of theological exposition provided us by Forsyth. Theologians must henceforth carry on their reflections within the wider context of reconciliation and with the aim of finding the unifying centre or the mutuality of the various Biblical aspects of the Cross.

Secondly, with regard to the atoning aspect of Christ's work on the Cross, we need to note three specific areas of similarity and difference between Forsyth's exposition and that of the Anselmic-Reformation tradition.

286

1. Both of these views are primarily objective views of the atonement, i.e. they ground the necessity and the goal of the atoning death of the Son in the nature of God. But in this similarity, fundamental differences are revealed. Anselm, thinking in feudalistic, medieval thought forms and against the background of the Church's sacrament of penance (*satisfactio operis*), defined God's nature in terms of honour. At the Reformation, this objective grounding was changed and God's nature was discussed in terms of retributive justice. The private honour of the feudal system was replaced by public law deriving from the Moral-Governor of the creation. Forsyth, however, grounds the objective necessity of the atonement neither in God's honour nor in his justice but in the Holiness of God. It is God's moral self-determination, his will to communion with his creatures or his intrinsic and purposed claim to be consciously glorified by his creation, that grounds the atonement. This purpose or self-determination to restore communion is a moral decision but it is deeper than justice. (See our discussion on pp. 35–6.)

2. In the Anselmic view, sin was the failure to render the obedience that man owed to God and man thereby incurred personal debt. Thus sacrifice was conceived of in terms of payment or merit. (Here Anselm draws upon Tertullian.) Christ's sacrifice was then the work of supererogation which gained him extra merit which he could place on the account of fallen man. (Cyprian has discussed the transferability of extra merit.) At the Reformation, sin was conceived of in terms of the transgression of God's law which incurred personal guilt. Christ's sacrifice was the vicarious or substitutionary acceptance of the penalty due to man for his trespasses. For Forsyth, sin is personal rebellion against God and guilty disobedience of his will, a disruption of communion which calls for God's moral victory over Satan and the re-establishment of communion for the hallowing of God's name. In this situation, Christ's sacrifice is the doxological confession of God's holiness by man under the conditions of sin and judgement. In the Son, God hallows his own Holy Name. This confession by Christ includes his substitutionary acceptance of the judgement upon sin—Christ's death; this is the once-for-all, the *extra nos* finality of the atonement provided by God himself to himself. But Christ's confession is also representative in that it proleptically includes the response which it evokes among men, i.e. the penitent confession by sinful man of God's holiness made from within the re-established communion with God. Thus Christ's sacrifice is the eternal confession of God as the God of Holy Love, that is, of God as he who wills to be in communion with his creatures and who absorbs the penalty in order to restore this communion and to destroy Satan.

3. The final comparison we wish to make is in reference to the appropriation of the atonement by man. Anselm was content to discuss this briefly and in terms of an external transfer of merit. At the Reformation, the act of faith was seen to be essential as the passive personal acceptance of the forensic judgement of God on the sinner in Christ. Here too Forsyth includes but seeks to go beyond the position of the Reformation. He places man's faith in closer relation to the

atoning Cross. The regenerative aspect of Christ's work is involved at this point. Holiness is only satisfied with personal communion, for only man's appreciative, obedient communion gives God the glory and appreciates the moral right of Lordship which is his. Man, however, participates in such communion only by penitent faith. Thus, while man's faith is not the ground of the atonement, not the substitutionary aspect, it does have a place in the atonement which is indicated by the representative function of Christ. So it is that Forsyth seeks to move beyond the Reformers by placing the work of the Spirit of the Cross in the closest connexion to the event itself. It is proleptically present. The atoning Cross is an eternal deed which extends itself in history.

Finally we wish to note that Forsyth seeks to overcome the basic objection to the Anselmic-Reformation interpretation of the Cross. This objection is that the love of God and the justice of God are defined independently of one another and then they are joined together rather artificially by the idea that 'what God's justice demands, his love supplies.' Forsyth offers us a twofold answer to this objection. On the one hand, he provides an exposition of the Cross which points out the unity of God's Holy Love and, on the other hand, he maintains the reality and necessity of the atonement for God as well as for man. Forsyth makes clear the unity of God's action in the atonement by discussing it in terms of God's holiness and not in terms of justice. The unity of God's Holy Love we observed in our discussion on pages 37–8 ff. Love is holiness in communion and grace is holiness in communion with sinful man. The atonement is grounded upon holiness—it is all of grace. The Son and the Father are of one heart and mind. There is no change in God's purpose or attitude before or after the atonement. Wrath does not change into grace but rather wrath and grace are aspects of the one movement of the Holy which culminates in the Cross for the reconciliation of God and man and the destruction of Satan. But in maintaining this, Forsyth does not make the atonement of no effect nor does he restrict its effect only to man. Rather he affirms, along with Anselm and the Reformers, its primary necessity and ground in God. There is not a change from wrath to grace, but there is a new relationship between God and man, effected by the Cross. In the Cross we have God's act in which he reconciles himself and man to himself. If the attitude of God to his creation does not change, the relationship does, for reconciliation is a personal communion and communion is mutual. God is free to act differently after he has restored communion than before. So too man is free to respond differently in reconciliation than outside of it. In such a manner Forsyth seeks to re-interpret the Anselmic-Reformation interpretation of the Cross, conserving its good points but advancing beyond it by viewing it in the larger context of the Scriptural witness to Christ.

Page 59
[95] Forsyth feels that an inadequate view of the Cross in history is reflected in confessionalism and Biblicism (an over-emphasis upon

the past) and in mysticism and idealism (an over-emphasis upon the present). See his discussion in *Faith and Criticism*, pp. 105–7.

Page 60
[96] P. T. Forsyth, *Socialism, the Church and the Poor* (London: Hodder & Stoughton, 1908), p. 47.
[97] Forsyth, *The Church and the Sacraments*, p. 91.
At this point we wish to indicate Forsyth's appreciation and criticism of Ritschl's use of the concept 'Kingdom of God.' Forsyth gives Ritschl the credit for bringing this Biblical theme to the forefront of dogmatic theology and thereby overcoming the individualism and amoralism of much handling of doctrine. He feels, however, that Ritschl failed seriously by separating the religious (redemption) and the moral (Kingdom of God) principles. This separation is indicated by Ritschl's analogy of the ellipse. Forsyth feels that, by such a separation, neither the religious nor the moral principle is properly understood. It leads to a subjective atonement on the one hand and moralism on the other. He feels especially that Ritschl ended up by placing his major stress on the moral side, thereby leading into moralistic anthropocentrism and transforming the Kingdom of God into social ethics. This also meant that the basic eschatological tension of the Kingdom which is come and not yet fully come is lost in Ritschl.
For Ritschl's discussion of the two principles related elliptically see his *Justification and Reconciliation*, pp. 10–12; for his separation of morality and faith where he claims that good works do not flow from faith, see ibid., p. 522; for Forsyth's critique of Ritschl see his *The Church and the Sacraments*, pp. 88 ff. and *Positive Preaching*, pp. 222–4.

Page 61
[98] Forsyth, *The Church and the Sacraments*, p. 92.
[99] ibid., p. 95.

Page 62
[100] Forsyth, *Justification of God*, p. 166. ibid., p. 30. ibid., pp. 126–7.
[101] ibid., p. 77.
[102] John 3:16; 16:33.

Page 63
[103] Forsyth, *Justification of God*, p. 220.
[104] Forsyth, *Work of Christ*, pp. 86–7. We note that Forsyth makes no real distinction between the Kingdom of God or the New Humanity and the Church. He does, however, make an eschatological qualification. 'And the saved Church is the earnest of a saved Humanity; it is the New Humanity in the making.' *The Church and the Sacraments*, p. 150. cf. ibid., p. 95; Forsyth, *The Christian Ethic of War*, p. 117. This identification must be understood as a broadening of the idea of the 'Church' and not a limiting of the idea of the Kingdom of God as takes place in Roman Catholicism. For Forsyth, the Church is the *communio sanctorum* which is

the eschatological earnest of the whole race. The Church is not to be thought of primarily as an institution.

[105] Forsyth, *The Church and the Sacraments*, p. 43. cf. Forsyth, *Work of Christ*, pp. 115–16.

[106] We note Forsyth's trinitarian basis for this theme. *Socialism, the Church and the Poor*, p. 26. Price feels that, due to Forsyth's personalism, he comes dangerously near to tritheism in such statements. Charles Price in unpublished lecture notes on *An Introduction to the Theology of P. T. Forsyth*.

Page 64
[107] Forsyth, *Work of Christ*, p. 122.
[108] Forsyth, *Justification of God*, pp. 20–1.
[109] cf. Forsyth, *The Christian Ethic of War*, p. 65.
[110] cf. Knight, op. cit., pp. 120–1.

Page 65
[111] Forsyth, *Theology in Church and State* (London: Hodder & Stoughton, 1915), p. 170.
[112] Forsyth, *Work of Christ*, p. 120.
[113] ibid., p. 121. cf. Forsyth, *Justification of God*, pp. 9–10.
[114] Forsyth, *Theology in Church and State*, p. 157.

Page 66
[115] ibid.
[116] Forsyth, *The Soul of Prayer*, p. 33.
[117] cf. Forsyth, *Justification of God*, p. 27; *The Christian Ethic of War*, p. 35.
[118] Romans 5:18.
[119] Galatians 2:20a.

Page 67
[120] Galatians 2:20b.
[121] Romans 8:6.
[122] Forsyth, *This Life and the Next*, p. 16. cf. A. M. Hunter's comments on Forsyth's rejection of 'universalism' in the article 'P. T. Forsyth Neutestamentler' in *The Expository Times*, LXXIII (January, 1962), p. 105.
[123] Forsyth, *Work of Christ*, p. 161. cf. Forsyth, *Justification of God*, p. 161 and *Faith, Freedom and the Future*, p. 125.
[124] See pp. 26–9.

Page 68
[125] See Brown, op. cit., pp. 131–2.
For a broad sketch of Forsyth's view of history see Brown, ibid., pp. 131–150.
[126] cf. Forsyth, *Christian Ethic of War*, p. 178.
[127] cf. Forsyth, *Justification of God*, p. 138.

Page 69
[128] Forsyth, *The Church and the Sacraments*, p. 98. cf. Forsyth, *Missions in State and Church*, p. 10.
[129] Forsyth, *The Christian Ethic of War*, p. 117.
[130] See Forsyth's discussion of Schiller, Lessing, Strauss and Nietzsche in *Justification of God*, pp. 199, 209, 212–14. For Forsyth on 'judgement in history' see ibid., pp. 178–85.
[131] ibid., pp. 28–9.
[132] ibid., p. 222.
[133] ibid., p. 130.

Page 70
[134] Forsyth, *Christian Aspects of Evolution*, pp. 24–5.
[135] Forsyth, *Justification of God*, p. 139.
[136] ibid., p. 151.

Page 71
[137] ibid., p. 191. cf. ibid., p. 47.
[138] ibid., p. 191.

Page 72
[139] Forsyth, *Work of Christ*, p. 130.
[140] Forsyth, *Justification of God*, p. 182.
[141] Forsyth, *Socialism, the Church and the Poor*, p. 48.
[142] Forsyth, *Justification of God*, p. 181.

Page 73
[143] Forsyth, *The Christian Ethic of War*, p. 104.
[144] Forsyth, *The Church and the Sacraments*, p. 126.

Page 74
[145] Forsyth, *This Life and the Next*, p. 63.
[146] Forsyth, *The Christian Ethic of War*, p. 188.

Page 75
[147] Forsyth, *Principle of Authority*, p. 198.
[148] Forsyth, *Justification of God*, p. 17. cf. Forsyth's repudiation of Troeltsch's position in *London Theological Studies*, pp. 133–66.
[149] Forsyth, *Christian Aspects of Evolution*, p. 16.

Page 76
[150] Hegel's view of the hope or assurance which we have in history is set forth in his famous statement; 'The only Thought which Philosophy brings with it to the contemplation of History, is the simple conception of *Reason*; that reason is the Sovereign of the World; that the history of the world, therefore, presents us with a rational process. This conviction and intuition is a hypothesis in the domain of history as such. In that of Philosophy it is no hypothesis. It is there proved by speculative cognition, . . .' *Hegel Selections* (ed., Loewenberg, New York: Charles Scribner's Sons, 1957), p. 348.

Kant, who does not have the same interest in history as does Hegel, rests all hope in history on the postulate of practical reason which requires a God who will make the proper balance of blessedness and goodness. *Kant Selections*, pp. 360–8.

151 Forsyth, *The Christian Ethic of War*, p. 122.

152 Forsyth, *Justification of God*, p. 192.

153 In Troeltsch we see the hidden idealism that often accompanies historicism.

Page 77

154 Forsyth, *Justification of God*, pp. 217–18. cf. Forsyth, *Christian Aspects of Evolution*, pp. 16, 19, 37–9.

Page 78

155 Forsyth, *Justification of God*, p. 41. ibid., p. 48. ibid., p. 155.

156 Forsyth, *The Christian Ethic of War*, p. 166. cf. Forsyth, *Justification of God*, p. 192.

157 ibid., p. 54.

158 Forsyth, *The Christian Ethic of War*, p. 122.

159 Forsyth, *Justification of God*, p. 42.

Page 79

160 Forsyth, *Faith and Criticism*, p. 140.

Footnotes to Chapter II

Page 82

1 cf. Ott, op. cit., p. 4; Denzinger, op. cit., p. 494, 1792; Michael Schmaus, *Katholische Dogmatik* (München: Max Huber Verlag, 1960), Band I, pp. 80–4; Emil Brunner, *Wahrheit als Begegnung* (Zürich: Zwingli-Verlag, 1938), *passim;* van Oyen, *Theologische Erkenntnislehre*, pp. 121–6 and Karl Barth, *Church Dogmatics*, V. I, first half-volume. (trans. Thomson, Edinburgh: T. & T. Clark, third impression, 1955), pp 309–15.

2 cf. Edward John Carnell, *The Case for Orthodox Theology* (Philadelphia: The Westminster Press, 1959), pp. 81–99; L. Harold DeWolf, *The Case for Theology in Liberal Perspective* (Philadelphia: The Westminster Press, 1959), pp. 19–45.

3 cf. William Hordern, *The Case for a New Reformation Theology* (Philadelphia: The Westminster Press, 1959), p. 53.

Page 83

4 Forsyth, *Theology in Church and State*, p. 24. cf. Forsyth, 'Higher Criticism' p. 575.

Page 84

5 cf. Forsyth, *Principle of Authority*, p. 61.

6 'the dogma which he is,' Forsyth, *Theology in Church and State*, p. xxv.

Page 85
[7] Forsyth, *Congregationalism and Reunion*, p. 12.
[8] Forsyth, *This Life and the Next*, p. 49.
[9] Forsyth, *Theology in Church and State*, pp. 13–14.

Page 86
[10] ibid., p. 61. Though Forsyth himself prefers the term 'dogma' to 'kerygma,' we have chosen for several reasons to use the term *'kerygma'* in our exposition. The most important one is that Forsyth himself equates the two terms (see page 90 of this study and the following places in Forsyth's writings: *Principle of Authority*, 126, 127, 134; *Positive Preaching*, 6; *Theology in Church and State*, 62).

To the writer's knowledge, Forsyth is the first theologian to have made such central dogmatic use of the concept *'kerygma.'*

Page 87
[11] Forsyth, *Principle of Authority*, p. 130. cf. Forsyth, *Faith, Freedom and the Future*, pp. 239–40.
[12] Forsyth, *Theology in Church and State*, p. 82.
[13] Forsyth, *Principle of Authority*, p. 259. cf. Forsyth, *Theology in Church and State*, p. 71.
[14] ibid., p. 13.
[15] cf. ibid., p. 35.

Page 88
[16] Forsyth, *Justification of God*, pp. 36–7.
[17] Forsyth, *The Church and the Sacraments*, pp. 80–1. cf. Bellarmine, quoted in Wilhelm Niesel, *Reformed Symbolics* (trans. Lewis, Edinburgh and London; Oliver and Boyd, 1962), p. 23.
[18] Forsyth, *Theology in Church and State*, p. 28. cf. ibid., pp. 27, 38.
[19] ibid., pp. 27–8.

Page 89
[20] ibid., p. 29.
[21] ibid., pp. 28–9.
[22] ibid., p. 9.

Page 90
[23] ibid., p. 62.

Page 91
[24] ibid., p. 63. It is important to point out at the beginning of this excursus Forsyth's relation to Harnack. Forsyth knew the writings of the great historian of the Ritschlian school well. He respected Harnack's abilities as an historian and often defended him against caricatures of his position. However, Forsyth felt that, as a theologian, Harnack was sadly lacking. This historical excursus will indicate just how widely they differed in their understanding of dogma and of the significance of the

293

history of dogma. Harnack may be considered typical of the Ritschlian School, though he is somewhat more extreme than either Ritschl or Kaftan would be. Harnack's position is well enough known and complex enough that we need not try to outline it here. Suffice it to say that at the following decisive points Forsyth differs from Harnack: For Forsyth, Dogma is Christ the Redeemer and Lord and, therefore, Christ is the object of faith and not simply the first believer and teacher: For Forsyth, the worship of God the Father is not separated from the worship of Christ as God and Son; Forsyth did not posit a distinction between the *kerygmatic* Christ of dogma and the historic Jesus; Forsyth sees the whole movement of the history of dogma down to his day as returning to the New Testament idea of *kerygma*, whereas Harnack ended his discussion of dogma with the Ikon controversy in the East and with Trent in the West, protestantism being non-dogmatic in its essence. This Harnack could do because he felt that dogma is not essential to Christian faith but is rather a metaphysical distortion of Christ's teaching. cf. Forsyth, *Positive Preaching*, p. 59.

For an excellent outline of his own position, see Adolf Harnack, *Outlines of the History of Dogma* (trans. Mitchell, Boston; Beacon Press, 1957), pp. 1–37.

[25] Forsyth, *Theology in Church and State*, p. 65.

Page 92
[26] ibid., p. 66.
[27] ibid., pp. 66–7.

Page 93
[28] ibid., pp. 68–71.
[29] ibid., pp. 72–3, footnote.

Page 94
[30] ibid., p. 73.
[31] Forsyth applies the same basic argument to the Anglo-Catholic or High-Church movement within Anglicanism, except that the episcopacy is substituted for the papacy.
[32] ibid., p. 75.

Page 95
[33] ibid., p. 77.
[34] ibid., p. 78.
[35] ibid., p. 78.
[36] ibid., pp. 79–80. We might summarize Forsyth's view of the Pope by referring to him as the incarnation of the self-sufficiency of the Church. In this sense we can understand why the Reformers referred to him as the 'anti-Christ.' Protestants see the Pope as a rival incarnation whereas Roman Catholics see him as the point at which the Church is the *Christus prolongatus*.

294

Page 96
[37] ibid., p. 82.

Page 97
[38] Forsyth, *The Church and the Sacraments*, pp. xv–xvi.

Page 98
[39] Forsyth, *Theology in Church and State*, p. xxiv.
[40] Forsyth, 'Revelation and Bible' in *Hibbert Journal*, X (1911–12), p. 239. Hereafter referred to as 'Revelation and Bible.'

Page 100
[41] Forsyth, 'Higher Criticism,' p. 583.
[42] cf. Forsyth, *The Church and the Sacraments*, pp. 135–6; *Theology in Church and State*, p. 81.
[43] Forsyth, 'Revelation and Bible,' pp. 243–4.

Page 101
[44] ibid., p. 243.
[45] Forsyth, *Positive Preaching*, p. 8.
[46] Forsyth, *The Church and the Sacraments*, p. 142. The term 'sacramental' is a favourite of Forsyth's. However, the reader should not allow himself to be misled by the term. Forsyth's usage is consistently the following: God uses persons, things, events and interpretations as the means for his personal communion with man; he himself comes to man in and through that which is not himself. It is this 'using' and this 'coming' on the part of God that Forsyth describes as sacramental. It is a broad usage and should not be thought of in too close a connexion with the complex discussions in the Church's history as to the nature of a sacrament. The reader is assured that Forsyth has the Gospel 'coming,' the moral or personal presence of God, always in mind. He is directly opposed to all forms of substance-sacramentalism. At the same time the term means more than just a reminder or a sign; God really uses someone or something to convey himself, to make his presence known. Forsyth, ibid., p. 229, *et passim*.

Page 102
[47] Forsyth, 'Higher Criticism,' p. 591.
[48] Forsyth, *Faith, Freedom and the Future*, p. 40.
[49] cf. John K. S. Reed, *The Authority of Scripture* (London: Methuen & Co. Ltd., 1957), p. 96.
[50] Forsyth, *Principle of Authority*, p. 299.
[51] Forsyth, 'Higher Criticism,' p. 591.

Page 103
[52] Forsyth, 'Revelation and Bible,' pp. 250–1. cf. Forsyth, 'Higher Criticism,' p. 594.
[53] Forsyth, 'Higher Criticism,' pp. 598–9. cf. our discussion of 'The Task of Theology' later in this chapter.

20—TTOPTF

Page 105

[54] Forsyth, 'Revelation and Bible,' pp. 242–3. cf. 'The revelation had to be interpreted for all time in order to act on time.' Forsyth, *Person and Place*, p. 152; ibid., pp. 149–52, 155, 159; Forsyth, 'Higher Criticism,' p. 583.

[55] Forsyth, *Person and Place*, p. 173. cf. Forsyth, *Theology in Church and State*, p. 40 and *Work of Christ*, pp. 53–4.

[56] Forsyth, *Person and Place*, p. 206.

[57] ibid., p. 150. cf. Forsyth, *The Cruciality of the Cross*, pp. 15–16.

Page 106

[58] Forsyth, *The Church and the Sacraments*, p. 135.

[59] Forsyth, *Person and Place*, pp. 112–13. cf. van Oyen, op. cit., pp. 199–202.

Page 107

[60] Forsyth, *The Cruciality of the Cross*, pp. 50–1.

[61] Forsyth, *Principle of Authority*, p. 133.

Page 108

[62] Forsyth, *Faith and Criticism*, p. 119.

[63] John 16:15.

[64] Forsyth, *The Cruciality of the Cross*, p. 49. cf. Forsyth, *Theology in Church and State*, p. 26; *Principle of Authority*, p. 133; van Oyen, op. cit., p. 213, *Evangelische Ethik I.*, pp. 13–30, *et passim*.

Page 109

[65] Forsyth, *God the Holy Father*, p. 18.

[66] Forsyth, *The Cruciality of the Cross*, p. 16.

[67] Forsyth, *Person and Place*, p. 151.

[68] One may question whether Forsyth makes a proper distinction between the Son and the Spirit; there can be little doubt, however, that in this connexion he follows St Paul. For a discussion of Paul's vision, see Forsyth, *Christ on Parnassus*, p. 249.

[69] Forsyth, *Person and Place*, p. 164.

Page 110

[70] Forsyth, *Work of Christ*, pp. 53–4. cf. Forsyth, *Person and Place*, pp. 162–3.

[71] ibid., p. 163.

[72] Forsyth, *Principle of Authority*, p. 131.

[73] Forsyth, *Person and Place*, p. 165.

[74] cf. Forsyth, *Principle of Authority* pp. 126–7; *Person and Place*, p. 44; *The Cruciality of the Cross*, pp. 11–15; and *Principle of Authority*, pp. 125–9.

Page 111

[75] cf. E. Basil Redlich, *Form Criticism: Its Value and Limitations* (London: Duckworth, 1956), pp. 26, 63–8.

[76] Forsyth, *Person and Place*, p. 103.

Page 112
[77] ibid., p. 139.
[78] Forsyth, *The Church and the Sacraments*, p. 143.
[79] Forsyth, *Positive Preaching*, p. 26.

Page 113
[80] ibid., p. 85.

Page 114
[81] Forsyth, *Christ on Parnassus*, pp. 243–4.
[82] Forsyth, *Person and Place*, pp. 138–9.

Page 115
[83] ibid., p. 140.

Page 116
[84] Forsyth, *Positive Preaching*, pp. 9–10.
[85] Forsyth, *Person and Place*, p. 155.

Page 117
[86] Forsyth, 'Revelation and Bible,' pp. 248–9.
[87] Forsyth, *The Christian Ethic of War*, pp. v–vi.

Page 118
[88] Forsyth, *Faith and Criticism*, p. 109.
[89] Forsyth, *Christ on Parnassus*, pp. 243–4.

Page 119
[90] Forsyth, 'Revelation and Bible,' p. 250.
[91] ibid., p. 245.

Page 120
[92] Forsyth, *Person and Place*, p. 172. cf. Forsyth, 'Revelation and Bible,' p. 244; ibid., p. 241; 'Higher Criticism,' p. 580.

Page 121
[93] Forsyth, *The Church and the Sacraments*, p. 137.
[94] ibid., p. 139.

Page 122
[95] Forsyth, *Faith and Criticism*, pp. 135–6.
[96] Forsyth, *The Church and the Sacraments*, p. 138.

Page 123
[97] Forsyth in *Priesthood and Sacrifice* (ed. Sandy, London: Longmans, Green & Co., 1900), p. 43.
[98] Forsyth, *The Church and the Sacraments*, p. 139.

[99] Forsyth, *Positive Preaching*, p. 1.
[100] ibid., p. 3.

Page 124
[101] ibid., p. 29.
[102] ibid., p. 55.
[103] ibid., p. 239.
[104] ibid., p. 56.
[105] Forsyth, *Principle of Authority*, p. 62. cf. *Faith, Freedom and the Future*, p. 33.
[106] For an excellent contemporary treatment of preaching which represents a view of preaching very similar to that of Forsyth, see Albert Schädelin, *Die Rechte Predigt* (Zürich: Zwingli-Verlag, 1953), pp. 20–42, *et passim*.

Page 125
[107] Forsyth, *Rome, Reform and Reaction*, pp. 217–18
[108] Forsyth, *Work of Christ*, pp. 40–1. cf. Forsyth, *Faith, Freedom and the Future*, p. 37.
[109] Forsyth, *Positive Preaching*, p. 26. cf. ibid., p. 20.

Page 126
[110] cf. ibid., pp. 112–13.
[111] Forsyth, *The Cruciality of the Cross*, pp. 42–3.
[112] Forsyth, *Positive Preaching*, p. 22.
[113] ibid., p. 5. cf. Forsyth, *The Church and the Sacraments*, p. 20.

Page 127
[114] Forsyth, *Positive Preaching*, p. 73.

Page 128
[115] ibid., p. 68.
[116] ibid., pp. 64–5.

Page 129
[117] ibid. pp. 60–1. cf. ibid., p. 70; Forsyth, *Principle of Authority*, p. 339.
[118] Forsyth, *The Church and the Sacraments*, p. 148.

Page 130
[119] Forsyth, *Person and Place*, p. 173.
[120] Forsyth, *Principle of Authority*, pp. 21–2.
[121] Forsyth, *Work of Christ*, p. 145. cf. Maurice, *Theological Essays*, p. 238; Karl Barth, *Church Dogmatics*, *V. I.* Part 2 (ed. Bromily and Torrance, Edinburgh: T. & T. Clark, 1956), p. 457.

Page 131
[122] Forsyth, *Person and Place*, p. 159.

Page 132
123 Forsyth, *Principle of Authority*, p. 250.
124 Forsyth, *The Church and the Sacraments*, p. 51.

Page 133
125 ibid., p. 34.
126 Forsyth, 'Higher Criticism,' p. 575.
127 Forsyth, *Rome, Reform and Reaction*, p. 108. cf. Forsyth, *The Church and the Sacraments*, p. 9; ibid., p. 25.
128 cf. Forsyth, *Theology in Church and State*, p. 181. ibid., p. 180.

Page 134
129 Forsyth, *Principle of Authority*, p. 230.
130 ibid., p. 316. cf. Forsyth, *Work of Christ*, p. 6. See also Herrmann at this point, *The Communion of the Christian with God*, pp. 189–95.

Page 136
131 Forsyth, *Theology in Church and State*, pp. 50–4. Forsyth uses 'doctrine' and 'creed' interchangeably. ibid., pp. 12–13.

Page 137
132 ibid., p. 107.

Page 138
133 Forsyth, *Faith, Freedom and the Future*, pp. 219–20.
134 cf. Forsyth, *Work of Christ*, pp. 46–7.
135 Forsyth, *Principle of Authority*, p. 338.
136 Forsyth, *Theology in Church and State*, p. 106.

Page 139
137 ibid. p. 260.
138 Forsyth, *Faith, Freedom and the Future*, p. 210. cf. Forsyth, *Theology in Church and State*, p. 21; for a similar position, van Oyen, *Theologische Erkenntnislehre*, pp. 84–8; and in contrast, see Barth's cautious refusal to allow the Church the phrase 'It seemeth good to the Holy Spirit and to us' in op. cit. V. I. Part 2, p. 592.
139 Forsyth, *Principle of Authority*, p. 291.

Page 140
140 ibid., pp. 326–7.
141 Forsyth, *Theology in Church and State*, p. 106.
142 ibid., p. 56.

Page 141
143 ibid., p. 99.
144 ibid., p. 101.

Page 142
145 cf ibid., p.23.
146 Rather than organic union Forsyth has in mind a federation of churches. cf. Forsyth, *The Church and the Sacraments*, pp. 45 ff.

Page 143
147 ibid., p. 62. cf. ibid., pp. 67–8; Forsyth, *Congregationalism and Reunion*, pp. 21–2.
148 Compare the difference of emphasis between Forsyth and Herrmann. Herrmann, op. cit., p. 13. We might express the difference in this manner: Forsyth is *kerygmatic* and Herrmann is moral-aesthetic.
149 Forsyth, *Principle of Authority*, pp. 258–9.

Page 144
150 Forsyth, *The Soul of Prayer*, p. 45. cf. ibid., p. 78; ibid., p. 27; Forsyth, *The Christian Ethic of War*, p. 177.

Page 145
151 Forsyth, *Principle of Authority*, p. 90. cf. Bo Reicke, 'Der Fleischgewordene' in *Der Historische Jesus und der Kerygmatische Christus* (ed. Ristow & Matthias, Berlin: Evangelische Verlagsanstalt, 1961), pp. 208–18; and Forsyth, *Positive Preaching*, pp. 69–70.
152 Forsyth, *Work of Christ*, pp. 176–7.

Page 146
153 Forsyth, *Positive Preaching*, p. 93. cf. Forsyth, *Work of Christ*, pp. 230–1.
154 Forsyth, *Principle of Authority*, p. 279.

Page 147
155 Forsyth, *Faith, Freedom and the Future*, p. 187. cf. ibid., pp. 25–6; and *Work of Christ*, p. xxx.
156 Forsyth, *Faith, Freedom and the Future*, p. 132.

Page 149
157 Forsyth, *Person and Place*, p. 216.
158 Forsyth, *Theology in Church and State*, p. 21.
159 Forsyth, *Person and Place*, p. 216.

Page 150
160 Ott, op. cit., p. 2. See van Oyen, op. cit., pp. 39–65.
161 The term 'possesses' would be misleading if it led one to think that the theologian, in his own strength, is able to grasp God. However, in the light of so much contemporary talk about the 'risk' of faith and the 'freedom' of God in his revelation, it might be valuable to use such a term to reflect the comfort given to the Church in God's free promise to be present with the Church in the Spirit.
162 Forsyth, *Faith, Freedom and the Future*, pp. 150–1.

Page 151
163 ibid., p. 119.

Page 152

[164] Forsyth, *Theology in Church and State*, p. 294.

[165] Forsyth, *Principle of Authority*, pp. 395–6. Forsyth also uses the fact that the theologian stands under the authority of his Object to repudiate the claim that in protestant theology we have nothing but individualism. Forsyth, ibid., p. 395.

[166] ibid., p. 211.

[167] Forsyth, *Theology in Church and State*, p. 300.

Page 153

[168] ibid., p. 19.

[169] Forsyth, *Positive Preaching*, pp. 202–3.

Page 154

[170] cf. Forsyth, *Principle of Authority*, pp. 219–21.

[171] Forsyth, *Positive Preaching*, p. 143; cf. ibid., p. 142.

[172] ibid., p. 158.

[173] ibid., p. 143.

[174] cf. Forsyth, *Faith, Freedom and the Future*, pp. 238 ff.

Page 155

[175] Forsyth, *Principle of Authority*, p. 212. cf. *The Church and the Sacraments*, pp. 304–5.

[176] Forsyth, *Positive Preaching*, p. 143. cf. ibid., p. 144.

Page 156

[177] ibid., pp. 138–9.

[178] cf. Forsyth, *Christ on Parnassus*, pp. 56–7.

Page 157

[179] Forsyth, *Positive Preaching*, p. 191. Material in parenthesis is the writer's.

[180] Forsyth, *Principle of Authority*, p. 213.

Page 158

[181] We have chosen the term 'Biblical interpretation' instead of 'Biblical hermeneutics' because of the wider connotation which the term 'hermeneutics' has today. By Biblical interpretation we mean the reading of the Bible in such a manner that proper communication occurs between the reader and the Object to which the Bible refers; in other words, the adequate interpretation (understanding) of the Biblical text. In the broader sense of hermeneutics as used today, Forsyth does offer an ontology. This will be dealt with in the next chapter and is dealt with more fully in the Appendix to this study.

The writer is indebted to Otto Weber for the basic structure of this excursus. While it does not come from Forsyth, it seems a most adequate pattern in which to organize and present his remarks on this subject. cf. Otto Weber, *Grundlagen der Dogmatik*, Erster Band (Neukirchen: Verlag der Buchhandlung des Erziehungsvereins, 1959), pp. 348–54.

Page 159

[182] cf. Maurice, *The Kingdom of Christ*, V. II, p. 167.

[183] cf. Forsyth's preface to J. Monro Gibson, *The Inspiration and Authority of Holy Scripture* (London: Thomas Law, 1908), pp. xv–xvi; Forsyth, *Work of Christ*, p. 55.

[184] These requirements suggested by Forsyth are now generally stressed as necessary to historical exegesis. cf. Forsyth, *Theology in Church and State*, p. xviii; and *Christian Aspects of Evolution*, p. 31.

[185] Forsyth, 'Higher Criticism,' p. 579.

Page 160
[186] Forsyth, *The Church and the Sacraments*, p. 284.
[187] Forsyth, *Positive Preaching*, p. 189.
[188] Forsyth, *Principles of Authority*, p. 283.

Page 161
[189] For Forsyth's view of the canon, see *Holy Christian Empire*, 1902 as quoted in Griffith, *The Theology of P. T. Forsyth*, p. 61. (To the writer's knowledge, Forsyth never dealt with the question of an open or a closed canon.) cf. *Person and Place*, pp. 128–9; *Faith, Freedom and the Future*, p. 27; *Rome, Reform and Reaction*, p. 224 and 'Higher Criticism,' p. 587.
[190] ibid., p. 588.
[191] Forsyth, *Positive Preaching*, p. 6.

Page 162
[192] Forsyth, 'Higher Criticism,' p. 588.
[193] cf. ibid., p. 595; Forsyth, *Work of Christ*, p. 34.

Page 163
[194] Forsyth, *Positive Preaching*, pp. 18–19. cf. Forsyth, *Rome, Reform and Reaction*, p. 103; cf. also: 'Revelation and the Bible,' p. 251; 'Higher Criticism,' p. 596; *The Cruciality of the Cross*, p. 94; *The Church and the Sacraments*, pp. 212–17; *Socialism, the Church and the Poor*, p. 69 and *Priesthood and Sacrifice*, p. 50.

Page 164
[195] Forsyth, *Christ on Parnassus*, pp. 240–1.
[196] Forsyth, *God the Holy Father*, p. 16. cf. Forsyth, *Theology in Church and State*, p. 31.

Page 165
[197] Forsyth, *Work of Christ*, p. 51.
[198] Forsyth, 'Higher Criticism,' p. 584.
[199] ibid., pp. 585–6.
[200] Forsyth, *The Church and the Sacraments*, p. 227. cf. Forsyth, *Christian Aspects of Evolution*, p. 38 and *Priesthood and Sacrifice*, p. 92.

Page 166
[201] cf. Forsyth, 'Higher Criticism,' p. 524.
[202] Forsyth, *Faith and Criticism*, p. 121. cf. Forsyth, *Rome, Reform and Reaction*, p. 134.

[203] Forsyth, *Principle of Authority*, p. 283. cf. Forsyth's lengthy treatment of Word and Spirit in Chapters 1, 7 and 8 of his *Faith, Freedom and the Future*, especially p. 211.

Page 167
  [204] Forsyth, *Person and Place*, p. 178.

Page 168
  [205] ibid., p. 169.
  [206] ibid., p. 49. cf. Forsyth, *God the Holy Father*, pp. 89–90.
  [207] Forsyth, *Principle of Authority*, p. 223. cf. Forsyth, *Justification of God*, p. 29.
  [208] Forsyth, 'Revelation and Bible,' p. 251. cf. Forsyth, 'Higher Criticism,' p. 596.

Page 169
  [209] cf. Forsyth, *Person and Place*, p. 160 and *Positive Preaching*, p. 256.
  [210] Forsyth, 'Revelation and Bible,' p. 252. cf. Forsyth, *Positive Preaching*, pp. 12, 187; 'Higher Criticism,' pp. 588–9; regarding the Holy Spirit as the Bible critic see ibid., p. 596.

Page 171
  [211] Forsyth, 'Revelation and Bible,' pp. 249–50. cf. Forsyth, 'Higher Criticism,' pp. 589–90 and *Positive Preaching*, pp. 13–15.

Footnotes to Chapter III

Page 174
  [1] Forsyth, *The Church and the Sacraments*, p. 60.
  [2] Forsyth, *Faith, Freedom and the Future*, p. 143. In the Ritschlian School, Herrmann is the most active opponent of rationalistic orthodoxy. See Herrmann, op. cit., Preface *passim* and pp. 1–18, *et passim*.
  [3] Forsyth, op. cit., pp. 29–30.

Page 175
  [4] ibid., pp. 11–13.
  [5] ibid., p.29. cf. ibid., pp. 33–4; *The Church and the Sacraments*, p. 223 and *Missions in State and Church*, pp. 23–4. We note Herrmann's agreement at this point. cf. Herrmann, op. cit., p. ix.

Page 176
  [6] Forsyth, *God the Holy Father*, p. 96. cf. Forsyth, *Work of Christ*, p. 170.
  [7] cf. Forsyth, *Principle of Authority*, pp. 64, 112.
  [8] Forsyth, *Justification of God*, p. 157. See our discussion in Chapter I, Part III, on the Cross as working itself out in history where the Cross is referred to by Forsyth as an 'eternal deed.' cf. ibid., p. 48.

Page 177
  [9] Forsyth, *Principle of Authority*, p. 113.
  [10] ibid., pp. 113–14.

Page 178
[11] ibid., p. 114.
[12] ibid., pp. 114–15.

Page 179
[13] ibid., pp. 116–17.
[14] cf. Forsyth, *Justification of God*, p. 48.

Page 181
[15] Forsyth, *Work of Christ*, p. 18. See ibid., pp. 11–30.
[16] The distinction which Forsyth makes throughout his writings between impression and regeneration is clearly expressed in *Faith, Freedom and the Future*, pp. 35–6.
[17] cf. Forsyth, *This Life and the Next*, p. 73.
[18] Forsyth, *Faith, Freedom and the Future*, p. 13. cf. Barth, *Church Dogmatics*, V. I, Part 2, p. 203.
[19] Forsyth, *Person and Place*, p. 222. cf. Our discussion of the interrelatedness of Christ's work on the Cross in Chapter I.

Page 182
[20] Forsyth, *Faith, Freedom and the Future*, p. 307.
[21] Forsyth, *Justification of God*, p. 128.
[22] Forsyth, *The Atonement*, p. 77.

Page 183
[23] ibid., p. 79.
[24] ibid.
[25] ibid., p. 76.

Page 184
[26] Forsyth, *Rome, Reform and Reaction*, pp. 92–3.
[27] Forsyth, *The Church and the Sacraments*, p. 199.
[28] cf. Forsyth, *Principle of Authority*, pp. 370, 388.

Page 185
[29] Forsyth, *Socialism, The Church and the Poor*, p. 25.
[30] Forsyth, *God the Holy Father*, pp. 126–9.

Page 186
[31] Forsyth, *The Soul of Prayer*, p. 32.
[32] ibid., p. 16.
[33] ibid., p. 78. cf. ibid., p. 46.
[34] ibid., pp. 11–12.
[35] ibid., p. 46. cf. ibid., p. 75.
[36] ibid., p. 48. cf. ibid., p. 35.

Page 187
[37] cf. ibid., pp. 90–1.
[38] ibid., p. 84.
[39] ibid., p. 70.

Page 188

⁴⁰ Forsyth, *Justification of God*, pp. 219–20. cf. Forsyth, *The Christian Ethic of War*, p. 182. This line of thought does not receive adequate emphasis in Forsyth's writings. But, at this point, we can see that for him the teleological emphasis did not require the exclusion of the cosmological. In this respect he seems to have overcome the fear of mechanistic-materialism which is prevalent in the Ritschlian School's attitude to nature. cf. Ritschl, op. cit., p. 17; ibid., *passim*.

Page 189

⁴¹ Forsyth, *Person and Place*, p. 339.

⁴² Forsyth, *The Christian Ethic of War*, p. 171. cf. ibid., pp. 52, 144, 177, and 182; *This Life and the Next*, pp. 68–9; *Justification of God*, p. 123 and *Principle of Authority*, p. 184.

Page 190

⁴³ cf. ibid., pp. 160, 164, 243 and 388; and *Work of Christ*, pp. 216–7.

⁴⁴ Forsyth, *Justification of God*, p. 123.

⁴⁵ ibid.

⁴⁶ cf. Forsyth, *The Christian Ethic of War*, p. 177.

⁴⁷ Forsyth, *This Life and the Next*, p. 69.

Page 191

⁴⁸ Contrast Ritschl, op. cit., pp. 6, 28 and 591.

Page 192

⁴⁹ cf. Forsyth, *Principle of Authority*, p. 35.

Page 193

⁵⁰ ibid., pp. 149–50. cf. Forsyth, *Christian Aspects of Evolution*, p. 13.

⁵¹ Forsyth, *Principle of Authority*, p. 100. Contrast Loewenberg, *Hegel Selections*, p. 380.

⁵² cf. Forsyth, *Theology in Church and State*, p. xlv.

⁵³ Forsyth, *Justification of God*, p. 47.

Page 194

⁵⁴ cf. Forsyth, *Principle of Authority*, pp. 154–5.

⁵⁵ Forsyth, *This Life and the Next*, p. 48. cf. ibid., pp. 37 and 42. We note the fact that knowing, election, and love inter-penetrate one another in Forsyth's thinking. We interpret this as an indication of his insight into and affirmation of Biblical ways of thinking. Forsyth's use of 'knowing' is best understood in reference to the Hebrew thinking surrounding *dabar* and its intimate interpersonal connotations. The Greek use of *logos* (not the New Testament usage) is the impersonal, observing type of thought which Forsyth refers to as 'scientific.' Van Oyen suggests the term *analogia communicationis* as expressive of this knowing in personal communion which is the background of the Biblical understanding of religious knowledge. For a fuller discussion of

this topic see van Oyen, *Theologische Erkenntnislehre*, pp. 121–6. Also cf. P. S. Minear, *Eyes of Faith* (London: Lutterworth Press, 1948), pp. 14–16.

Page 195
[56] Forsyth, *Principle of Authority*, p. 151.

[57] It is true that God in his divine Self-hood lives in a light unapproachable by finite man and therefore he must express and reveal himself to man in a way which his creatures can receive. But Forsyth is concerned to stress that it is not simply the Creator-creature line that God must overcome in his revelation; there is also perverted, distorted man who is not able to stand before God and live as he is. To know God is to know oneself regenerated.

Page 196
[58] ibid., p. 2.
[59] Forsyth, *Positive Preaching*, p. 27.

Page 197
[60] Forsyth, *Principle of Authority*, pp. 58–9. cf. ibid., p. 61.
[61] cf. Forsyth, *Positive Preaching*, pp. 39–40, 43; *Principle of Authority*, pp. 11–12.
[62] cf. Forsyth, *Person and Place*, p. 230; and *Principle of Authority*, p. 53.

Page 198
[63] ibid., pp. 12–13.
[64] ibid., pp. 158–9. cf. Forsyth, *Positive Preaching*, pp. 43–4; *Theology in Church and State*, p. 96; *Principle of Authority*, p. 13.

Page 199
[65] ibid., p. 287; cf. ibid., pp. 289–90.
[66] Forsyth, *Positive Preaching*, p. 44. cf. Forsyth, *Principle of Authority*, pp. 254–5.

Page 200
[67] ibid., p. 49.
[68] ibid., p. 81–2.
[69] cf. Paul Tillich, *Systematic Theology*, V. I, (London: Nisbet & Co. Ltd., 1953), pp. 67–73.
[70] Forsyth, *Principle of Authority*, p. 54.

Page 201
[71] ibid., p. 39. cf. ibid., p. 352.
[72] ibid., p. 46. cf. ibid., p. 345.

Page 202
[73] ibid., p. 213. Forsyth, *Faith and Criticism*, p. 124. cf. ibid., pp. 111–12
[74] It is for this reason that Forsyth prefers to use such terms as 'person,' 'community,' etc. and avoids scholastic terms such as 'substantia,'

'essentia,' 'attributio,' etc. It is our opinion that, in using these more personalistic, more modern terms, Forsyth was careful to define them in the light of Christ. He did not take them uncritically from the culture.

[75] Forsyth, *Principle of Authority*, p. 350. Here Forsyth stands in disagreement with Tillich. cf. Paul Tillich, *Systematic Theology*, V. II, (Chicago: The University of Chicago Press, 1957), pp. 72–3; cf. also the agreement between Forsyth and Brunner at this point in Brunner, *Revelation and Reason*, pp. 207–18.

Page 203
[76] Forsyth, *Person and Place*, pp. 346–7. cf. Forsyth, *The Church and the Sacraments*, pp. 242–4.

Page 204
[77] Forsyth, *Principle of Authority*, p. 389. Here we see clearly his basic difference from Herrmann. cf. ibid., p. 65.
[78] Forsyth, *God the Holy Father*, p. 148.
[79] Forsyth, *Person and Place*, p. 332.
[80] Forsyth, *Faith and Criticism*, p. 139.
[81] Forsyth, *Positive Preaching*, p. 47.

Page 205
[82] Forsyth, *Principle of Authority*, p. 325.

Page 206
[83] Forsyth, *The Cruciality of the Cross*, pp. 62–3.
[84] cf. Forsyth, *Principle of Authority*, p. 5.
[85] ibid., p. 240. cf. Hendrik van Oyen, *Botschaft und Gebot* (Gutersloh: Verlagshaus Gerd Mohn, 1962), p. 18. Contrast Kant, Greene, *Kant Selections*, pp. 281–5.

Page 208
[86] Forsyth, *Missions in State and Church*, pp. 64–5. cf. Forsyth, *Justification of God*, p. 81.
[87] Forsyth, *Rome, Reform and Reaction*, p. 120.

Page 209
[88] Forsyth, *Principle of Authority*, p. 372. cf. Forsyth, *Work of Christ*, pp. 50–1; *The Church and the Sacraments*, p. 216.

Forsyth was well aware of the danger of using the term 'experience' in connexion with religion. Forsyth, *Principle of Authority*, p. 74.

It is possible that Ritschl surrendered to psychology. Ritschl, op. cit., p. 20. ibid., p. 22.

The following places in Forsyth's writing point out the intensity with which he was called upon to fight differing forms of introspection: Against psychologism—*Positive Preaching*, p. 176; *Principle of Authority*, pp. 74–6, 91–2. Against romantic pietism—ibid., pp. 331–4, 337, 346; *God the Holy Father*, pp. 101–2; *Faith and Criticism*, pp. 100–1; *Faith*,

Freedom and the Future, pp. 96–7; *The Church and the Sacraments*, p. 16. Against romantic idealism—*Principle of Authority*, pp. 105–6.

The earlier statement by Maurice represents Forsyth's later view. Maurice, *The Kingdom of Christ*, V. I, p. 256.

[89] Johnson, *Authority in Protestant Theology*, p. 100. This is the most perceptive theological evaluation of Forsyth in the contemporary literature concerning Forsyth.

[90] Forsyth, *Principle of Authority*, p. 75.

Page 210

[91] See ibid., pp. 23–33 and 177–97.

[92] cf. Forsyth, *The Church and the Sacraments*, p. 230; *Work of Christ*, pp. 49–51; *Justification of God*, pp. 80–1; *The Christian Ethic of War*, p. 140.

[93] cf. Forsyth, *Person and Place*, pp. 192–3; *Principle of Authority*, p. 50; *God the Holy Father*, pp. 88–9; *Positive Preaching*, pp. 46–7.

[94] cf. Forsyth, *Principle of Authority*, p. 52.

[95] cf. ibid., pp. 188, 414; Forsyth, *This Life and the Next*, p. 71.

[96] cf. ibid., p. 70; Forsyth, *Positive Preaching*, pp. 136, 211.

[97] cf. Forsyth, *Principle of Authority*, p. 181.

Page 211

[98] cf. ibid., pp. 24–6; Forsyth, *The Church and the Sacraments*, p. 216.

[99] cf. Forsyth, *God the Holy Father*, p. 108; *Principle of Authority*, pp. 24, 374.

[100] Forsyth, *Positive Preaching*, p. 46. cf. Forsyth, *Work of Christ*, p. 41; *Faith, Freedom and the Future*, p. 219.

Page 212

[101] Forsyth, *Work of Christ*, p. 49. cf. Forsyth, *God the Holy Father*, p. 88; *Person and Place*, pp. 56–8.

[102] Forsyth as quoted in Escott, op. cit., p. 122, (unpublished material).

[103] Forsyth, *Positive Preaching*, pp. 31–2. cf. Forsyth, *Christ on Parnassus*, pp. 158–9.

[104] Forsyth, *The Church and the Sacraments*, pp. 220–1. cf. Forsyth, *Principle of Authority*, p. 55, pp. 49 and 331.

Page 213

[105] ibid., pp. 399–400. cf. Forsyth, *The Church and the Sacraments*, p. 24. Forsyth, *Principle of Authority*, p. 71.

[106] ibid., p. 163.

Page 214

[107] ibid., p. 20. cf. ibid., pp. 17–19; Forsyth, *Faith and Criticism*, p. 111.

[108] The same holds true for eschatology. Forsyth, *Faith, Freedom and the Future*, p. 252.

[109] The centrality of the will takes its place within the context of a voluntaristic ontology which is based on the Redemptive as the Real.

Page 215

[110] One of the characteristics of liberal theology was its intellectualism. See Forsyth, *Faith, Freedom and the Future*, p. 99. cf. ibid., pp. 89–90.

[111] Forsyth, *Principle of Authority*, p. 212. cf. ibid., pp. 178–9; Forsyth, *Cruciality of the Cross*, p. 17; *Justification of God*, p. 197.

Page 216

[112] cf. Forsyth, *Principle of Authority*, p. 179. cf. Forsyth, *Theology in Church and State*, p. 43; 'Higher Criticism,' p. 587; *Congregationalism and Reunion*, p. 66.

[113] cf. Forsyth, *Justification of God*, pp. 136–9, 140–6, 154–5 and 185–6; *Principle of Authority*, p. 267.

Page 217

[114] cf. Forsyth, *Positive Preaching*, pp. 201–2; *Person and Place*, pp. 305–6; *The Soul of Prayer*, pp. 59, 64 and 86.

[115] cf. Forsyth, *Theology in Church and State*, p. xviii; *Justification of God*, p. 217.

[116] Forsyth, *Principle of Authority*, pp. 295–6.

Page 218

[117] ibid., p. 300.

Page 219

[118] ibid., p. 147.

[119] ibid., p. 101.

[120] cf. 'We are not called on to sacrifice our intellect, if only we do not idolize it.' Forsyth, *Person and Place*, p. 284.

[121] Forsyth, *Principle of Authority*, pp. 94–5.

Page 220

[122] ibid., p. 179.

[123] ibid., pp. 35–6.

[124] Forsyth, *Positive Preaching*, p. 209.

Page 221

[125] Forsyth, *Principle of Authority*, pp. 108–9.

[126] ibid., p. 103.

Page 222

[127] ibid., p. 100.

Page 223

[128] ibid., pp. 101–2.

[129] Forsyth rejects both views. See ibid., p. 399.

[130] cf. ibid., p. 148.

Page 224

[131] Forsyth, *God the Holy Father*, pp. 17–18. cf. Forsyth, *The Cruciality of the Cross*, p. 42. cf. also Forsyth, *Principle of Authority*, pp. 412–13, 84–8.

Page 225

[132] ibid., p. 293.

[133] Forsyth, *Positive Preaching*, pp. 87–8. cf. ibid., pp. 86–7; Forsyth, *Justification of God*, p. 32.

Page 226

[134] Forsyth, *Principle of Authority*, p. 214.

[135] Forsyth, *Person and Place*, pp. 355–6. cf. Forsyth's remarks about Ritschl on this point in *Principle of Authority*, p. 205.

Page 228

[136] Forsyth was not implying moralism. See ibid., p. 336. We remind the reader of Forsyth's peculiar usage of the word 'Gospel' at this point. For other statements regarding moralism, see our discussion in the excursus in Chapter I and Forsyth, *Justification of God*, pp. 112–16; *Faith and Criticism*, p. 133; *Principle of Authority*, p. 389; with Ritschl's moralism particularly in mind see ibid., p. 380.

Page 229

[137] Forsyth, *God the Holy Father*, p. 7.

Page 230

[138] Forsyth, *Principle of Authority*, p. 63. cf. ibid., pp. 299–300, 368.

[139] Forsyth, *London Theological Studies*, p. 160. cf. Forsyth, *The Old Faith and the New Theology*, p. 60. See Barth, *Church Dogmatics*, V. I, Part 1, p. 213 and the discussion following on pp. 213–83. cf. the summary statements in ibid., V. II, Part 1, pp. 3, 63, 179.

[140] Forsyth, *Principle of Authority*, pp. 315–16.

Page 231

[141] ibid., pp. 333–4. cf. ibid., pp. 55, 118, and 121–2.

[142] ibid., p. 118.

[143] Forsyth, *Positive Preaching*, p. 34. cf. Forsyth, *The Cruciality of the Cross*, p. viii. Whereas Forsyth allows no judgement by man on revelation outside of faith, Herrmann sees a criterion in man. Herrmann, op. cit., p. 355; or ibid., p. xi. cf. ibid., especially pp. 63–4, but also pp. 110, 142 and 190.

[144] Forsyth, *Faith and Criticism*, p. 109.

Page 232

[145] ibid., pp. 99–102.

Page 233

[146] Forsyth, *Principle of Authority*, p. 168.

[147] ibid., pp. 174–5.

Page 234

[148] ibid., p. 168.

[149] ibid., p. 146. ibid., p. 145.

Page 235
[150] ibid., p. 119.
[151] ibid., p. 60.
[152] Forsyth, *The Church and the Sacraments*, p. 44.

Page 236
[153] Forsyth, *Principle of Authority*, pp. 236–7. cf. ibid., p. 247.
[154] ibid., p. 60.
[155] Forsyth, *The Church and the Sacraments*, p. 10.

Page 237
[156] Forsyth, *Missions in State and Church*, p. 19. cf. Forsyth, *Justification of God*, p. 84; *Cruciality of the Cross*, p. 24.
[157] Forsyth, *Rome, Reform and Reaction*, p. 226. cf. '. . . we must *become* sacraments to men, and not merely use them.' ibid., p. 227.
[158] Forsyth, *The Christian Ethic of War*, p. 24.

Page 239
[159] Forsyth, *The Empire for Christ*, Sermon preached in the City Temple, 8th May, 1900, as quoted in Escott, op. cit., pp. 58–9.

Footnotes to Chapter IV

Page 242
[1] For Brunner's remarks about Forsyth see A. M. Hunter, *Introducing New Testament Theology*, (London: SCM Press Ltd., 1957), p. 100. For Mozley's comments see his *The Heart of the Gospel*, pp. 66 and 69.

Page 255
[2] See *Faith, Freedom and the Future*, passim.

Page 256
[3] Forsyth, *Person and Place*, p. 327.

Page 257
[4] This practice was used by Schleiermacher, Ritschl and many of his followers, i.e., Kaftan, Haering, etc. cf. Ritschl, op. cit., pp. 193–203; Haering, *Der Christliche Glaube Dogmatik* (Stuttgart: Calwer Vereinsbuchhandlung, 1922), pp. 33–82.
[5] cf. C. H. Dodd, *The Apostolic Preaching and Its Developments* (New York: Harper and Brothers Publishers, 1936, reprint, 1954) and Hunter, op. cit., This thesis is defended in both of these short studies. We do not mean to imply, however, that Forsyth would be in agreement with the somewhat over-simplified separation of *kerygma* and didache in Dodd, or with his one-sided emphasis on realized eschatology.

Page 259
[6] As we noted in the study earlier, Ritschl had separated man's moral and religious responses to God. Forsyth rejected this. Faith is a unified, moral response of trust in God's redeeming grace in Jesus Christ. Most

significant is Barth's treatment (*Church Dogmatics*, 1, 2, pp. 782–6) in which he indicates how such a separation has, throughout the history of dogmatics, always led to the importation of foreign norms into Christian ethics. This in turn has acted upon dogmatics to intellectualize and distort it as well. We are in full agreement with the material connexion which Forsyth and contemporary theologians such as Barth, Brunner, van Oyen, Althaus, see existing between Christian dogmatics and Christian ethics. We are not convinced, however, that this material unity makes it imperative or even desirable to treat the two in formal unity, that is to include the ethical material in dogmatics. cf. Paul Althaus, *Die Christliche Wahrheit* (Gutersloher Verlagaus, Gerd Mohn, 1959), pp. 255–7 and *Grundriss der Ethik* (Gutersloh: C. Bertelsmann Verlag, 1953), pp. 11–12; van Oyen, *Evangelische Ethik I*, pp. 15–20.

7 Forsyth, *The Christian Ethic of War*, p. 85.

Footnotes to Appendix

Page 265

1 cf. Forsyth, *Positive Preaching*, chapters 4, 6 and 7, especially pp. 168–98. His most philosophically written book is *Principle of Authority*.

Page 267

2 No doubt Forsyth was acquainted with this school since he cites the writings of T. H. Green. However, he seems to have been little influenced by it except in so far as British idealism mediated a Kantian influence in England.

3 We are indebted for this insight, and for much help in organizing this section, to I. M. Bochenski's book, *Contemporary European Philosophy* (English trans. Los Angeles: University of California Press, 1961). Also L. B. Elliott-Binns, *The Development of English Theology in the Later Nineteenth Century* (London: Longmans, Green & Co., 1952), especially chapter 2, and Clement C. J. Webb, *A Study of Religious Thought in England from 1850* (Oxford: Clarendon Press, 1933) were helpful in offering a general review of the period as it affected the English scene.

Page 268

4 He does make one basic exception. See the introduction to his book on theological aesthetics, *Christ on Parnassus*, in which he points to Hegel's genius and indicates that he accepts the main position of Hegel's aesthetics.

Page 270

5 cf. Forsyth, *Principle of Authority*, pp. 329 and 173.

Page 271

6 To include the terms '*Geschichte*' and '*Historie*' at this point, we must include Wobbermin among the Life-philosophers, for Forsyth indicates his reliance on Wobbermin for this distinction. cf. ibid., p. 112.

Page 273
  [7] ibid., p. 184.
  [8] cf. ibid., pp. 179–80. cf. ibid., p. 4.

Page 274
  [9] cf. Emil Brunner, *Man in Revolt, A Christian Anthropology* (trans. Wyon, London: Lutterworth Press, 1939), pp. 300–17.
  [10] Forsyth, *The Atonement*, p. 80.
  [11] Forsyth, *Principle of Authority*, p. 179. Forsyth seems to have been acquainted with Butler's writings—perhaps Butler's cautious restriction of the role of reason assisted Forsyth in giving expression to his own view. cf. Joseph Butler, *The Analogy of Religion Natural and Revealed to the Constitution and the Course of Nature* (London: George Routledge & Sons, Ltd., 1890), pp. 161–5, 173–4. Also Butler's stress on the moral relation between God and man would not have gone unheard by Forsyth, cf. ibid., pp. 278–83.

Page 275
  [12] Forsyth, *Positive Preaching*, p. 76.
  [13] ibid., p. 82. cf. Forsyth, *Justification of God*, pp. 69 and 168.
  [14] cf. Forsyth, *Person and Place*, p. 193.

Page 276
  [15] Forsyth, *Positive Preaching*, p. 170.

BIBLIOGRAPHY

This is not meant to be a complete list of the writings of Peter Taylor Forsyth nor of the other literature used in the preparation of this study. We have listed only those books which have been directly referred to or cited in our study.

BOOKS BY FORSYTH

Christ on Parnassus. Lectures on Art, Ethic and Theology. London: Independent Press Ltd., second impression, 1959.

Christian Aspects of Evolution. London: The Epworth Press, reprint 1950. (First published in the *London Quarterly Review*, 1905).

Christian Ethic of War, The. London: Longmans, Green and Co., 1916.

Church and the Sacraments, The. London: Independent Press Ltd., fifth impression, 1955.

Congregationalism and Reunion. Two Lectures. London: Independent Press Ltd., reprinted, 1952.

Cruciality of the Cross, The. London: Independent Press Ltd., third impression of second edition (1948), 1955.

Faith, Freedom and the Future. London: Independent Press Ltd., second impression, 1955.

God the Holy Father. London: Independent Press Ltd., re-issued, 1957.

Justification of God, The. Lectures for War-time on a Christian Theodicy. London: Independent Press Ltd., second impression, 1957.

Missions in State and Church. London: Hodder and Stoughton, 1908.

Person and Place of Jesus Christ, The. London: Independent Press Ltd., eighth impression, 1955.

Positive Preaching and the Modern Mind. London: Independent Press Ltd., fifth impression, 1957.

Principle of Authority in Relation to Certainty, Sanctity and Society, The. An Essay in the Philosophy of Experimental Religion. London: Independent Press, second edition, 1952.

Religion in Recent Art being Expository Lectures on Rossetti, Burne Jones, Watts, Holman Hunt and Wagner. London: Simpkin, Marshall and Co., 1889.

Rome, Reform and Reaction. Four Lectures on the Religious Situation. London: Hodder and Stoughton, 1899.

Socialism, the Church and the Poor. London: Hodder and Stoughton, 1908.

Soul of Prayer, The. London: Independent Press Ltd., fourth impression, 1960.

Theology in Church and State. London: Hodder and Stoughton, 1915.

This Life and the Next. The Effect on this Life of Faith in Another. London: Independent Press Ltd., fourth impression, 1953.

Work of Christ, The. London: Independent Press Ltd., second edition, 1958.

ESSAYS BY FORSYTH IN COLLECTIONS

Atonement in Modern Religious Thought, The. London: James Clarke and Co., 1902. pp. 59–88.
Faith and Criticism. Essays by Congregationalists. London: Sampson Low Marston and Company Ld., second edition, 1893. 'Revelation and the Person of Christ,' pp. 95–144.
London Theological Studies by Members of the Faculty of Theology in the University of London. London: University of London Press, 1911. 'Christ and the Christian Principle,' pp. 133–66.
Old Faith and the New Theology, The. Charles H. Vine, ed., London: Sampson Low Marston and Company, Ld., 1907. 'Immanence and Incarnation,' pp. 47–61.

ARTICLES AND MISCELLANEOUS WRITINGS BY FORSYTH

'Evangelical Churches and the Higher Criticism, The,' *Contemporary Review*, Vol. LXXXVIII, July–December, 1905. pp. 574 ff.
'Revelation and the Bible,' *Hibbert Journal*, Vol. X, 1911–12. pp. 235 ff.
Priesthood and Sacrifice. A Report of a Conference. W. Sanday, ed., Longmans, Green and Co., London, 1900. pp. 174 ff.
Gibson, J. Monro, *The Inspiration and Authority of Holy Scripture.* London: Thomas Law, 1908. Introduction by Forsyth, pp. vii–xviii.

EVALUATIONS OF FORSYTH

Bradley, William Lee, *P. T. Forsyth, The Man and His Work.* London: Independent Press Ltd., 1952.
Brown, Robert McAfee, *P. T. Forsyth: Prophet for Today.* Philadelphia: The Westminster Press, 1952.
Escott, Harry, ed., *Peter Taylor Forsyth 1848–1921 Director of Souls.* London: The Epworth Press, 1948.
Griffith, Gwilym O., *The Theology of P. T. Forsyth.* London and Redhill: Lutterworth Press, 1948.
Hunter, A. M. 'P. T. Forsyth Neutestamentler,' *The Expository Times.* Vol. LXXIII, No. 4, January, 1962, Edinburgh: T. and T. Clark. pp. 100–6.
Price, Charles, 'Introduction to the Theology of P. T. Forsyth.' Unpublished notes of lectures given at the Protestant Episcopal Theological Seminary in Virginia, Alexandria: 1960.
Rosenthal, Klaus, 'Die Bedeutung des Kreuzesgeschehens für Lehre und Bekenntnis nach Peter Taylor Forsyth,' *Kerygma und Dogma Zeitschrift für Theologische Forschung und Kirchliche Lehre.* Vandenhoeck und Ruprecht, Göttingen, 7 Jahrgang, Heft 3, Juli, 1961. pp. 237–59.

OTHER BOOKS

Althaus, Paul, *Die Christliche Wahrheit. Lehrbuch der Dogmatik.* Gerd Mohn: Gutersloher Verlagshaus, 1959.

——, *Grundriss der Ethik*. Gutersloh: C. Bertelsmann Verlag, 1953.

Barth, Karl, *Church Dogmatics* Vol. I, part I. (trans, Thomson) Edinburgh: T. and T. Clark, third impression, 1955.

——, *Church Dogmatics* Vol. I, part II. (trans. Thomson, Knight) Edinburgh: T. and T. Clark, 1956.

——, *Church Dogmatics* Vol. II, part I. (ed. Bromily and Torrance) Edinburgh: T. and T. Clark, 1957.

——, *Evangelische Theologie im 19 Jahrhundert*. Heft 49 of *Theologische Studien*, (ed. Barth and Geiger) Zollikon-Zürich: Evangelischer Verlag AG., 1957.

Berkhof, Louis, *Systematic Theology*. London: The Banner of Truth Trust, reprint, 1949.

Bochenski, I. M., *Contemporary European Philosophy*. Berkeley: University of California Press, 1961.

Brunner, Emil, *Revelation and Reason. The Christian Doctrine of Faith and Knowledge*. (trans. Wyon) London: Student Christian Movement Press Ltd., 1947.

——, *The Christian Doctrine of God. Dogmatics*. Vol. I. (trans. Wyon) London: Lutterworth Press, second impression, 1955.

——, *Man in Revolt. A Christian Anthropology*. (trans. Wyon) London: Lutterworth Press, sixth impression, 1962.

——, *Wahrheit als Begegnung. Sechs Vorlesungen über das Christliche Wahrheitsverständnis*. Zürich: Zwingli-Verlag, 1938.

Butler, Joseph, *The Analogy of Religion, Natural and Revealed, to the Constitution and the Course of Nature*. London: George Routledge and Sons, Ltd., fourth edition, 1890.

Carnell, Edward John, *The Case for Orthodox Theology*. Philadelphia: The Westminster Press, 1959.

Denzinger, Henrici, *Enchiridion Symbolorum*. Freiburg: Herder, 1960.

DeWolf, L. Harold, *The Case for Theology in Liberal Perspective*. Philadelphia: The Westminster Press, 1959.

Dodd, C. H., *The Apostolic Preaching and its Developments. Three Lectures with an Appendix on Eschatology and History*. New York: Harper and Brothers Publishers, reprint, 1954.

Elliott-Binns, L. B., *The Development of English Theology in the Later Nineteenth Century*. London: Longmans, Green and Co., 1952.

Haering, Th., *Der Christliche Glaube. Dogmatik*. Stuttgart: Calwer Vereinsbuchhandlung, 1922.

Harnack, Adolf, *Outlines of the History of Dogma*. (trans. Mitchell) Boston: Beacon Press, 1957.

Hegel Selections. (ed. Jacob Loewenberg) New York: Charles Scribner's Sons, 1957.

Herrmann, Wilhelm, *The Communion of the Christian with God*. (trans. Stanyon and Stewart) London: Williams and Norgate Ltd., 1930.

Hordern, William, *The Case for a New Reformation Theology*. Philadelphia: The Westminster Press, 1959.

Hunter, A. M., *Introducing New Testament Theology*. London: SCM Press Ltd., 1957.

316

Johnson, Robert Clyde, *Authority in Protestant Theology*. Philadelphia: The Westminster Press, 1959.

Kant Selections. (ed. Theodore Meyer Greene) New York: Charles Scribner's Sons, 1957.

Kennedy, H. A. A., *The Theology of the Epistles*. London: Gerald Duckworth and Co. Ltd., reprint, 1952.

Knight, George A. F., *A Christian Theology of the Old Testament*. London: SCM Press Ltd., 1959.

Maurice, Frederick Denison, *The Kingdom of Christ or Hints to a Quaker Respecting the Principles, Constitution, and Ordinances of the Catholic Church*. London: SCM Press Ltd., 1958. (New edition based on the second edition of 1842. Edited by Alec R. Vidler, 2 Vols.)

——, *Theological Essays*. London: James Clarke and Co. Ltd., 1957.

Minear, Paul Sevier, *Eyes of Faith. A Study of the Biblical Point of View*. London: Lutterworth Press, 1948.

Moore, Edward Caldwell, *An Outline of the History of Christian Thought since Kant*. London: Duckworth, second impression, 1947.

Mozley, J. K., *The Heart of the Gospel*. London: Society for Promoting Christian Knowledge, 1927.

Niesel, Wilhelm, *Reformed Symbolics. A Comparison of Catholicism, Orthodoxy, and Protestantism*. (trans. Lewis) Edinburgh and London: Oliver and Boyd, 1962.

Orr, James, *The Progress of Dogma*. Grand Rapids, Michigan: Wm. B. Eerdmans Publishing Company, 1952.

Ott, Ludwig, *Fundamentals of Catholic Dogma*. (trans. Lynch) Cork: The Mercier Press, Limited, 1960.

Otto, Rudolf, *The Idea of the Holy. An Inquiry into the Non-Rational Factor in the Idea of the Divine and its Relation to the Rational*. (trans. Harvey) New York: Oxford University Press, reprint, 1958.

Redlich, E. Basil, *Form Criticism, Its Value and Limitations*. London: Duckworth, reprint, 1956.

Reed, John K. S., *The Authority of Scripture. A Study of the Reformation and Post-reformation Understanding of the Bible*. London: Methuen and Co. Ltd., 1957.

Ristow, Helmut and Karl Mattiae, eds., *Der Historische Jesus und der Kerygmatische Christus. Beiträge zum Christusverstandnis in Forschung und Verkundigung*. Berlin: Evangelische Verlagsanstalt, 1961. Bo Reicke, 'Der Fleischgewordene. Zur Diskussion über den "historischen" Jesus und den Kerygmatischen Christus,' pp. 208–18.

Ritschl, Albrecht, *The Christian Doctrine of Justification and Reconciliation*. (ed. Mackintosh and Macaulay) Edinburgh: T. and T. Clark, 1900.

Robinson, H. Wheeler, *The Religious Ideas of the Old Testament*. London: Duckworth, third impression, 1926.

Schädelin, Albert, *Die Rechte Predigt. Grundriss der Homiletik*. Zürich: Zwingli-Verlag, 1953.

Schmaus, Michael, *Katholische Dogmatik*, Band I. München: Max Huber Verlag, 1960.

317

Tillich, Paul, *Systematic Theology*, Vol. I. London: Nisbet and Co. Ltd., 1953.

van Oyen, Hendrik, *Botschaft und Gebot*. Gerd Mohn: Guterslöher Verlagshaus, 1962.

——, *Evangelische Ethik I. Grundlagen*. Basel: Verlag Friedrich Reinhardt AG., no date.

——, *Evangelische Ethik II. Liebe und Ehe*. Basel: Verlag Friedrich Reinhardt AG., no date.

——, *Theologische Erkenntnislehre. Versuch Dogmatischer Prolegomena*. Zürich: Zwingli-Verlag, 1955.

Webb, Clement, C. J., *A Study of Religious Thought in England from 1850*. Oxford: Clarendon Press, 1933.

Weber, Otto. *Grundlagen der Dogmatik*, Band I. Neukirchen: Verlag der Buchhandlung des Erziehungsvereins, 1959.

THE AUTHOR

John Hewitt Rodgers was born in Clayton, Missouri, on June 13, 1930, to John H. Rodgers, a departmental head in a printing firm, and Amanda Hancock *née* Rich. He attended the Clayton and Kirkwood public schools until 1948. He then attended Central College in Fayette, Missouri, 1948–49, the University of Missouri, 1949–50, and the United States Naval Academy in Annapolis, Maryland, 1950–54. Upon graduation from the Naval Academy he served with the United States Marine Corps as a Second Lieutenant in the infantry. He attended the Protestant Episcopal Theological Seminary in Virginia, 1955–58. Upon graduation he served the congregation of the Church of the Epiphany in Washington, D.C., as an assistant minister with collateral responsibility as a college chaplain. In 1960 he and his wife, Blanche Inez Kostka, whom he married in 1959, travelled to Basle, Switzerland, where he studied under Professors Hendrik van Oyen, Karl Barth, Oscar Cullmann, Bo Reicke, Max Geiger, and Heinrich Ott. In 1963 he graduated summa cum laude and returned with his wife and son, Mark Daniel, born while in Basle, to take up his present position as assistant professor for systematic theology at the Protestant Episcopal Theological Seminary in Virginia, located in Alexandria, Virginia. On 29 July, 1964 a daughter, Sarah Christine, was born to the Rodgers.

INDEX

322